PUBLIC DIPLOMACY

PUBLIC DIPLOMACY:
USA Versus USSR

Richard F. Staar, Editor

Foreword by W. Glenn Campbell

HOOVER INSTITUTION PRESS

Stanford University   Stanford, California

The Hoover Institution on War, Revolution and Peace, founded at
Stanford University in 1919 by the late President Herbert Hoover,
is an interdisciplinary research center for advanced study on
domestic and international affairs in the twentieth century. The
views expressed in its publications are entirely those of the
authors and do not necessarily reflect the views of the staff,
officers, or Board of Overseers of the Hoover Institution.

Hoover Press Publication 345

First printing, 1986

Manufactured in the United States of America

90 89 88 87 86   9 8 7 6 5 4 3 2 1

Library of Congress Cataloging in Publication Data

Public diplomacy.

   Includes index.
   1. United States—Foreign relations—Soviet Union—
Congresses.   2. Soviet Union—Foreign relations—United
States—Congresses.   I. Staar, Richard Felix, 1923–
JX1428.S65P82   1986   327.73047   86-15194
ISBN 0-8179-8451-8 (alk. paper)

CONTENTS

FOREWORD

      The idea for this workshop originated at a luncheon attended by, among others, former U.S. Information Agency (USIA) director Frank Shakespeare and former Radio Free Europe/Radio Liberty (RFE-RL) president Sig Mickelson. Frank has been confirmed as American ambassador to Portugal and cannot be here; Sig, who has given willingly of his time and advice, is on the program.[1]

      We begin our discussion with a look at what the USSR is doing. In Soviet terminology, the "correlation of forces" assessment is reached after examining and comparing all aspects of relative national strength. Usually, this means the relationship between the USSR and the United States and their respective military alliance systems.

      However, one of the most important elements in this "correlation of forces" is the power of ideas. Whether right or wrong, accurate or misleading, penetrating or shallow, ideas have a cumulative and potent impact in the competition between the two superpowers. If the resources expended serve as a barometer in this regard, the Soviet Union recognizes the field as highly important to its global ambitions. The USSR annually spends at least $3.5 billion for what we would term "public diplomacy."[2]

      According to an unclassified 1978 study by the U.S. Central Intelligence Agency (CIA), the Soviet Union has

> developed a worldwide network of assets second to none, consisting of an extensive shortwave radio system, broadcasting in many languages; two news agencies; the pro-Soviet communist parties; the in-

ternational communist fronts; bilateral friendship societies and other quasi-official instrumentalities; a large corps of foreign correspondents, many of them Soviet Intelligence officers; the foreign clandestine propaganda assets under the control of the KGB; and the intelligence services and assets of Cuba and Moscow's East European allies.[3]

Besides enormous differences in their order of magnitude, the public diplomacy programs of the United States and the Soviet Union differ sharply in other important respects. The USSR combines facts with distortion, disinformation, and outright falsehood. Where the United States presents a cacophony of voices from every viewpoint, the system of centralized control allows Moscow to speak with a single voice and to orchestrate campaigns without fear of internal contradiction or criticism. Over the past seven decades, the Communist Party of the Soviet Union (CPSU) has developed and used its network of international front organizations and foreign communist parties to disseminate its propaganda line.

Currently, the war of words, or more generally of ideas, is being fought throughout the world. It behooves the United States to be aware of the "correlation of forces" in this specific confrontation and to alter that relationship to one which at least approaches parity. Nearly all of the gains that the Soviet Union has made in the post–World War Two period have been accomplished without the use of armed force in combat. A clearer indicator of the importance attached to the war of ideas could hardly be imagined.

The existence and missions of USIA and the U.S. Advisory Commission on Public Diplomacy, both of which we are pleased to have represented at this workshop, bear testimony to official recognition of this fact. National Security Decision Directive 77, signed by the president of the United States on 14 January 1983, also formally acknowledged this fact and established a special planning group to coordinate various aspects of U.S. public diplomacy.[4]

It is a great pleasure to welcome all of you to the Hoover Institution, especially our guests from Western Europe. I wish you a productive conference.

W. Glenn Campbell
Director
Hoover Institution on War, Revolution and Peace

NOTES

1. Sig Mickelson's book about the radios remains a classic, *America's Other Voice: The Story of Radio Free Europe and Radio Liberty* (New York: Praeger, 1983).

2. Paul A. Smith, Jr., "Propaganda: A Modernized Soviet Weapons System," *USIA World* 2, no. 10 (November 1983): 9, gives $3.5 billion as the annual budget (as cited by Richard F. Staar, *USSR Foreign Policies After Detente* [Stanford: Hoover Institution Press, 1985], p. 63). See also U.S. Congress, House, Permanent Select Committee on Intelligence, Subcommittee on Oversight, *Hearings on Soviet Covert Action: The Forgery Offensive*, 96th Cong., 2d sess., 1980, p. 60.

3. Quote from CIA study cited by United States comptroller general, *Report to the Congress of the United States on the Public Diplomacy of Other Countries: Implications for the United States*, ID-79-28 (Washington, D.C.: General Accounting Office, 23 July 1979), p. 25.

4. *Management of Public Diplomacy Relative to National Security*, National Security Decision Directive 77 (Washington, D.C.: The White House, 14 January 1983). See Appendix for the full text of this document.

INTRODUCTION

Richard F. Staar

This volume is the result of a workshop, sponsored by the Hoover Institution at Stanford University, which assembled representatives from U.S. government agencies, retired officials, professors and other academicians, Radio Free Europe/Radio Liberty and Voice of America executives, and several prominent West Europeans, most of whom work for the media in their respective countries. All those who subsequently submitted written comments are identified at the end of the book.

Our thanks go to Mrs. Margit N. Grigory for her many hours of work as assistant conference coordinator and to my colleague Richard T. Burress for his support as chairman of the publications committee. We are also grateful to the Tinker Foundation and the United States Information Agency for their financial support. USIA funds made it possible to invite nine West Europeans to participate at this workshop. Six later sent written comments, which provide a unique perspective and appear in Part Three of this volume.

* * *

The introductory chapter offers a *tour d'horizon* from the perspective of a historian versed in both the past of Imperial Russia and the present of the Soviet Union. James Billington suggests that an effective U.S. public diplomacy "must be rooted in broad forces that endure" and that today "the power and importance of ideas . . . is greatly enhanced." One might disagree with his suggestion that the USSR export of authoritarian regimes to Central America, Southeast Asia, and southern Africa during the past 45 years has not been impressive. That statement, however, can be contrasted with the fact that the "real dynamism in postwar social, economic, and political development lies in constructive evolution toward democracy" rather than vice versa.

Unfortunately, the United States has been unable to devise an acceptable rationale for its international cultural policy. The speaker suggested that exported institutions, like the one at Yenching, too often become recruiting grounds for communist cadres. Foreign students should be brought to the United States (especially those from the USSR), a suggestion that may have influenced President Reagan's proposal to establish a U.S.-USSR annual exchange of 50,000 students. Such a program might help erode the Soviet commitment to a global mission that, the leadership believes, will result in a worldwide victory. Dr. Billington concludes his paper with four general suggestions for improving United States foreign policy.

The next essay, by a senior policy analyst at the Voice of America, deals with USSR propaganda, whose origins date back to Lenin's time. Mrs. Lisa Jameson interviewed important Soviet defectors who had operated under journalistic cover. Her insights offer primary source documentation on the modus operandi of foreign propaganda dissemination by the International Department. Utilizing its network of so-called research institutes, front organizations, and foreign communist parties, this unit of the Central Committee receives information from all pertinent government agencies, including the KGB. It dispenses white, gray, and black propaganda, examples of which include commentary about the September 1983 shooting down of the Korean civilian passenger airliner by a Soviet fighter plane and the Summer 1985 youth festival in Jamaica.

Wittingly or unwittingly, the media in the United States have been exploited by the USSR. *Time* magazine provides Mikhail S. Gorbachev with a cover story, and the best known purveyor of disinformation (Georgii Arbatov) claims on U.S. television that "freedom of the press in America is a myth." The latter was also given space on the opinion/editorial page of the *New York Times* on 10 January 1986. In the scramble to interview leading Soviet propagandists, the lack of reciprocity seems to be ignored.

Two illustrations of the techniques used by the Kremlin in its attempts to subvert Western Europe are examined in the next presentation. Michael Ledeen discusses KGB establishment of the daily newspaper *Ethnos* in Greece for disinformation purposes. The Soviets use most of the profits from this enterprise to support their other dubious publishing activities. The second case study deals with the peace campaign, directed against deployment of American intermediate-range missiles in NATO countries, and thoroughly documents USSR activity in the Federal Republic of Germany, Denmark, Norway, and the Netherlands.

Stanton H. Burnett's paper focuses on U.S. informational and cultural programs, which have difficulty competing with those of the Soviet Union where media are totally regime-controlled. President Reagan's five-minute broadcast on 1 January 1986 over Moscow television had been neither announced in advance nor repeated thereafter. The battleground seems to be everywhere else except in the USSR; for instance, the U.S. Information Agency's WORLDNET is linked to 50 countries, not one of which is communist-ruled. Moreover, the Soviets and their East European client regimes have been jamming the Voice of America ever since August 1980, despite the Helsinki agreement five years earlier. The 74 percent budget increase for USIA between 1981 and 1985 cannot overcome the jamming, unfortunately.

It is vital, however, to expand the United States' exchange-of-persons program by inviting more midcareer professionals from the developing countries and by enlarging the number of American experts sent abroad. Through the efforts of USIA, however, the U.S. government can only do so much. Assistance must come from the private sector, because all exchange programs ultimately depend on the American citizen for success. Mark Blitz provides a thoughtful analysis of this issue.

Recently retired foreign service officer Gifford Malone discusses the roles, relationships, and operation of diplomatic organs involved in the practice of U.S. public diplomacy, which he indicates is now an instrument of foreign policy rather than a "neutral process of interaction." Apart from USIA, major actors include the White House and the National Security Council, the Department of State, and more limited participants, such as the Department of Defense and the Agency for International Development.

Announced during January 1983, National Security Decision Document 77 (NSDD-77), entitled "Management of Public Diplomacy Relative to National Security" (reprinted in the appendix) coordinates all activities in this field through four interagency committees. A separate National Endowment for Democracy, established as a private and nonprofit corporation, functions separately from USIA. A new emphasis on public diplomacy led the Department of State to allocate three senior positions to this area (by late 1985, however, one of these—special advisor to the secretary—had been abolished).

Examples of special issues that have required the Department of

State to appoint coordinators in the field of public diplomacy have included the modernization of intermediate-range missiles in Western Europe and the crisis in Central America. Attempts to induce foreign service officers abroad to engage in public diplomacy, however, have not encountered much success. Meanwhile, back in Washington, D.C., "there is no single focal point for public diplomacy" at the Department of State, whose performance in this area is characterized "by confusion and lack of coherence."

Exchanges with the USSR are another important aspect of public diplomacy and, in the long run, may weaken social controls in the USSR. In his paper, Nils Wessell suggests that nurturing the Soviet intelligentsia's feeling of separateness from the communist party rulers should be the main objective of the United States. He discusses the different types of exchanges. The principal benefits to the United States include exposure to our standards and ideas, informational access within the USSR, and training of American academic and governmental specialists. Dr. Wessell discusses the National Academy of Sciences' (NAS) 1982 decision to curtail major symposia (but not individual exchanges) with its Soviet counterpart because of Andrei Sakharov's internal exile to the city of Gorky; after two years the ban was lifted, since the NAS boycott evidently proved ineffective.

In his paper on new broadcasting techniques, Professor Allen Peterson explains some of the problems regarding noise levels and jamming. These may be overcome through the use of satellites, although higher power already can be achieved for conventional transmissions at high-frequency levels. The VOA objective is to overcome jamming so that 90 percent of the message will become intelligible for the same ratio of listeners. The development of special jam-resistant antennas is leading to further receiver system enhancement.

In his presentation, Richard E. Bissell, a former head of research at USIA, makes the astute observation that $1 million spent on updating listener figures is inexpensive compared with the cost of new Voice of America transmitters that, otherwise, would be broadcasting to unknown audiences. Other problems include the change in radio listening habits from use of short to medium waves, the explosion in the number of video cassette recorders, new information and data processing techniques, and the computer revolution within the Soviet bloc.

Philip Habib, a former undersecretary of state and again a special presidential envoy in 1986, commended the workshop mix, that is, the presence of active bureaucrats as well as persons without government responsibility. He outlined the foreign policy process and the role of various agencies in this process. Although the United States can deal with overt Soviet public diplomacy, it needs an institutionalized way to counter the covert type. During the 1950s and 1960s, when a small group doing so reported directly to the undersecretary of state, this kind of activity had been easier for the United States to counter. Ambassador Habib recounted his own involvement in this process at the time, namely, the specialized U.S. action in the 1960–61 Congo crisis. As structured under the terms of NSDD-77, a committee would not have viewed such problems on an issue-by-issue basis.

Dr. Habib also gave an overview of foreseeable world developments. Although competition with the USSR will continue, the United States and its allies must discover a way to manage these relations more effectively. Apart from the foregoing, functional issues will face the United States, and crisis management remains unavoidable. Fortunately, the public understands foreign policy, more than it is given credit for, and this may be America's greatest asset.

PART ONE

SOVIET VERSUS AMERICAN PUBLIC DIPLOMACY

1

AMERICAN FOREIGN POLICY AND THE NEW ISOLATIONISM

James H. Billington*

Paradoxically, the United States is steadily and simultaneously becoming more deeply involved in the external world, yet more psychologically detached from it. A host of seemingly separate developments may soon converge into a new isolationism: the erosion of language study and international education, the protectionist passion among politicians, the inability to deal rationally with illegal immigration, and the seeming promotion of selfishness into a virtue (the glorifying of economic aggrandizement on the right, special interest on the left, and self-centered self-indulgence everywhere).

Our drift toward a new isolationism is basically a reaction against the technocratic liberal internationalism of the postwar foreign policy establishment. After Vietnam, confidence eroded in the elite conceit that power plus applied intellect could control outside events. Most Americans either lost interest in foreign policy or tried to find ways to reassert closer to home their traditional and undiminished sense of self-esteem. But no new definition of the United States's role in the world was forthcoming, and American world commitments were sustained more out of sheer inertia than fresh conviction. A political willingness to flirt with a withdrawal to fortress the United States underlay the Nixon Doctrine, the Mansfield Amendment, and the initial Carter proposal on Korea. Even President Reagan's major new idea for interna-

---

*Copyright © 1985 by James H. Billington; printed with permission.

tional security, the Strategic Defense Initiative, may unintentionally contribute to neoisolationism by seeming to give cosmic, high-tech respectability to the idea that America may eventually retreat into simply protecting itself.

Although the Reagan administration has helped the United States to recover a sense of self-confidence—a feeling for *who* we are—there has been no comparable gain in understanding *where* we are. The basic questions of where we stand in the world and how we should relate to it have not been seriously addressed, let alone answered; writers on foreign policy increasingly tend to repackage partial perceptions of the world or recycle ideological preconceptions. Over the long term in a healthy, skeptical democracy, the net result will almost certainly be the growth of even greater isolationist sentiment.

Only a new, tough-minded look at where the United States really fits into a changing world will provide the needed underpinnings for continued American involvements abroad. Sound policy must be based on essentials about America and the world as a whole—not on the undue fascination with the methods of our opponents or with any of the transitory challenges we face. If we basically define our involvement in the world as mobilization against a particular enemy, we unwittingly nurture the illusion that we can withdraw from all of the world later if we only throw ourselves into part of it now. Illusion leads to disillusionment, and resigning agenda-determination to an opponent involves losing initiative and ultimately self-respect. We define ourselves best in terms of what we are and may become, not in terms of what others have become or of what we are not. Effective public diplomacy for the long term must be rooted in broad forces that endure, not on narrow preoccupation with opponents and issues that may not.

In the twentieth century the entire globe has been awakened to political and economic aspirations that were, in the previous two centuries, largely confined to Europe and North America. This awakening has been channeled politically into a proliferation of new national states without any parallel development of any overall framework for international order. Politically, the balance of power among sovereign, secular states established in Europe at the end of the religious wars could not survive two world wars; economically, the open world market based on the American dollar could not continue to play the integrating hegemonic role it assumed in the postwar era. In retrospect, the era between Westphalia and Sarajevo may be seen as an exceptional period in which a relatively homogeneous and small group of French-speaking European Christians secured a monopoly of the means of violence for a few of their own territorially defined sovereign states—and held violence between states to acceptable limits as they spread their own ambitions and many of their goods and ideas to the rest of the world. But for the real problems of today, the more ideological (even apocalyptical) perspectives of the preceding era of renaissance, reformation, and religious conflict may be more relevant and instructive.

In the second half of the twentieth century, two superpowers armed for Armageddon seem to have replaced a multiplicity of lesser states with finite forces. The destructive power of the principals transcends borders; the rise of private violence through crime and terrorism threatens central authorities; and the dramatic global increase in population, education, and mass communication sharply increases the numbers of people who are hungry for and responsive to the direct appeal of ideas and symbols that can make sense of change and give new legitimacy to leaders.

The passions of the Reformation were fueled by gunpowder and Gutenberg into broad and bitter religious wars that were fought ostensibly over the narrowest questions of doctrine. So the passions of our time, fueled by the missile and the microchip, instill fears of some new apocalypse that are not dispelled by the arcane, theological redefinitions of strategic doctrine.

At such a time of uncertainty and apprehension, the power and importance of ideas and the political relevance of ultimate beliefs is greatly enhanced (hence, the growth of activist fundamentalism within all three of the great prophetic monotheisms: Judaism, Christianity, and Islam). Given the power and diffusion of weapons and the volatility of the world, the danger grows that we may be playing with fire if we are not careful in the definition and declamation of ideas in the public arena.

How, then, can we responsibly do what we cannot responsibly avoid unless we return to isolationism and abdicate world leadership to others? What ideas can we properly project into a world that presents us so inescapably with both danger and opportunity (like the famous Chinese character)—a world where Newtonian certainties have vanished along with the security of living in the balanced, Westphalian community of states secure in both their legitimacy and their limitation? How do we live in the age of relativism and indeterminacy about the universe, social Darwinism in society, and the growing belief that we may have to settle for the spread of a totalitarian peace in order to avoid the risk of a total war?

We must accept the uncertainty that the world presents and ground our foreign policy on a positive, inclusive affirmation of what Americans are—on ideas generated by America rather than on any ideology of

Americanism, or for that matter globalism or any "ism" in between. The reality of America mixes material accomplishment and spiritual aspiration and continues to annoy intellectuals bent on forcing reality into the straitjacket of ideology, that twilight zone of political illusion that cuts people off from either concrete productive reality, on the one hand, or personal moral responsibility, on the other.

Effective communication with the world necessarily involves the projection of one's own subjective values into others' objective reality. We need to be clear and honest about both before presuming to open our mouths abroad—secure in our own values but conscious of our ignorance about others' realities. Unfortunately, much of our intellectual elite has it just the other way around: They see our values as problematic and in need of endless dissection, whereas impersonal material trends in the outside world are their sources of both certainty and legitimacy. Articulate anguish about ourselves and miscellaneous certainties about the alleged forces of our times and inevitabilities of history are elegantly recycled through the tenured ranks of our national media and national universities and tend to intimidate even those who are not altogether seduced or persuaded. But most Americans instinctively believe (a) in freedom that is to be exercised both in the mundane material world and in a higher spiritual one and (b) in America, not as a perfect model, but as the partial realization of some universal ideals.

To speak effectively to the outside world, however, Americans must do a better job of sorting out what may simply be a peculiarity (however cherished) of our own development from the genuinely universal part of our ideals. In our public diplomacy, we should not be embarrassed to proclaim those higher goals to which we have aspired in our collective experience: democratic capitalism and the Judeo-Christian tradition. Yet, however central to our experience, these ideals may not be optimally effective with the global audience we must address. It may not be possible to state our essential ideals in ways that will seem both authentic to ourselves yet relevant to others—let alone to all the varied societies now striving for a place in the sun and often looking to us for some kind of guidance. We can isolate and affirm two sets of basic ideals arising from our own experience that can and should be shared by all: One set, basic to dignified human life, is *freedom and responsibility;* the other set, essential for civilized human society, is *plurality and participation.*

In our experience, freedom is essentially the liberation of man from oppressive external authority—above all, that of arbitrary political power. The limitation of political power is an American ideal of far wider appeal, but freedom is not license unless divorced (as it sometimes is in our indulgent culture) from its Siamese twin of responsibility.

In order to be free from external authority, the individual must be deeply, internally accountable to a higher moral norm that for most of us comes from God. If responsibility implies transcendent belief, a respect for the plurality of such beliefs is essential to the preservation of a free and civil society. Once again, the American experience in accommodating religious and racial plurality (however scarred and imperfect) provides elements of hope and even guidance for a world that must learn to accommodate such variety in the crowded global conditions that lie ahead. I would speak of plurality or plural communities rather than pluralism, since the American experience celebrates a variety of authentic beliefs rather than a monism of indifference or an ideology of relativism. The United States is a multiplicity of live experiences and convictions—not some arid monument to the proposition that all beliefs are equally relevant.

Perhaps the most important of these general ideals is participation. It provides a more universally applicable and verifiable political goal than democracy, the institutions of which are often unfamiliar and the rhetoric of which is so often co-opted or debased by tyrants. Maximizing the numbers of people who can run for office and participate in both choosing leaders and exercising power—these are standards that can be applied to all kinds of political systems. The criterion of participation in real political choice (like that of expanding individual freedom) is intrinsically threatening to dictatorships of all kinds, but particularly to communist ones that are controlled by a *nomenklatura* and have generally been superimposed on lands with weak traditions of liberal democracy.

Turning from the general definition of our own goals to the particular problem posed by rival Soviet objectives, we should perhaps take note of another way in which history and socioeconomic development may make our ideals more relevant than their ideology. Objective reality itself may be rendering anachronistic one of the favorite clichés of our time: that we live in an age of revolution. Social revolution has taken Leninist shape in some authoritarian societies, such as Cuba, Nicaragua, and Ethiopia; and Leninist leaders have scavenged part of the French transition from colonialism in Southeast Asia and of the Portuguese transition in southern Africa. In addition, a new kind of Islamic revolution has triumphed in Iran. But this is not a very impressive inventory for the long postwar era with all its disruptive change and Soviet investment in subversion.

The real dynamism in postwar social, economic, and political development lies in constructive evolution toward democracy rather than in destructive revolution leading to dictatorships. In Western Europe and Japan, south Asia, southern Europe, and South America, democratic evolution rather than totalistic revolution has increasingly become, not just the pattern for change, but the source of political legitimacy. The most profound challenge to a Soviet-type regime in Eastern Europe has come, not from any revolutionary (or counterrevolutionary) elite driven by any secular ideology, but from a spontaneous popular movement in Poland calling for *evolutionary* change and sanctioned by the Catholic Church. As the revolutionary fire burns itself out on peripheral killing fields and historians catalog the horrors perpetuated in the name of revolutionary ideologies, humanity seems increasingly inclined to look to evolution rather than revolution for constructive change. To such a world, the meliorate American model with all its compromises and improvisations may have more to say than the absolutist models with all their public myths and private murders.

In some respects, we may be living in an age of evolution in which revolution is a dying ideal. Another aspect of objective reality favorable to America is the rising importance of education and intellectual leaders in world politics. The life of the mind has a vested interest in freedom and an inherent bias toward free societies. In this country, we have yet to understand fully the immense political importance of the rapid, unprecedented spread of education worldwide in the postwar era—let alone the decisive leadership role played by small educated elites in developing societies. Full realization of this might enable us at last to make the hard case for the "soft" part of our international relations: the seemingly amorphous complex of exchanges, short-term visitors, cultural exports, and information transfer. It is tragic that we continue to be confused about the value of these programs. Those who participate in them (who are often academic) tend to view their cultural activities as so intrinsically noble that they are almost demeaned by any attempt at justification to the broader society. That society, in turn, tends to the practical view that any publicly subsidized international activity must have a demonstrable "bottom line" of immediate benefit to the nation.

Unfortunately, a coherent, broadly acceptable rationale for our international cultural policy has not yet been developed, or at least effectively communicated. Despite all their recurrent problems with budgets, programs in this area have, in fact, often been better supported than they have been understood. The Fulbright program—which is, quite simply, the largest exchange program in the history of the world and which, on the Stanford campus, Arnold Toynbee called one of the two most important American programs of the postwar era (along with the Marshall Plan)—has been the centerpiece of an amazing network of American associations with rising intellectual elites in dozens of countries throughout the postwar world. Yet it receives little serious public attention or, for that matter, intellectual analysis from its intellectual beneficiaries. As the program approaches its fortieth anniversary, the America that created it has not even compiled a simple list of its astonishingly influential global alumni.

Our commitment to higher education is the largest, both relatively and absolutely, that the world has ever seen—both a magnet and an example for much of the world. The confident spread of the unlimited pursuit of truth is one of the most powerful and inexhaustible forms of assault against any system, such as that of the USSR that claims (in the very name of the communist party's official newspaper, *Pravda*) already to possess and express the truth in its state policy. More important, the pursuit of truth tends to keep us all from the pursuit of each other; since such a pursuit is ultimately noncompetitive, since all can be free if more are responsible, and since in an age of increased physical constraints (rising population and finite resources) it may be that only in the ever-expanding life of the mind and the spirit can the horizons of our most cherished ideal, freedom, remain truly infinite.

Spreading this activity and sharing this commitment through exchanges, and immersion experiences in American culture and academia are probably more effective aspects of American foreign policy even in the short run, and incontestably so over the long term, than most of the more advertisement- and product-oriented efforts to package and distribute American policy messages to opinion makers abroad. In most cases, it is better to bring foreigners to America so that they can see the full richness of the American experiment and make their own adaptations rather than to attempt to replicate American institutions abroad. Those Asian leaders from Japan and Korea who came to the United States to study in the early part of this century, before there was a Fulbright program, proved among the fastest friends of the United States. Exported American institutions, on the other hand, like Yenching—despite all the noble mix of missionary idealism and Ivy League cerebral input—ultimately proved among the most important recruiting grounds for communist cadres.

The rationale for higher exchange programs should not be confused with the very different rationale for technical-assistance programs, which are also much needed and still absent from our public discourse. These are properly concentrated on areas where there are great need and important national interests requiring special training and specific skills. Higher academic exchanges and nationally sponsored cultural programs and exchanges, however, establish the very identity of our civilization with liberty by stressing liberal learning and free creativity.

It is in our national interest not to let them become abused into narrow technical training and technology-transfer programs, as authoritarian regimes of all kinds inevitably try to do.

The greatest long-range potential of exchange programs lies precisely with authoritarian regimes, for whom the exercise of individual freedom is an inherently subversive act. In recent years the most important aspect of our opening to Communist China may well prove to lie, not in the economic or even the political and geopolitical sphere, but in the simple act of bringing some 12,000 Chinese students of the post–Cultural Revolution era to study at United States universities. One of the most important new initiatives that we could and should take to try to reach the new postwar and post-Stalinist generation inside the USSR would be to propose a comparably dramatic increase in Soviet students coming to the United States. Massively increasing the numbers would remove the heavy control that the *nomenklatura* elite inevitably holds over a small program. Although it would pose problems for our security, it would pose even greater problems for theirs, since they would be forced either to permit far more people from far more places in the USSR than they could effectively control to experience the United States for themselves or to be put in the position of refusing to let their own people take advantage of an educational opportunity of immense inherent appeal.

There is a historical opportunity to propose a massive increase in this area at a time of generational change in the USSR. It would be unfortunate if we moved timidly and incrementally because of our continued penchant to view negotiation on cultural exhibits and scholarly exchanges as if they were warheads and delivery systems. In public diplomacy, we should always be on the side of openness and increased numbers in all directions since they bring long-run gains, whatever the short-term embarrassment. A dramatic increase in educational exchanges could finally reach Soviet society as a whole and not simply offer further travel benefits for propagandists and vacuum cleaners of the *nomenklatura*.

So far, I have tried to argue that we have a stronger basic hand to play in world affairs than we often seem to realize, and that this strength is not simply dependent on our material power (military or economic). Our greatest strength lies in ideas and ideals that are embedded in, but more universal than, our institutions. These ideas and ideals are more relevant to the coming era than outmoded ideologies of the early industrial era, such as Marxism. The broader relevance of the American experience to the present derives not only from the growing appeal of an evolutionary example to a largely postrevolutionary world but also from the importance of religion in American development.

This statement may shock many American academics who generally view religion as the polar opposite of the features that I have stressed so far: the United States' free, critical pursuit of higher learning and openness to information, innovation, and change. The distinctive co-existence in the United States of a continued, deep, and widespread belief in revealed religion alongside our belief in natural reason gives the American experience a kind of potential resonance with much of the world that the profoundly secular opinion-making community in the university-media complex of this country may be incapable of appreciating. Far from becoming irrelevant with rapid modernization and change, in many parts of the world religion has become a resurgent element in that change. The most original (and most unforeseen) developments of the last decade in the Third and Second worlds respectively, the rise of Khomeini in Iran and Solidarity in Poland, are both examples of political movements deeply rooted in a prophetic monotheistic faith. Much of both radical and conservative politics in the Western world is increasingly linked with religion and religious leaders.

No less than our hospitality to genuine plurality, our individual faith commitments enable us to identify with an entire dimension of human experience that communists can relate to only in the most egregiously insincere and manipulative of manners—committed as they are to a monolithic atheism. The force of religion, of course, may prove a positive element within the otherwise ominous nationalist and nativist revival currently occurring in the Soviet Union. The forthcoming anniversary in 1988 of the millennium of Russia's conversion to Christianity may serve as a quiet catalyst. The virtually requisite secularism of American higher academia has left the otherwise sophisticated analysts of society, which we incubate in our universities, frequently insensitive to the importance of religion in general and of religion in the USSR, in particular. In this area, one cannot expect much understanding, let alone sympathy, from the mainstream media. A recent survey of 140 randomly selected leaders of television showed that 93 percent had a religious upbringing but that the same percentage seldom or never attended religious services.

I am arguing for a foreign policy more deeply grounded in our own values rather than one that has to be continually reshaped to ever-changing external crises and opponents. To shape a policy that translates enduring values into present reality, however, we need a fundamental diagnosis of what is wrong with our present national policy. One of the sad features of our times is that, in general, those with the experience and judgment to make diagnoses do not take the time away from often profitable private activities to perform this important public service. Academics who have the time and training for diagnostic work, on the other hand, often lack either the experience or judgment intelligently to apply learning to reality. In both groups, there is a failure to share responsibility for the common concerns of the civilization.

We are haunted by the late Roman syndrome: the decadent erosion of shared values in the West, in general, and the United States, in particular. In terms of the two pairs of values already defined, we claim freedom without responsibility, plurality without participation. In our passive, television-oriented consumer culture, no one cares much about the public agenda any more. Common purposes, civil decencies, and civic involvement are all undermined by a medium that encourages spectatorism and destroys interest in issues and participation in their resolution—increasingly relying on sex, violence, and sheer noise to arouse us from our self-indulgent stupor. It is increasingly respectable to be indifferent to one's neighbor and preoccupied with narrow issues and self-centered interests. All of this ultimately poses a survival issue for our type of society.

Since this syndrome has more serious and immediate political implications for the more vulnerable states of Europe than for the United States, it might be advisable to have the next summit of leaders of the industrial democracies discuss values rather than economics. I have more confidence in the marketplace to deal with economic problems than with the underlying value problems. On the basis of the real accomplishments of the postwar free world, there might even be real opportunity to etch out for our times some declarations of principles similar to the Atlantic Charter and Four Freedoms of the wartime era. These should be developed jointly and should not be the product of unilateral lectures on our part. In avoiding preachy moralism, we must not be afraid to affirm moral ideals, because in a truly democratic society the deepest values of a people cannot be shut out of foreign policy and should not be unduly intimidated by the relativism of much of the university-media complex.

Out of hostility or simple boredom with traditional values, the elite culture often tends to substitute aesthetic for moral criteria in human affairs and judgment. People in Washington, D.C., tend to be preoccupied with the aesthetics of power rather than the substance of policy, the marketing of slogans rather than the generation of ideas, "beautiful" rather than good people, and style rather than substance. The corrosive effects of this moral decay, accompanied by aesthetic spectatorism in world affairs, can be seen in the Western media's remarkable suspension of serious hard questioning, let alone moral judgment, about Afghanistan or anything else amidst the initial aesthetic enthusiasm for Gorbachev's youth, clothing, and new style of discourse.

If the first basic problem of U.S. foreign policy is the internal one of the erosion of shared values, the second problem follows logically from the first. It is the failure to recognize the elementary external problem that a free society must heed for its survival: the locus of what Holmes called the "clear and present danger." There could hardly be anything more clear and present than the ability an adversary possesses for the first time in American history to destroy totally, in a matter of minutes, our entire country. They can also blackmail, if not overrun, our allies in a matter of days and incite or intimidate, if not subvert, many others over a period of months and years.

At some level of consciousness, most people recognize the destructive nature of our weapons, but many do not understand that the "danger" comes from the men who man the weapons and, ultimately, from the ideology that legitimates their power. However little they really believe it, however much they cynically manipulate it, the Soviet leaders continue to justify their political legitimacy in terms of the historical, global mission of their party and of the belief in the eventual global victory of their cause. Traditional Russian imperialism never applied to the Caribbean, Vietnam, and Africa.

Like other transnational movements based on belief, Soviet communism may be entering the particularly dangerous phase that dying religions sometimes go through: the attempt to compensate for the loss of inner faith among the believers by projecting and asserting external authority over others. As a protégé of Suslov and Andropov, Gorbachev is part of this richly entrenched priestly class. Even if he were inclined to do so, he would find it difficult to resist using this weapon for internal control in an otherwise fissiparous and anachronistic empire—providing both totalistic legitimation of his authority and total flexibility in its exercise.

But how can one pass from diagnosis to prescription? How can we shape a more effective modern foreign policy, in general, and deal with this kind of opponent, in particular? One must begin with basic facts about the two societies: The USSR is a strong central state with a weak civil society; America is just the opposite. The United States has a strong civil society, a powerful polity but a relatively inept foreign policy. The Soviet Union is an inept polity with, however, a powerfully focused foreign policy.

It is not only ironic but also inexcusable that the United States, which has such a powerful basic polity, cannot get its policy act together. We face a problem that is intrinsically easier than the Soviet problem of doing something about their unproductive and repressive polity. Ideas and economics are the approaching fields of competition: In terms of basic strengths, these are precisely the areas in which America has the greatest advantage over the USSR. Yet these seem to be the areas of our greatest confusion and ineptness in terms of national policy. They will thus figure prominently in the general suggestions I shall make for a better United States foreign policy.

1. Since there is an overarching importance of dealing with the Soviet Union for the conduct of U.S. foreign policy, there must be a central mechanism for dealing with it comprehensibly and on a governmentwide basis. Australia does this in dealing with Japan. Perhaps the United States should as well; with the USSR, it seems essential. Whether in the White House or in the State Department, the nerve center of such a mechanism must be headed by someone in whom the president has full confidence, and it should include two quite separate and distinct top figures: (a) someone in charge of coordinating and implementing all government policy toward the USSR and (b) someone totally divorced from policymaking to be in charge of continuous assessment of overall Soviet capabilities, strategy, and tactics.

Such a top-level leadership team is needed not only to bring the act together but also to check the dangerous intrusion into U.S. policymaking recently of two types of structural deformations: (a) the tendency of political-level figures, seeing dialogue as a status symbol without bringing any expertise to the exercise, to be seduced by the aphrodisiac of elite contact with Soviet professionals and (b) the tendency of the foreign policy bureaucracy, being forced to deal repeatedly with the Soviet professionals, to subtly accommodate themselves to Soviet procedures and thus become, in some ways, a symbiotic extension of the Soviet system.

2. A second need is for a central coordinating body (also with the confidence of the president) to define and implement national economic policy, in general, and economic policy toward the USSR, in particular. Economic policy must be closely coordinated with our allies and with the U.S. private sector—both of whom desperately need a single, reliable reference point in the United States government. Such a body is needed, not so much to revive the illusion of manipulation through boycotts and the like, but to reap a different kind of benefit from the expected increase in East-West trade. Such

a body could help frustrate the unfair advantage that the USSR often gains by manipulating our open competitive system. Such a body could encourage business leaders, not to hold back, but to conduct their business boldly without becoming frightened appendages of the Soviet system huddled in Moscow waiting for favors from the Ministry of Foreign Trade or some other central control point.

American and Western businessmen could be encouraged to insist on access to end users, full inspection of construction sites, and information on reserves—in short, on the business conditions they would expect elsewhere. There may be a considerable potential for stimulating change in the USSR through on-site exposure of its emerging new generation to the creative abrasions of entrepreneurial capitalism and matrix management. A serious problem of technology transfer in the military field continues to exist. Our general posture and that of our allies, however, should be to open up, not hold back. The hard point will be the need to insist on genuine openness on their side and an end to the funneling of U.S. contacts through the usual Moscow manipulation centers.

3. A third and related need is for real reciprocity in our bilateral diplomacy. The scandal of the inequality between the physical facilities and ambassadorial access in Moscow and Washington is nothing short of a national disgrace—one that has yet to be fully acknowledged, let alone rectified. We should insist that the Central Committee of the Communist Party of the Soviet Union is the equivalent of the United States Congress—not the USSR Supreme Soviet, since decisions are made and divisions recorded in the Central Committee. We should insist that on academic exchanges the Soviets send real scholars and not *nomenklatura* officials. Moreover, we should move toward regional, professional, and even purely randomized exchanges to ensure that visits to the United States are part of a broadening dialogue and not merely a form of political patronage for party officials. We must also demand reciprocity in the private sector. It is important to repeat and sustain such demands, not out of petulance or solely for pedagogy, but as encouragement for those inside the Soviet system who may be arguing for a policy change but who cannot argue it themselves.

4. Finally, we must form a clearer idea of what we really want and might reasonably expect from the USSR. The answer is quite simply to cease posing a clear and present danger, not only by controlling and reducing arms but also by terminating the Soviet ideologically-based commitment toward indefinitely expanding their political control.

There are other legitimate matters for our concern: changing their internal political and economic system and improving the status of subject nationalities. Since the Helsinki agreements, greater civil and cultural liberties have been part of their international obligations. Our proper focus, however, must be on ending their international danger, not on propounding any aim of internal revolution or imperial breakup of the Soviet Union. If we insist—persistently and consistently—on the repudiation of the totalistic Leninist-Stalinist ideology internal changes will result. If we focus our attention on ending, rather than adjusting to, the international danger posed by this kind of armed ideological adversary, we need to bear in mind two seemingly contradictory considerations.

First, the United States may have more influence than it suspects in a period between the new generation's consolidation of power and the proclamation of new policies. This is one of those rare periods when the Soviets are considering change, and we may be more of a potential model than we realize. The United States is the only nation by which they can measure themselves and the only one that can destroy them.

The Russians have historically had a peculiar love-hate relationship with their principal foreign adversary. The Eastern Slavs took their first religious and artistic models from Constantinople after raiding it, their first modern governmental institutions from the Swedes after fighting them, and their first industrial models from the Germans as they were preparing to fight them in two world wars. The postwar Soviet Union has sought to "overtake and surpass" the United States; forty years of postwar propaganda have created far more curiosity than enmity toward America; and a new generation might well secretly borrow even more from the other multiethnic, continentwide civilization that they publicly oppose.

At the same time, however, we must understand that the decisive factor in the immediate future of Soviet development will be the Russian majority within the multinational Soviet state. If a new leadership in the USSR seems more flexible and Western in style, it is predominately Great Russian in composition and deeply seized by the need to find a post-Stalinist identity for the Russian people. This question has political origins and will require a political resolution. De-Stalinization was put on the agenda by Khrushchev, shelved by Brezhnev, but will almost certainly have to be faced by Gorbachev and his post-Stalinist generation.

The need to learn anew from foreign examples heightens the psychological importance to the Russians of finding their own cultural identity based on their own rich culture. The rise of the village writers, the renewal of religious interests, and other aspects of the cultural ferment of this generation remind us that there is probably more to this nationalist revival than a merely xenophobic chauvinism. Although the dissidents' ferment of recent years has been cruelly destroyed, their unofficial search for a more worthy, non-Stalinist identity for the Russian people may, in the long run, anticipate deeper changes in the official culture. Beyond the rise in education and the need for new energy in the economy lies the inner psychological need to make some sense out of the immense human suffering that Russia has undergone in this century, much of it self-inflicted during the Stalin era.

If the West can remain tough and united without being provocative, and if the United States can undertake new initiatives without reviving old illusions, there may be reasons for cautious hope that in the long run the USSR may move beyond the nationalism of the military-police establishment (the current fall-back position from a decaying communist faith for the ruling oligarchy) and develop some new identity by the twenty-first century that is presently unforeseen by either them or us. This could be a constructive evolution that draws both on old Russian tradition and on recent outside experience rather than on the destructive revolutionary ideology and the dangerous international politics of recent Soviet history.

2

SOVIET PROPAGANDA: ON THE OFFENSIVE IN THE 1980S

Lisa Jameson*

He gradually became aware that this intolerable gap between outer pretense and inner reality was only a single reflection of something broader and more serious still . . . This was the terrible, cynical, demeaning contempt for the truth that seemed to pervade Russian government and society. The behavior of the entire governing establishment appeared to be based on a series of massive fictions— fictions not just subconsciously and innocently appropriated into the minds of the bearers, but deliberately conceived, perpetrated, and enforced.[1]

To almost any student of the Soviet Union, George Kennan's description of the Marquis de Custine's disillusionment with the regime of Nicholas I must seem uncannily prophetic. There is reason to believe—and Kennan emphasizes this—that many of Custine's observations were exaggerated. Yet how ironic that nearly 70 years after the Bolsheviks seized power the tendentious duplicity evident in virtually every realm of Soviet life and international behavior seems a monstrous but logical extension of what Custine perceived in 1839.

Lenin foresaw that the future of his social revolutionary movement would ultimately depend on controlling the minds and the spirits of men. His weapon, at home and abroad, was propaganda. In *What Is To Be Done*, his most seminal work on communist tactics, Lenin wrote that

---

*The views expressed in this paper are those of the author and do not necessarily reflect official positions of the United States government.

the "principal thing is propaganda and agitation among all strata of the people."[2] Lenin drew a distinction between propaganda and agitation; both were essential to effective political indoctrination and education, but to Lenin, propaganda was expressed in writings, and agitation exploited the spoken word.

In his time, of course, there was no radio or television, and movies were silent pictures. Were Lenin planning revolution today, cognizant of the enormous power of modern telecommunications, he most certainly would call for an all-out war of images, using every type of medium. This, in fact, is what his contemporary disciples have been doing—to an extent even Vladimir Ilich could not have imagined.

To the Soviets, propaganda is the face of ideology and the arm of policy. It is the central element in what Soviet theorists have always referred to as the ideological struggle—the struggle between East and West, between the forces of progress and reaction, between socialism and imperialism, or between champions of peace and makers of war. During his brief reign as general secretary, Iurii Andropov made the Soviet position unquestionably clear in a 1983 speech: "Our time is marked by a confrontation, unprecedented in the entire postwar period, by its intensity and sharpness, between two diametrically opposed world outlooks, the two political courses of socialism and imperialism. A struggle is going on for the minds and hearts of billions of people on our planet."

In the Soviet Union, propaganda is an instrument of both foreign and domestic policies that, in turn, are justified by the ideological interpretations of the Communist Party of the Soviet Union (CPSU). Only in rare circumstances (usually when propaganda is used for deception operations) do underlying messages of Soviet foreign propaganda differ substantially from those of the domestic variety. Immediate goals of particular propaganda actions may vary, but ultimate objectives remain constant. Moreover, techniques and tools of both domestic and foreign Soviet propaganda are frequently the same, and overall direction of propaganda, though translated into action by various agencies, is centrally carried out in the Central Committee Secretariat.

THE PROPAGANDA APPARAT

Domestic Propaganda and Propaganda Policy

In its myriad forms, propaganda invades almost every aspect of Soviet activity. Used to an unlimited information supply of differing bias,

Westerners have difficulty grasping the vast scope of tailored, officially controlled communications that greet Soviet citizens at each turning. Yet, if we are to understand how the Soviet regime designs propaganda for foreign audiences, some appreciation of the massive process of internal propagandization is necessary. Soviet émigré writer Vladimir Voinovich has summed it up well: "Comparing Soviet propaganda with the American sort or with Western propaganda in general is difficult, perhaps even impossible, because Soviet propaganda is the basic product of the system—a product whose output significantly exceeds the combined total of goods produced by agriculture, light industry, heavy industry, and even the arms industry."[3]

I once interviewed Viktor Belenko, the air defense pilot who flew his MiG-25 into Hokkaido nine years ago. I asked him to tell me his main reason for defecting: He answered with one Russian colloquialism—*beliberda!* Accurately translated, this means "claptrap," and Belenko had used it to summarize his disgust with the all-pervasive propaganda that oppressed his life in the Soviet Union.[4] Again, Voinovich's discourse is appropriate:

> All Soviet newspapers, magazines, television and radio stations, cinemas, theaters, writers' unions, composers' unions, and even the official Orthodox Church are hard at it. The output of propaganda is equally a responsibility of all factories, collective farms, hospitals, construction enterprises, and the military. Every director, manager, department head, chairman, or unit commander has to ensure that his bailiwick is kept supplied with portraits of Lenin and of the current members of the Politburo (of course, if one of them is sacked, then his portrait must disappear instantly and forever); then there are the banners proclaiming . . . meaningless slogans . . . the ubiquitous wall newspapers . . . and the countless posters that shriek appeals, quotations, figures, and percentages promising over-fulfillment of production plans.[5]

In his entertaining and thought-provoking series of essays, *Armageddon in Prime Time,* George Bailey describes what had to be the height of this folly: "The most significant episode in the history of the *Great Soviet Encyclopedia*," he writes, "remains that day in 1953 when each subscriber received a razor blade through the mail along with instructions to cut out the two pages on Lavrenti Beria, who had just been liquidated, and replace them with enclosed pages on the Bering Strait."[6]

Direction of propaganda and agitation (agitprop) activities within the Soviet Union is the responsibility of the Propaganda Department of the Central Committee, and subordinate agitprop units in republic, oblast, and city party organizations. Agitprop functions include indoctrination of the masses through multifarious means (the gamut of devices Voinovich described): lectures, sloganeering, collective meetings, rallies, and management of domestic media at every level. The targets of propaganda are Soviet citizens and not those of foreign countries. As one might expect, domestic propaganda has remained less sophisticated, more predictable, and more blatantly distorted than the foreign variety. When it comes to paeons to Soviet science and industry, idealization of workers, and appeals for vigilance against the infection of Western ideas and culture, there is still little to choose between today's internal propaganda and that of earlier eras.

Since the Gorbachev ascendancy, however, several significant changes in the ideological sector may presage a remodeling of internal propaganda. The first clue came in early December 1984, when Gorbachev, three months before he became general secretary, made the closing speech at a major Moscow conference on party ideology:[7]

> It is impossible not to agree with the comrades who have noted that the forms and methods of ideological work under present-day conditions should be more varied and flexible and more fully suited to the innovative character of the tasks to be resolved . . . Searching and creativeness, sensitivity to new phenomena and processes, decisive rooting out of formalism, red tape, and empty talk are the demands of life for all workers on the ideological front . . . We must continue to develop in Soviet people's consciousness a clear understanding of the historical importance of our huge social triumphs and at the same time expose existing difficulties and real contradictions . . . and show the work of the Party and people in resolving them. In this, one must remember that leaving questions unanswered opens a gap for hostile propaganda.[8]

This speech indicated to some observers that Gorbachev's reformist instincts would likely be directed not only to the Soviet economy but also to party cadres and ideological work. In this and later pronouncements, Gorbachev said that the Communist Party of the Soviet Union (CPSU) needed to give more information to the people, an implied criticism of the quality of political indoctrination (or agitation) at lower levels of party organization.[9] This, of course, does not mean we can expect the Soviet regime to move toward pluralism, or to tolerate frank, open-ended discussion in party circles. Instead, it appears Gorbachev's administration will take measures to increase the dissemination of communiqués and policy studies, and to encourage party instructors to allow more informed, less obfuscatory exchanges in party meetings. It is unlikely that Soviet citizens will really hear anything more than the party line; by referring to actual facts and events and not just Leninist platitudes, however, agitators may give listeners the illusion they are hearing something new.

Radio Liberty analyst Elizabeth Teague points out that this effort may be a return to the program launched by Andropov in late 1982 to "revamp outmoded techniques of political indoctrination."[10] Gorbachev, Andropov's protégé, probably shares his mentor's conclusion that the party had lost much of its attractiveness to growing numbers of the Soviet population, especially young people. His actions to increase party participation at lower levels and inject creativity into the indoctrination process seem to fit with his stated intentions to rejuvenate moribund layers of the party/state bureaucracy. In this, he seems to have taken up where Andropov left off—a process that almost came to a grinding halt under Chernenko.[11]

Gorbachev's first major personnel move came in late April 1985, just five weeks after Chernenko's death, at the first regular Central Committee Plenum at which he presided. Including KGB chief V. M. Chebrikov, five promotions within the top Soviet leadership took place. More important, Party Secretary Egor Ligachev was directly elevated to full membership in the Politburo. Ligachev had served as Gorbachev's secretary in charge of party cadres during the former's tenure as second secretary and chief party ideologue under Chernenko. Ligachev has now assumed this mantle for himself and may be considered the second most powerful man in the Kremlin.

In fulfilling the same role when directed by Mikhail Suslov in his long tenure as overlord of ideology, Ligachev's secretariat functions encompass top-level supervision of foreign policy, culture, science and education, party cadres, and the entire propaganda apparatus (domestic and foreign). Ligachev's deputies, all considered junior secretaries, include Mikhail Zimianin (former editor of *Pravda*) for culture and propaganda and Boris Ponomarev for foreign policy and foreign communist parties. On the rung below are the heads of respective Central Committee departments: Vasilii Shauro (culture), Leonid Zamiatin (international information), and the newly appointed Aleksandr Iakovlev (propaganda). Iakovlev—who had headed the Institute for World Economics and International Relations (IMEMO), one of the Kremlin's main think tanks for policy studies—was chosen to replace Boris Stukalin, who has since been sent off as ambassador to Hungary. Stukalin is thought to have been the personal protégé of Zimianin; his demotion may, therefore, herald a similar fate for Zimianin as well.[12]

Stukalin's demise has been the subject of considerable speculation, since it was Gorbachev's only known demotion to date of a Central

Committee department head appointed under Andropov. If Gorbachev's December 1984 speech was a clue, Stukalin may have been sacked for failing to execute Andropov's planned modernization of Soviet internal propaganda. Ligachev, who probably gave Stukalin the coup de grace, is reported to have complained that Soviet press and television "still have not managed to drop their clichés and sloganeering."[13]

We have already witnessed a few signs of change in Soviet internal media. *Pravda*, for example, published most of Gorbachev's *Time* interview, and Moscow Radio broadcast it.[14] For Soviet audiences, one of its most refreshing characteristics was the absence of tiresome ideological rhetoric, the slogans and buzz words of what we have come to identify as typical Soviet propaganda. Even Gorbachev's references to Lenin as the model for his own political style avoided traditional quotations from Lenin's works. Gorbachev's invocation of "God on high," his citations from American periodicals unavailable to Soviet readers, and his characterization of both President Reagan and himself as "politicians placed in office by the people," were—as might be expected—deleted. More important, although dismissed by Gorbachev as aggressive and impossible, a long passage that revealed much of the American argument for the Strategic Defense Initiative (SDI) was retained.

In the past, Soviet internal media seldom quoted the nonsocialist foreign press. Today, this is commonplace: *Pravda* regularly cites Western newspapers, especially prominent United States dailies, such as the *Washington Post* and the *New York Times*, when their negative commentary on American actions or socioeconomic conditions serve to buttress positions taken by the USSR, or when they have quoted critics of American policy. For example, on 31 August 1985, the second anniversary of the shooting-down of Korean Air Lines (KAL) flight 007, *Pravda* cited an article in the *Washington Post* as confirmation of the Soviet contention that the plane had been on a spy mission. The *Post* article was quoted out of context, and of course, *Pravda* did not bother to include material from Western periodicals that refuted Soviet claims.[15]

Yet this type of obvious counterpropaganda serves a useful purpose. Today's Soviet readers are often so jaded by a lifetime of propaganda that they may tend to believe the opposite of what official organs have told them. In many cases, they have also been exposed to Western versions of events through broadcasts of the Voice of America (VOA), the British Broadcasting Corporation (BBC), or other foreign radio stations that, despite heavy jamming, still manage to be heard. Skillful use of material from the Western press—even distorted, out-of-context, or one-sided—can provide a certain patina of credibility to otherwise dismissible Soviet boilerplate.

Foreign Propaganda

Western Kremlinologists sift through Soviet newspapers and periodicals like panners for gold—a laborious exercise that often yields enlightened nuggets about Soviet policymaking and the party/state hierarchy. However, gleaning the Soviet press for insights into the makeup and chain of command of the Soviet foreign propaganda apparatus has been disappointingly unproductive. Until recently, other sources (émigrés, defectors, foreign diplomats, and journalists) have rarely added more than well-informed opinions to the body of knowledge we have in this area.

In preparing this paper, I interviewed two recent defectors, both of whom possess unique information from personal experience about the direction and execution of Soviet foreign propaganda.[16] Stanislav Levchenko had been a KGB disinformation specialist, who defected in 1979 while serving undercover as a *Novoe vremia* correspondent in Tokyo. Early in his career, Levchenko worked as an interpreter for the Central Committee's International Department and, later, for the Soviet affiliates of two front organizations: the World Peace Council and the Afro-Asian People's Solidarity Organization.

Ilia Dzhirkvelov worked in both the First and Second Chief Directorates of the KGB, under journalistic cover. After 1957, he served in the International Department (with *nomenklatura* status); later, as deputy secretary general of the USSR Union of Journalists (concurrently as delegate to the international front group to which it is affiliated, the International Organization of Journalists); and, finally, as chief editor of the final editing desk of TASS. Where their individual experiences corresponded, Levchenko and Dzhirkvelov corroborated one another in almost every respect. With regard to policy decisions, responsibilities, and the chain of command within the foreign propaganda organs, their first-hand information differed from some of the conclusions of Western analysts.

Both Levchenko and Dzhirkvelov stressed that management of Soviet foreign propaganda is essentially monolithic, because the same body, namely, the Central Committee Secretariat, directs both Soviet foreign policy and foreign propaganda. Finalization of policy is the prerogative of the Politburo, but policy guidelines are staffed out in the Secretariat. This centralization of foreign policy and propaganda planning within the highest organs of the party explains why propaganda lines on different issues are so consistent and, conversely, how they can be adjusted quickly to meet specific needs. Foreign propaganda can be an expression of policy and a catalyst for the realization of policy goals.

In a perverse sense, the Soviet leadership may be a prisoner of its own policy and propaganda axis. In his *Time* interview, Gorbachev complained that the United States was not taking Soviet disarmament initiatives seriously. "We keep hearing one and the same answer," he lamented. "No, no, no, it's propaganda, propaganda, propaganda!" Zhores Medvedev, an exiled Soviet dissident scientist and writer, may have provided the best formula for separating pure propaganda from that which really reflects Soviet intentions: "The only test to distinguish propaganda from realistic and serious proposals," he wrote, "is negotiation."[17]

Both Levchenko and Dzhirkvelov claimed that overall action strategies were issued over the signatures of Central Committee secretaries. In fact, Dzhirkvelov said such orders were invalid unless signed by *all* the secretaries, including the general secretary. If the general secretary were ill—as was the case during Brezhnev's final years and during much of Andropov's and Chernenko's respective tenures—the order had to be carried to him in the hospital or sanitarium. Since Levchenko recalled seeing action directives signed by Brezhnev, he confirmed this to an extent (occasionally, however, they were signed by Suslov). It seems probable that general orders for foreign policy support activities, which include all types of propaganda, must come from the Secretariat and be personally approved by, at least, the general or second secretary.

Excluding Gorbachev, the present head of Soviet propaganda is Egor Ligachev, most senior of the remaining Central Committee secretaries. Below Ligachev is 80-year-old Boris Ponomarev, de facto head of the International Department for more than 30 years. During that period, Ponomarev may have more directly influenced the course of Soviet foreign policy and propaganda than any other man, including former Foreign Minister Andrei Gromyko.[18] Ponomarev has been a fixture for so long that everyone seems to take him for granted. The deaths of Brezhnev, Andropov, Chernenko, Suslov, and Ustinov; the accession of Gorbachev; and the current rise of relatively younger Kremlin leaders, such as N. I. Ryzhkov, indicate a change in the tides of the generational sea in the Soviet Union. When his longtime mentor, Suslov, died in 1982, it seemed that Ponomarev's power base might slip away; however, to date Ponomarev somehow remains, like a dinosaur in the age of mammals.

Ponomarev's career spans more than 50 years. From 1936 to 1943, he was a Soviet representative on the Comintern's Executive Committee. When the Comintern was dissolved and the International Department organized by Andrei Zhdanov in 1943, Ponomarev probably became its first deputy chief.[19] Having served in the Comintern, Ponomarev had established expertise in dealing with foreign communist parties. Apparently, he had also served as a propagandist: In 1938 the Comintern published a pamphlet recounting the confession of Bukharin, with an introduction by B. Ponomarev. In his voluminous work, *The Bolshevik Revolution*, E. H. Carr noted that the "initiative in introducing propaganda as a regular instrument of international relations must be credited to the Soviet Union . . . Soviet Russia was the first modern state to establish, in the form of the Communist International, a large-scale, permanent international propaganda organization."[20]

As the linear descendant of the Comintern, the International Department is the most powerful unit within the support apparatus of the CPSU Central Committee. From all accounts, it is the hub of foreign policy, foreign propaganda, and public diplomacy planning within the Secretariat. It has never relinquished responsibility for Soviet relations with foreign communist parties, and it supervises the operations of all major international front organizations. Soviet representatives and functionaries of these fronts work under the immediate direction of the International Department, even those who are, concurrently, KGB officers. This provides limitless opportunities for generating propaganda: publishing books and pamphlets; financing demonstrations; issuing petitions, appeals, and open letters; and organizing elaborate international festivals.

Area specialists in the International Department receive information from all foreign agencies of the Soviet government: the KGB, the Ministry of Foreign Affairs, the Ministry of Foreign Trade (in the United States this is generally referred to as "raw intelligence"). A network of research institutes, staffed by academic specialists and globetrotting experts, provides policy-support studies directly to the International Department. These include such familiar names as the Institute for the Study of the USA and Canada and the Institute for the Study of the Peoples of Africa and Asia (formerly the Institute for Oriental Studies). In addition, the International Department has its own representatives in key Soviet embassies abroad, usually listed as members of the political section.

In processing so much information, the International Department has a continuous supply of material on which to base recommendations for propaganda campaigns and foreign diplomatic strategies. Both Levchenko and Dzhirkvelov have confirmed that ideas for propaganda originate in the International Department, the KGB, or the Politburo itself.[21] They seldom, if at all, seem to originate in the International Information Department (IID), which, contrary to the opinions of some observers, appears to function almost entirely as a support unit. Headed by former

TASS director Leonid Zamiatin, the IID was created in 1977 in response to a major Central Committee decision. It was felt—probably with justification—that Soviet propaganda responses to events or Western initiatives took too long to coordinate. The Politburo decided that a quick response mechanism was needed: The IID was the result.[22]

The IID is staffed almost entirely by professional journalists recruited from major Soviet media organs such as TASS, Radio Moscow, and *Pravda*. These experienced propagandists prepare guidance outlines, and even whole articles and scripts, which are then distributed to various media outlets and Soviet embassy information departments. The topics and themes for IID production are determined on a daily basis at a high-level morning meeting in the Secretariat. According to Dzhirkvelov, this meeting is chaired by the ideology chief (now, Ligachev or, in his absence, Ponomarev) and includes Zamiatin; possibly V. F. Shauro, head of the Central Committee Culture Department; senior officials of the Ministry of Foreign Affairs and the KGB; and the directors of all major Soviet media organizations (*Pravda, Izvestiia, Sovetskaia Rossiia, Literaturnaia gazeta*, TASS, and Novosti). Daily propaganda guidance is based on the general directives discussed earlier, and these are approved by the Politburo. New ideas for major campaigns may come up in these meetings, but they must be worked out in the Secretariat and submitted for authorization by the Politburo before they can be enacted.[23]

Material provided by the IID may be used repeatedly in both Soviet foreign and domestic propaganda outlets. The stories may be different in style and language, and updated with recent examples, but the substance is generally the same. Propaganda for Western consumption, especially in recent months, may have fewer Marxist-Leninist stock phrases and seem less vituperative than material for domestic, Third World, or Soviet bloc audiences. Only top-level organs, such as *Pravda*, have the right to originate foreign policy pieces on their own. Usually signed by senior political commentators or special correspondents, these articles must be cleared in advance of publication. Dzhirkvelov said that V. G. Afanas'ev (the editor of *Pravda*) would have to personally call the Secretariat, probably Ponomarev, for permission to proceed.

Recently, several Western analysts have suggested that Gorbachev's housecleaning broom may sweep out Zamiatin, a holdover from the Brezhnev era. At least one analyst predicted that the IID would be disbanded, and the Central Committee's International Department and the Press Department of the Ministry of Foreign Affairs (MFA) would absorb its functions.[24] The primary justification for this belief is the increase of on-the-record MFA press conferences, hosted by the highly visible Vladimir Lomeiko, and a corresponding decrease in the number of official announcements made by Zamiatin. The press conference is one of the newer Soviet foreign propaganda techniques (discussed below), and Lomeiko fits the mold of the smiling, cooperative Soviet official of the 1980s.

Nevertheless, there does not seem to be any hard evidence for rumors about the IID's immediate dismemberment, and TASS confirmed Zamiatin in his post as recently as September 1985. In the past year we have seen an increase in the number of Soviet television Studio Nine productions, starring Zamiatin and political commentator Valerian Zorin; these are tedious expositions of Soviet foreign policy positions or anti-Americanisms, intended primarily for the internal Soviet audience. I am inclined to think that, like other devices for foreign consumption, the MFA press conferences are arranged in response to decisions taken at the Secretariat's morning meeting. Zamiatin's days may be numbered, and Lomeiko may be heir to his position; to date, however, we have no reason to assume this.

Principal Techniques of
Soviet Foreign Propaganda

Overt Foreign Propaganda

"Your task is simple," says Gletkin to Rubashov: "To gild the Right, to blacken the Wrong. The policy of the opposition is wrong. Your task is, therefore, to make the opposition contemptible."[25] In a sense, this dialogue from Arthur Koestler's *Darkness at Noon* describes the key purposes of overt Soviet foreign propaganda: to enhance the image of the USSR and further its goals; and at the same time, to diminish the reputation of the USSR's opponents and, in doing so, to prevent their goals from being realized.

In their overt propaganda (that is, "white" propaganda openly attributed to its sponsor), the Soviets employ accurate, semiaccurate, embellished, or, sometimes, totally false information or outright denial. They frequently denigrate or accuse others (usually the United States) of engaging in unacceptable behavior for which the Soviet Union more justifiably can be blamed. A typical example is the continuing campaign to charge the United States with aggression and support of terrorism. The current line names Grenada, Nicaragua, and Afghanistan as America's victims. Constant repetition of such charges can eventually make an impression, even on indifferent audiences; it may also deflect atten-

tion from international condemnation of the Soviet's military adventur-
ism in Afghanistan and other countries. The USSR spreads overt propaganda more widely and in greater quantities than the "gray" or "black"
propaganda used for specific deception or influence operations. Its pur-
veyors include all media mechanisms at home and abroad, not to mention thousands of human outlets since almost any Soviet official or journalist can be considered a walking propagandist.

Before the Reagan-Gorbachev summit in November 1985, the Soviets measurably toned down the virulence of their anti-American rhetoric, especially in their dispatches, broadcasts, and pronouncements to
Western Europe and America—a sudden softening to serve as an over-
ture to the Soviet summit symphony. This permitted Gorbachev to claim
that his government is reasonable and flexible and to fault the Reagan
administration for following its anti-Soviet course, thus preventing real
progress toward arms control and an improvement in relations. Even as
the number of direct barbs decreased, subtle anti-American messages
remained; Soviet propaganda especially concentrated on arousing anx-
iety in the West by alleging that Soviet-American relations were dan-
gerously unhealthy and might be irreparably damaged, primarily because of the recalcitrance and warmongering of the American side.

In August 1985, Gorbachev had threatened to walk out of the Geneva arms negotiations if the United States did not abandon the Strategic Defense Initiative (SDI). By September, in his *Time* interview, Gorbachev did not speak of turning his back on Geneva but did say that
"the train might leave the station" if something was not done to stabilize
relations. Throughout this period, the Soviets continued to propose
counterpropaganda programs (such as the "Star Peace" initiative) and
moratoria on testing and on intermediate-range nuclear missile deployment. All part of the continuing anti-SDI and Soviets-for-peace campaign, these proposals were designed to place the United States on the
defensive. The United States was making its proposals within diplomatic channels in Geneva, as Foreign Minister Andrei Gromyko and
Secretary of State George Shultz had agreed to do in January 1985; however, Soviet propaganda was floating trial balloons in the public arena.
By the time the new USSR foreign minister, Eduard Shevardnadze, arrived in Washington and presented President Reagan with a concrete
counterproposal for arms reductions, the stage had long been set to
portray the Soviet Union as the bastion of peace and Gorbachev its
champion.

The increasing openness, fluency, and knowledgeability of Soviets
in the West has enhanced the credibility of Soviet news reporting,
which, of course, is based on official propaganda. Western television,

radio, and newspapers have provided a forum for Soviet journalists, officials, and experts and presented them as the equals of their Western counterparts. Over the past few years, this growing aura of equivalence has finally extended to Soviet foreign media as well. We increasingly find well-intentioned American journalists citing TASS dispatches, Moscow press conferences, and even articles in Soviet journals as sources for stories they file as objective news reports.

Disinformation

Disinformation has become a fashionable term: In the United States it is bandied about in everything from *Foreign Policy* to *Playboy*. Writers frequently use the term interchangeably with propaganda to describe any Soviet actions that involve the use of media, or simply as a catchall label for active measures. Moreover, the word has been popularly adopted to categorize what the American press perceives as anybody's self-serving publicism: administration disinformation, Pentagon disinformation, CIA disinformation, and even the tobacco lobby's disinformation. It seems that not all people who use the term actually understand it.

Perhaps the most accurate translation of the Russian word *dezinformatsiia* is deception. In KGB operational parlance, it refers to the use of partially accurate or totally false information to deceive individuals, groups, or governments into believing or acting in ways that will advance the interests of the sponsor, and to do so in such a way that the sponsor's identity is concealed and the target does not realize he is being deceived. Thus, disinformation is a special, usually covert, means of persuasion that utilizes propaganda as its resource material.

Stanislav Levchenko emphasized that *dezinformatsiia* was a term he used only within the KGB. Central Committee instructions never spelled out specific types of operations; they called for various executive agencies to take whatever "measures or actions" (*mery ili aktsii*) were needed to accomplish agreed upon policy strategies. In carrying out propaganda and counterpropaganda operations, disinformation is a tactic used with considerable frequency by the KGB; its military counterpart, the Main Intelligence Directorate (GRU); and functionaries of the Central Committee's International Department through agents of influence, front organizations, and foreign communist and the left wings of socialist parties.[26]

For the most part, disinformation operations use black or gray propaganda (previously mentioned). Black propaganda is information attributed to someone other than the actual purveyor; in the case of gray propaganda, the identity of the information source is concealed or obfuscated. Even overt (white) propaganda can be used. A Soviet newspaper may replay a story that was planted in the Indian press by a KGB co-optee. Sometime later, in Mexico City, a KGB officer under journalistic cover may suggest that his contact report the story in a local daily. He will insist, however, that the Mexican item be sourced to the original Indian story: How else could a Soviet journalist in Mexico know about an article in a Hindu newspaper?

Two recent examples illustrate how the USSR employs disinformation. When Soviet fighter planes shot down KAL flight 007 in September 1983, killing all 269 passengers and crew members aboard, the USSR was greeted with worldwide opprobrium. Six days passed before the Soviets even admitted they had intercepted the airliner; until then, official propaganda maintained that KAL 007 had left Soviet airspace before it inexplicably crashed into the sea. Faced with a rash of criticism detrimental to the peacemaker image they were trying to portray, the Soviets set out to diffuse it with counterpropaganda: They began an offensive that has continued for over two years, charging the United States with sending the passenger plane over the USSR on a spy mission. To support this claim, which they have maintained in the face of an authoritative report to the contrary by the International Civil Aviation Organization, the Soviets have used a variety of propaganda techniques, including disinformation. Soviet fabricators, almost certainly the KGB, published a glossy booklet entitled *The President's Crime*, allegedly authored by one Akio Takahashi. It was supposedly written first in Japanese and then translated into Russian—although the reverse is probably true. It has since been translated and distributed in several Western languages, including English. And no one has been able to prove that Akio Takahashi even exists.[27]

During April 1985, in connection with the United Nations' International Youth Year, the Jamaican Government hosted a youth festival attended by hundreds of delegates from more than 50 countries. The attendees represented the left, right, and center of the political spectrum; had spirited arguments and discussions; but, at last, issued a manifesto calling for international observance of human rights and the preservation of the democratic process. Even before the festival took place, the Soviets sought to disrupt it and diffuse any publicity that might contrast unfavorably with their own controlled, regimented youth extravaganza held at Moscow in late July. Predictably, official Soviet propaganda portrayed the Jamaica festival as a CIA-sponsored reactionary powwow. In addition, the KGB attempted to prevent young people from the Third World from attending; one scurrilous effort was a leaflet in bad French warning prospective delegates that Acquired Immune Deficiency Syndrome (AIDS) was rampant in Jamaica.

Exploitation of Foreign Officials and Journalists

George Bailey has described a key difference between the approaches of American and USSR journalists: "As contradistinct from the Soviet media, the American media are out to criticize the government, not to praise and popularize it."[28] This is a phenomenon the Soviets have long understood. The post-Vietnam/Watergate era has produced what Bailey calls a "mediacracy," a community of television, radio, and newspaper personalities that exerts powerful influence on public opinion and, thereby, on the policies of the United States government. The Soviets are well aware of the seminal role of the American media and, during the past five years, they have highly exploited their accessibility to it.

The KGB may have many agents among foreign journalists, ready at any time to place prepared stories in their national media; yet, according to Dzhirkvelov, the majority of Soviet press placements are *not* accomplished via officially recruited or co-opted sources. As a KGB operative posing as a journalist, Dzhirkvelov simply offered information to his Western counterparts, making no secret that he knew it would be reported. He generally used the following approach: "I would say, for example, that I am a Soviet journalist and no one will believe me if I write this story. But if you write it, it will be believed." Often, this was enough to pass along what the KGB referred to as "rumors" that would whet the professional appetites of foreign journalists. Occasionally, foreign contacts would accept payment—not agreeing to any long-standing relationship but simply on a one-time basis.

Any Soviet official, scholar, or journalist abroad may indulge in such "rumor-planting"—another euphemism for spreading propaganda— even if he is not a member of the KGB. This is especially true in the United States, where the Soviets seem to have a fertile field for implantation. The increasing visibility of Soviet officials and journalists on American television screens and newspaper pages has given them new respectability; to an uncomfortably large number of unsuspecting viewers, it has lent credence to their pronouncements, even when these Soviet spokesmen are guilty of distorting reality, or of downright untruthfulness.

In mid-September 1985, a week after Gorbachev's *Time* interview appeared on the newsstands and two weeks before Shevardnadze's visit to Washington, the ubiquitous Soviet specialist on the United States,

Georgii Arbatov, appeared on a nationwide U.S. television talk show. Viewers from around the country called in with questions, some quite provocative in nature. Arbatov fielded each query with practiced aplomb, answering with such ingenuous sincerity and good humor that even those who recognized his mendacity were forced to admire his skill. Asked whether an American official could appear on Soviet television to explain U.S. policies to the Soviet public, Arbatov replied: "Many Americans have appeared on Soviet television." At the end, after a few more, equally difficult questions, Arbatov lamented that the American people have misconceptions about the policies of the Soviet Union. He said this is because the Reagan administration feeds them misinformation through the press: "Freedom of the press in America is a myth."[29]

CONCLUSION

Soviet foreign propagandists of the 1980s are knowledgeable and sophisticated. They have at their disposal an empire of media, agencies, and experts; a supportive government structure; and a legacy of experience unmatched anywhere else in the world. The democratic traditions and open society of the West, especially in the United States, afford them unlimited opportunities to spread influence and information that serves the interests of Soviet foreign policy—an advantage obviously not shared by Western officials and journalists in the Soviet bloc. Smiling, polished, and confident, they have come a long way since the commissars and the Comintern and since Khrushchev used his shoe to drive home his challenge to the West.

Yet we must never forget that the affable correspondents and seemingly flexible officials are still bound by the ideological underpinnings of Soviet-style communism and that their overriding goals have not changed since the time of Lenin. Although we can appreciate and even welcome the well-tailored suits and smooth rhetoric of Mikhail Gorbachev, we should remember what Nikita Khrushchev said in 1955: "Our smiles are genuine. We wish to live in peace and tranquility. But if anyone believes that our smiles involve abandonment of the teachings of Marx, Engels, and Lenin, he deceives himself poorly. Those who wait for that must wait until a shrimp learns to whistle."[30]

Discussion

Walter F. Hahn

I agree with Lisa Jameson's implication that we tend to trivialize the Soviet version of the phenomenon when we call it "propaganda," let alone when we refer to it in the same breath as American "public diplomacy." As a society, we first became aware of the term *propaganda* in the context of Nazi Germany and Dr. Josef Goebbels. Based on that experience, in the United States the word still connotes a shady practice of propagating untruths. Open (ergo honest) democratic systems do not engage in such practices: They convey the truth through information services and public diplomacy. As was demonstrated by the defeat of Nazi Germany and its propaganda, truth ultimately prevails. Among the idealistic luggage we tote into the international arena, this is only one piece.

We denigrate Soviet propaganda if we equate it with public diplomacy, an activity that is, by definition, "aboveboard." As Michael Ledeen has pointed out, in the Soviet phenomenon we confront a seamless web that stretches from pronouncements in *Pravda* to influence operations and other covert activities. Most of the phenomenon functions because of its lack of visibility. Even if we designate propaganda as the more-or-less visible part of the Soviet spectrum of political and psychological warfare, we are dealing with something that is completely integrated into the Soviet external modus operandi.

The editor of *Problems of Communism*, Paul Smith, has characterized Soviet propaganda as a "strategic weapons system." The description is apt in several salient respects. First, there is the technological dimension. Until World War II, the effectiveness of the instrument was limited by its reach. Even the advent of radio and, particularly, shortwave transmission—which were seized upon by Goebbels in his pioneering work on a "science of propaganda"—largely restricted the impact of the weapon to a tactical arena of neighboring target societies. Since in the German case these societies were the principal objectives of deception and conquest, the weapon's range was effective enough.

Today, the intervening revolution in communications has given the propaganda weapon both extended range (that is, intercontinental dimensions) and the multiplier of the "echoing" effect within the target society. This revolution has also dramatically raised the stakes of propaganda warfare. It is not only a generalized process of persuasion and deception aimed at target societies but also a "precision-guided" process to penetrate to the heart of a nation's policy mechanism. It can be targeted over time to effect changes in its public mind-set. The chief orchestrators in the CPSU Central Committee's International Department use this instrument in such a comprehensive manner.

However, the weapons system of propaganda is strategic in a more direct military sense. Although peace campaigns have been a staple of Soviet propaganda since the Bolshevik Revolution, the current peace offensive (in its truly offensive case, distinguishing it from past efforts) dates back to the Twentieth Party Congress in 1956 and is integrally related to the Soviet buildup in strategic forces that has unfolded since that time. At that congress, Nikita Khrushchev not only banished the ghost of Stalin but also modified the heretofore sacrosanct Leninist tenet of the "inevitability of war with capitalism." The Khrushchevian revision was clearly mandated by the advent of nuclear weapons and its implications for the fate of the "homeland of socialism" in an "inevitable" conflict. Yet the revision did not deviate from Lenin's prediction that capitalism would ultimately lash out before succumbing to socialism; instead, it held that such a reaction could not be permitted with nuclear weapons.

It is from this doctrinal platform that Khrushchev inaugurated his "new look" policy of emphasis on nuclear weapons and launched the Soviet buildup that gathered such massive momentum in the late 1960s. Behind all this is the doctrine of what I like to call the overwhelming counterdeterrent. The objective was, and remains, to assemble the kind of vastly superior nuclear arsenal that would, in the best case, deter even an irrational lashing out by capitalism in its death throes or, in the worst case (that is, "if imperialism nevertheless unleashes a war"), bring the conflict to a rapid and victorious conclusion with minimum damage to the Soviet base.

Khrushchev and his immediate successors realized that the Soviet Union could not aspire to the ultimate objective of overwhelming strategic superiority in the face of determined competition from the United

States, with its inherent technological advantages. The imperative, therefore, was to invoke all possible means of psychological warfare both to cover the thrust of the Soviet buildup, which the USSR did successfully until at least the early 1970s, and to inhibit United States responses. The peace offensive—which Aleksei Kosygin summoned already at the Twentieth Party Congress and which was subsumed under the concepts of "peaceful coexistence" and "détente"—became an essential part of the total strategy. The doctrinal nexus explains why the offensive is markedly escalated at the slightest indication of a U.S. countermilitary effort, as it has been during the Reagan administration.

There is nothing ingenious in Soviet propaganda thrusts in the strategic arena. They trade upon crude themes and their repetition—unmindful of, or uncaring about, the manifold contradictions in those themes. The current, frenzied Soviet campaign against President Reagan's Strategic Defense Initiative (SDI) is a prime example. In Soviet anti-SDI pronouncements, two themes are presented, without any adequate transition between them: (1) it is inherently impossible for the United States to put up an effective defense against ballistic missiles and (2) "Star Wars" represents the road to a United States "first-strike" posture against the Soviet Union.

The contradictions are partly a function of the "playback" phenomenon. Soviet propaganda campaigns directed against particular U.S. weapons systems capitalize strongly on Western arguments. In the process, they apparently pay little attention to sorting out the contradictions among such arguments. Occasionally the Soviet playback technique reflects a veritable bonanza of ammunition delivered to them from the West; for example, the issue of "yellow rain" and evidence that the Soviets have been practicing chemical warfare in Southeast Asia and Afghanistan. When evidence came to light in 1982, and the issue was pressed by the United States, the Soviets were clearly on the defensive, responding with contemptuous denials. A group of American academicians headed by Professor Matthew S. Meselson of Harvard University proposed the much-publicized thesis that yellow rain was attributable, not to chemical warfare, but to the innocuous phenomenon of bee feces. The Soviets adopted this thesis with alacrity. In the meantime, the substantial samplings of bee feces collected in Southeast Asia by Meselson and his colleagues reportedly did not contain any of the mycotoxins that were present in the original evidence of yellow rain. The bee feces thesis has thus collapsed, but the Soviets continue to promote it, aided by the fact that U.S. "public diplomacy" fails even to elevate the discredited information on which they trade.

This playback technique has been even more blatant in the case of the so-called "nuclear winter." In the last several years, a group of American scientists (prominent among them the "popularizer" Carl Sagan) have advanced the hypothesis that the detonations in a nuclear war would generate climatic effects with devastating consequences for human life and its sustenance. This nuclear winter hypothesis has rested thus far on tenuous assumptions and computer models; nevertheless, it gained wide publicity in the West. The Soviets were quick to encourage the theme: They dispatched a group of their own scientific experts (all with somewhat questionable credentials) to various Western forums to provide ostensibly "independent confirmation" of the findings of Sagan and others. But as Leon Gouré has pointed out in a well-documented article in *Strategic Review* (Summer 1985), the Soviet "scientists" have failed to submit any independent analysis or findings: Their presentations have almost completely mirrored Western data, scenarios, and computer models.

The function of these scientists-propagandists indicates an institutional incentive behind the playback technique. Since information, especially that relevant to policy, is tightly compartmentalized in the secrecy-obsessed Soviet system, it is presumably easier for propagandists to operate with Western sources than with the leadership's carefully doled out information. This does not change the fact, however, that Soviet propaganda battens on and magnifies our "propaganda against ourselves."

There are vulnerabilities in the Soviet propaganda offensive. The contradictions are there to be exploited: This applies fully to the larger contradiction inherent in the Soviet peace offensive. As a closed society, the Soviets can carefully craft their propaganda issues for export and domestic consumption. Thus, the peace offensive has been directed strictly outward, with the obvious fear that its spillage into the domestic arena could prove debilitating to the leadership's policies and intentions, particularly with respect to the Soviet military buildup. Indeed, the peace offensive abroad has been counterpointed by a conspicuous martialization at home, focused especially on Soviet youth.

This insulation between outward and inward theme projections has not been completely successful. There are no indications of even the stirrings of a peace movement in the Soviet Union comparable to those that have sprouted in the West. Yet there are signs of problems (for example, increasing evasion of military conscription) that could be attributed to some small measure of backlash from the peace offensive.

The target of any potential Western counteroffensive is clear: to break the hermetic seals that bar the Soviet population from the outside world, from a true assessment of their leadership and its policies, and from a contemplation of their own lot. The technological means for such breakage may be increasingly apparent. But more than the means, we need a comprehensive recognition of the propaganda arena into which we have been placed, despite our societal preferences, and of a strategy to cope with it, even one that heeds our ideal of the truth.

Wallace Spaulding

I would like to comment on Mrs. Jameson's brief allusion to the use of Soviet-line international communist front organizations as propaganda vehicles in discussing the front technique and some recent developments. Fronts serve to unite diverse elements in the pursuit of a common goal and/or to provide an organizational framework that conceals the true control element. Between ten and fifteen Soviet-line worldwide fronts do both. Communist participation is not concealed because demonstrating that such groups can work together with noncommunists is an important (though not paramount) goal of their activity.

The paramount objective of these Soviet-line fronts is to enhance the credibility of the USSR foreign policy line by having it put forward by those who are, apparently, less self-serving and more objective than the communists themselves. For this reason, the president/chairman (titular head) and secretary general (working head) of such organizations are never Soviets. Although the main targets and best possibilities are afforded the USSR by left-wing socialists (developed world) or semicommunist "revolutionary democrats" (Third World), there is an ever present reach toward the political right. Having a centrist enunciate the Soviet line is more effective; a conservative playing such a role is "pure gold."

The primary problem for the USSR in this activity has been a gradual erosion in the fronts' credibility, both as different groups have withdrawn when they came into conflict with the Soviets (for example, the Yugoslavs, the Chinese, and the Albanians) and as the fronts themselves took a pro-Moscow line or remained silent when the more unseemly aspects of USSR foreign policy surfaced (for example, Hungary in 1956, Czechoslovakia in 1968, Afghanistan in 1979, and Poland in

1981–82). Although the old fronts still continue in their traditional activity (they have no effective "free world" competition, except in the trade union field), their personnel are being used in a new and seemingly more effective way; that is, as core cadres in informal groupings and new organizations, wherein the Soviet hand is not so evident.

A recent example is the attack on the Strategic Defense Initiative (SDI, currently the primary Soviet propaganda theme) sponsored by 36 world-renowned personalities whose names appeared in the 5 July 1985 issue of the *International Herald Tribune*. World Peace Council (WPC) president Romesh Chandra was noted as being connected with the WPC, the most important of the Soviet-line worldwide fronts. Six other signatories were identified with national WPC affiliates: half are members of the WPC's Presidential Committee (top 200 plus); two-thirds (24) are members of the WPC per se (2,000 plus members); and the remaining one-third are new persons, drawn in to give the appeal an even more enhanced credibility.

Currently, the major Soviet propaganda theme for the Third World involves a certain interpretation of the U.N.-sponsored New International Economic Order, a plan to redress the imbalance between the developed and underdeveloped worlds. A subcategory focuses on the campaign to have Latin American countries unilaterally cancel their foreign debts. Although led by Fidel Castro, the initiative is strongly endorsed by the Soviets. Castro's landmark statement on the subject in an interview with Mexico City's *Excelsior* (21 March 1985) was replayed by Moscow's TASS (28 March) and by the WPC's monthly *Peace Courier* (July, no. 7), and bimonthly *New Perspectives* (July, no. 4). Castro suggested that Western governments reimburse their respective creditor banks for the debts incurred by Latin American countries from funds saved by cutting defense expenditures about 10 to 12 percent. It represented a perfect complement to the above-mentioned anti-SDI campaign and the concurrent one to keep American intermediate-range nuclear forces (INF) out of the Netherlands; if any such defense cutback were to be made by the United States, it is logical that these newly planned programs would be the first to suffer.

Castro's use of fronts in the antidebt campaign has been innovative. Castro organized two conferences, held in Havana, of Latin American regional fronts to promote the debt proposal: the Continental Front of Women (June 1985) and the Federation of Latin American Journalists (FELAP, July 1985). Although these relatively new organizations have a core group of persons also involved in their worldwide Soviet-line counterparts (the Women's International Democratic Federation and the International Organization of Journalists, respectively), they incorporate more than just the Latin Americans involved in FELAP and are less identified in the popular mind as Soviet-controlled organizations.

Two other Havana conferences—one for Latin American trade unionists (July 1985) sponsored by the World Federation of Trade Unions, the other for Latin American youth (September 1985) sponsored by the World Federation of Democratic Youth—also included more than just the Latin American adherents of the sponsoring fronts in advocating nonpayment of external debts.

Finally, Castro hosted a Havana conference with more than 1,200 Latin American political personalities in late July and early August 1985 to promote nonpayment of international debts. Although this conference was dominated by leftists—for example, of the 134 speakers, there were eight communist party chiefs, ten WPC members, other front leaders, and notable out-of-power Latin American politicians—centrists and even conservatives attended.

Castro's techniques in these five conferences were the same. He personally attended virtually every session, mingled with the delegates on the floor, answered questions from the audience, gave extensive statements to the press, and made at least one of the major addresses at each conference. By doing all this, he tended to dominate openly the proceedings and thus went against the front "spirit." This spirit was provided, however, by having the noncommunist leftists, centrists, and even the few conservatives address and/or chair sessions. Although they did not always agree with the Castro line, they were nonetheless identified in the mind of the Latin American publics with the conference and its antirepayment theme. In addition to the absence of direct sponsorship by well-known Soviet-line worldwide fronts, this certainly appeared to enhance the credibility of the theme.

Harriet Fast Scott

The Trojan Horse, with its deadly cargo, was welcomed at first. None of the Trojans were suspicious when they rolled the Greeks' "gift" horse into their midst. For nearly twenty years, the Soviet Union has been using a contemporary version of the Trojan Horse to further Soviet foreign propaganda aims, namely, the institutes of the USSR Academy of Sciences, particularly those like Georgii Arbatov's Institute of the USA and Canada.

A great deal has been written about Arbatov's institute. Hundreds of Americans, from congressmen to visiting students, have been processed through his organization. Arbatov and his stable of *Amerikanisti* researchers are frequent participants in seminars and conferences throughout the United States, Canada, and Western Europe. They are polished, urbane, smiling, and confident; they have memorized the party-approved answers to any number of questions; and they speak English with charming accents. What is their origin and what are their missions?

TRAINING THE HORSE

The institute propagandists are not new. There is even information on how they are trained. Although the role of Boris Ponomarev and the late Mikhail Suslov in Soviet foreign propaganda has been discussed in an earlier paper, it was not mentioned that they were both trained at the Institute of Red Professors. This special school prepared social science teachers to serve in Soviet higher schools; and workers, in scientific research institutes or in central government and party organs. Organized by Lenin on 11 February 1918 in Moscow, the Institute of Red Professors was given general direction by the Agitation and Propaganda Department of the party Central Committee. The department's primary concern was to give the social sciences the correct Marxist-Leninist orientation.

Initially a single institute, by 1921 the Institute of Red Professors had three sections: economics, history, and philosophy. In 1928 several more were added, and in 1931 the original institute was divided into several independent institutes: history, history of the party, natural sciences, economics, and philosophy. Instructors at the Institute of Red Professors included A. S. Bubnov, E. S. Varga, A. M. Deborin, A. V. Lunacharskii, and E. M. Iaroslavskii. In addition to Ponomarev and Suslov, the graduates have included N. A. Voznesenskii, I. I. Mints, P. N. Pospelov, and A. Ia. Pelshe.

The institute was originally located in Moscow at 53 Ostozhenka Street (in the 1930s this street was renamed Metrostroevskaia). Today the Moscow State Institute of International Relations (MGIMO) is in the building that once housed the Institute of Red Professors. MGIMO was founded in 1946 and graduated its first class in 1949, which included Georgii Arbatov; Nikolai Inozemtsev, the late director of the Institute of World Economy and International Relations (IMEMO, the parent institute of Arbatov's think tank and other similar ones); and Vadim Zagladin, first deputy head of the International Department of the Central Committee. Among later graduates were Iurii Bobrakov (1950), Vitalii Zhurkin (Arbatov's deputy), Genrikh Trofimenko, and Vladimir Krestianov (1951). Another 1951 graduate was Dzherman Gvishiani, son-in-law of the late Aleksei Kosygin.

One of the early post–World War II instructors at MGIMO was Anatolii Dobrynin, the Soviet ambassador to the United States since 1962. Presently, MGIMO is a favorite school for the sons and daughters of the *nomenklatura* members. As a rule, graduates receive very favorable assignments, both domestically and abroad. Throughout their careers, graduates utilize the MGIMO old-school network.

THE STABLES

After the horse has been thoroughly trained by MGIMO, he needs a place to practice his skills. Initially, the primary stable was the Communist Academy (founded in 1918 as the Socialist Academy) located at 14 Volkhonka, adjacent to the present Pushkin Museum of Fine Arts. Unlike the Institute of Red Professors, which trained students, the Communist Academy performed research functions. It housed a number of institutes, including those on world economy and world politics, economics, history, and philosophy. In 1936, to gain a cloak of respectability outside the USSR, the institutes of the Communist Academy were placed under the USSR Academy of Sciences, where they have remained through the present.

During Stalin's purges of the 1930s, the institutes experienced shake-ups. Many disbanded. The Institute of World Economy and World Politics finally closed in 1947; its remnants became incorporated into the Department of Contemporary Capitalist Economy within the Institute of Economics of the USSR Academy of Sciences. The department was the base for the Institute of World Economy and International Relations (IMEMO), formed in 1956.

In 1967 the CPSU Central Committee adopted a resolution to revamp the social sciences, and subsequently, a number of new institutes were formed: the Institute of the International Workers' Movement, the Institute of Scientific Information for the Soviet Sciences (INION, in the same building that once housed the library of the Communist Academy), and the Institute of the USA (later, the USA and Canada). In addition, other institutes were revitalized: the institutes of the Far East, Oriental Studies, Africa, Latin America, and the Economics of the World Socialist System.

THE GOAL

In 1972 Vadim V. Zagladin delineated the purpose of the Trojan Horse:

> The CPSU Central Committee orients the Academy of Sciences' scientific collectives toward elaboration of urgent questions concerning world development, primarily, the entire world revolutionary process. The Resolution (of 1967) stressed that these problems need to be elaborated not only for scientific purposes but also for practical Party activity and *for determining the most effective ways and means to insure socialism's victory over capitalism.*[31] (Emphasis added.)

In other words, the real race of the Trojan Horse focuses on winning the jewels of horse racing, the Triple Crown—that is, spreading Soviet propaganda in the foreign, domestic, and summit arenas.

In the foreign arena, Ambassador Dobrynin has already been mentioned in relation to fulfilling this function abroad. Arbatov's institute and IMEMO are well known in practically every West European capital. Genrikh Trofimenko is as familiar to defense intellectuals in Paris and Bonn as he is to those in Washington and San Francisco.

In the Soviet domestic arena, visiting VIPs are funneled through the Institute of the USA and Canada. Presidential hopefuls, American research institute directors, university presidents and professors are escorted by young polished Soviet graduate students in tailored suites, if male, or in fashionable dress, if female. General M. A. Milshtein, a former faculty member of the General Staff Academy and presently a member of Arbatov's staff, whispers dire warnings about military matters into eager ears, with disarming ease and apparent frankness.

But the jewel of the Triple Crown is the summit meeting of the general secretary, at which the Trojan Horse runs hardest to win. Whereas he can use interviews with leading newspapers or journals of the other side's domestic territory, his counterpart is denied reciprocal access to the Soviet media. He places full-page advertisements in leading Western newspapers that promote Moscow's current line. He appears on television news shows, rising early in the morning, if necessary, for a live appearance; all questions are fielded with the skill of a juggler; and there are always clever answers, some to questions that were not asked.

The Trojan Horse particularly likes to refer to God. Knowing somehow that godless communism has been a thorn in the side of many people abroad, he takes pains to say "God forbid" (Khrushchev); "God will never forgive us" (Brezhnev in Vienna, 1979); or "God on high" (Gorbachev, *Time*, 1985). Many people are convinced that even a good communist secretly believes in God. With the Trojan Horse inside the walls, the populace was quickly overcome.

NOTES

1. George Kennan, *The Marquis de Custine and His "Russia in 1839"* (London: Hutchinson, 1972), pp. 80–81.

2. V. I. Lenin, *What Is to Be Done*, in Robert C. Tucker, ed., *The Lenin Anthology* (New York: W. W. Norton, 1975), p. 52.

3. Vladimir Voinovich, "Soviet Anti-Soviet Propaganda," *The Spectator*, 24 August 1985, p. 9.

4. Author's interview with Viktor Belenko in September 1983.

5. Voinovich, "Soviet Anti-Soviet Propaganda," p. 9.

6. George Bailey, *Armageddon in Prime Time* (New York: Avon Books, 1985), p. 64.

7. Gorbachev's presence at this conference was the fullest confirmation up to that time that he had assumed supervision of ideology and culture within the Secretariat of the Central Committee. See Archie Brown, "Gorbachev: New Man in the Kremlin," *Problems of Communism* 34, no. 3 (May–June 1985): 1–23.

8. Closing speech to All-Union Conference on "The Perfecting of Developed Socialism and the Ideological Work of the Party in the Light of the Decisions of June 1983 Plenum of the Central Committee," *Pravda*, 12 December 1984.

9. See Archie Brown, "Gorbachev."

10. See Elizabeth Teague, Radio Liberty Research Report 237/85, summarized in *RFE/RL Soviet East European Report* 2, no. 31 (10 August 1985).

11. In the December 1984 speech, Gorbachev used the same Leninist formulation that Andropov had quoted in an address to the Central Committee Plenum of 22 November 1982, one week after Brezhnev's funeral. Revealing reformist tendencies, Gorbachev said it was "important to run ahead of the times" and that "one should not confuse what has already been attained with that which is desired." For a more complete discussion, see Elizabeth Teague, RL 474/84, summarized in *RFE/RL Soviet East European Report* 88, no. 8 (20 December 1984).

12. See Teague (RL 474/84) and an excellent short study of the CPSU Central Committee Secretariat by Alexander Rahr in *Radio Liberty Research*, RL 439/84, 16 November 1984.

13. Quoted in *The Economist*, 10 August 1985; the source for Ligachev's comments was not given.

14. *Time*, 9 September 1985, pp. 22–29.

15. *Pravda*, 31 August 1985.

16. Interviewed by author: Stanislav Levchenko on 7 September 1985; and Ilia Dzhirkvelov on 18 September 1985.

17. Zhores Medvedev, *Andropov* (New York: W. W. Norton, 1983), p. 185.

18. "Ponomarev at Eighty," *Soviet Analyst* (London, 23 January 1985), p. 8.

19. Robert W. Kitrinos, "The International Department of the CPSU," *Problems of Communism* 33, no. 5 (September–October 1984): 49.

20. Edward H. Carr, *The Bolshevik Revolution*, vol. 1: 137–38, as quoted in Roy Godson, ed., *Intelligence Requirements for the 1980s: Covert Action* (New Brunswick, N.J.: National Strategy Information Center, 1981), p. 169.

21. Personal interviews with Levchenko and Dzhirkvelov, previously cited.

22. Dzhirkvelov related this information in a personal conversation on 18 September 1985.

23. Personal interview with Dzhirkvelov. See also John Barron, *The KGB Today* (New York: Reader's Digest Press, 1984), p. 447.

24. *The Economist*, 10 August 1985.

25. Arthur Koestler, *Darkness at Noon* (New York: Bantam Classics, 1975), p. 193.

26. Disinformation is discussed in great detail in U.S. Congress, House of Representatives, Permanent Select Committee on Intelligence, *Hearings on Soviet Active Measures*, 13 and 14 July 1982, 97th Cong., 2d sess. (Washington, D.C.: Government Printing Office, 1982).

27. For a full discussion of the Soviet KAL campaign, see Thomas Maertens, "Tragedy of Errors," *Foreign Service Journal* 62, no. 8 (September 1985): 24–31.

28. Bailey, *Armageddon*, p. 92.

29. Larry King interview with Arbatov, Cable News Network, 17 September 1985.

30. *International Affairs* (Moscow), January 1956, p. 2, quoted in N. H. Mager and Jacques Katel, comps. and eds., *Conquest Without War: An Analytical Anthology of the Speeches, Interviews, and Remarks of Nikita Sergeyevich Khrushchev, with commentary by Lenin, Stalin, and others* (New York: Pocket Books, 1961), p. 310 n12.

31. V. V. Zagladin, "The Revolutionary Process and the International Policy of the USSR," *Kommunist*, no. 13 (September 1972): 15.

3

THE POLITICAL SUBVERSION OF WESTERN EUROPE

Michael A. Ledeen

The Greek operation of the USSR Committee on State Security (KGB) from the mid-1970s to the present may eventually be recognized as the most ambitious example of political subversion of a West European country. The Greek case exposes the KGB at its most arrogant and aggressive, generally not even bothering to carefully hide its own direct involvement in the internal affairs of Greece. Even today, without the usual lag in our understanding of such matters, we can see the broad outlines of the design and many of the details of the operational plan: first, restructuring the national political debate in such a way that all discussion occurs within the comfortable context of Moscow's worldview; to achieve this, establishing maximum possible control over the mass media; and, once this has been accomplished, ruthlessly attacking those who dare to challenge this cultural hegemony.

The window through which we have been able to view the KGB's Greek operation is the Paul Anastasi Affair, in which a distinguished journalist for the *New York Times* and the *London Telegraph* wrote a book about the KGB's involvement in Greece's most popular daily newspaper, *Ethnos*, and was subsequently sued for libel by the paper. In the course of Anastasi's research and his ensuing legal and political woes, a remarkable amount of information has been acquired. Unfortunately, his book on the KGB's involvement has been published only in Greek, and although there has been a fair amount of Western press coverage of the affair, this has tended to focus primarily on the legal cases rather than on the data that Anastasi presented in his published work. My analysis is based on a rough English version of his book, on interviews with

Greeks involved in one way or another in the affair, and on published accounts in both Greek and English.[1]

THE GENERAL FUND:
GREECE'S RUSSIAN SUGAR DADDIES

The Soviets decided to mount a massive disinformation operation in Greece by the mid 1970s, and they systematically established a "legitimate" publishing house in Athens and arranged for its funding—independent of the local communist party or official Soviet businesses. It may be that this operation stemmed from their considerable success during the same period in combating the proposed deployment of American neutron weapons in Western Europe. Although the Greeks did not play a major role in the debate over the neutron bomb, the Soviet campaign was directed against all NATO publics, and thus something had to be done in Greece and in the more important Central European nations such as Germany, France, and Italy. In any event, the themes that the Soviets developed in the Greek effort were strikingly similar to those used to fight Carter's proposed deployment, and they remain the same themes that the Soviets are now using against "Star Wars": Soviet weapons are defensive and not threatening, except when Soviet spokesmen threaten to use them against Europe if the Europeans do not accommodate Soviet politics, whereas American weapons are considered to be offensive and disruptive to efforts to achieve peaceful East-West relations.

In many respects, the business phase of the Soviet Greek operation resembles the methods they used in Italy in the years following the end of World War Two, when a plethora of communist activities was financed through import-export companies and otherwise normal businesses.[2] In the Italian case, the import-export firms paid commissions at each end: generally 3 percent to the communist-bloc country or cooperative with whom the transaction was performed and another 3 percent to the Italian cooperative, or front company, or directly to the Italian Communist Party (PCI). Ironically, this occasionally made some businessmen wealthy enough to break their ties with the PCI and even with the Soviet Union (as in the celebrated case of Dino Gentili), but their gratitude to the Soviets was generally sufficient to guarantee their public silence about the overall operation.

In Greece, the Soviets adopted similar methods, with mixed results: A great deal of money was produced, and a new newspaper, which has achieved superlative results, was launched. In the process, however,

Yannis Yannikos, a member of the pro-Soviet Communist Party of Greece (KKE) and one of the original partners in the operation, had to be bribed after he made damaging revelations. In May 1976, Yannikos signed an agreement with the Soviet Copyright Agency (VAAP) that gave him the right to publish the *Great Soviet Encyclopedia* in Greece. As in subsequent negotiations, top KGB officer Vasilii Romanovich Sitnikov was the key Soviet official in this agreement. Anastasi and Yannis Dimitriades, the authors of *The Soviet Infiltration of Greece*, both claim that Sitnikov was the deputy director of the KGB's Disinformation Department of Service A.[3]

From the beginning, the Soviets were interested in pursuits larger than the publication and distribution of the *Great Soviet Encyclopedia:* The contract with Yannikos, in his own written court evidence some years later, "included the publishing of newspapers and other publications." Moreover, the Soviets were not content to have this operation run by an overt member of the KKE, and they insisted from the beginning that Yannikos find himself a "legitimate" business partner—someone with considerable financial assets. Yannikos initially approached the owner of the largest publishing group in the country, Lambrakis, who was intrigued by the proposal and signed an agreement with Yannikos that led to the creation of a company called Akademos, S.A. The following year, however, Lambrakis withdrew from the venture, upon discovering that the funding for the new publications was to be drawn from a series of commercial deals that the Soviets wanted to pass through Akademos. This was a serious setback for the KGB, and Sitnikov personally sat down with Lambrakis in an attempt to convince him to reconsider. Sitnikov failed, however, and Akademos was dissolved at the end of 1977, leaving Yannikos with the original rights (that is, he was entitled to use the name "Akademos").

At this point, George Bobolas, a shipping tycoon with a variety of commercial interests, appeared on the scene. In a few months, he and Yannikos had signed a series of agreements that laid the groundwork not only for the ultimate launching of *Ethnos*, the newspaper that would eventually be declared "the KGB's first fully owned and operated newspaper in Western Europe," but also for the commercial operations that apparently financed *Ethnos* and other publishing ventures that the Soviets found attractive.

The first agreement was dated 7 December 1977 and stipulated that Yannikos would share equally with Bobolas the rights under the original 1976 agreement, which had provided for the publication of the *Great Soviet Encyclopedia* and other commercial deals. In return, Bobolas agreed to finance both the encyclopedia publication and other ventures that would be arranged with the Soviets. It was also agreed that profits from the commercial ventures would be used for publication projects.

These details were spelled out with greater precision in the second agreement between Bobolas and Yannikos, this one dated 24 February 1978. In that agreement, the two promised that a publishing royalty of 8 percent of gross sales of the encyclopedia would be paid to VAAP and that Yannikos would assign publication rights to Akademos. Despite this agreement, however, no royalty was ever paid to the Soviets; instead, they signed an agreement with Akademos that provided for the company to conduct other publishing activities.

In March, there were two additional agreements between Bobolas and Yannikos. These spelled out Bobolas's obligations: 5 million drachmas to the company and 5 million, in the form of a loan, to Yannikos for his equity in Akademos. In addition, there were two intriguing details: All commercial deals with the Soviets had to be carried out through a new company (Overseas Trade and Transport, Inc.), and the profits that Akademos realized from these ventures were not to be removed but were to be rolled over into new publishing ventures. Finally, Yannikos and Bobolas were only entitled to a total of 30 percent of the profits from the commercial ventures, and the remaining 70 percent was to go entirely to financing Akademos's publishing activities.

In other words, the Soviets had swung their usual business deal with Western entrepreneurs: All of the hard cash came from the Greeks (in this case, from Bobolas), and the money was used exclusively to conduct activities approved by the Soviets. They would enable Bobolas and Yannikos to make profits through commercial deals that, incidentally, were quite useful to the Soviets in the area of technology transfer. The lion's share of these profits, however, did not go into the pockets of the Greek businessmen but were rolled over to finance the disinformation activities of the Soviet Union in Greece. Once Yannikos had served his function of organizing the operation and bringing Bobolas into the deal, he was summarily purged, with that cheerful disregard for loyalty that is the trademark of the Kremlin. Yannikos was a bit of an embarrassment to the KGB because he was a known communist, and the Soviets vastly preferred the successful capitalist Bobolas to manage their finances.

The break with Yannikos—significant because he would subsequently become one of the prime sources of information about these activities—occurred after a June 1978 meeting in Moscow that got the venture into high gear. Bobolas and Yannikos were present at this meeting as well as their "interpreter" Maria Beikou, the wife of a prominent Greek communist who served as the Moscow correspondent of the official communist party newspaper. The meeting produced several agreements, including one that provided for the publication of a volume entitled *Peace Is the Priceless Belonging of All People.* The highlight of this book was Brezhnev's introduction, in which he praised Akademos for its service in the promotion of Soviet ideals.

In August, Bobolas took a cruise on a chartered yacht with some of his Soviet friends, including Soviet ambassador Ivan Dachov and press attaché Evgenii Chistiakov, who was subsequently expelled for espionage. Yannikos was not invited, and just two days after the cruise ended, Bobolas forced through an increase in the capitalization of Akademos. This was clearly an effort to squeeze out Yannikos, a hypothesis that was confirmed when Bobolas failed to lend the necessary funds to him, even though their agreement required the loan. This established a pattern whereby Yannikos was eventually driven out of Akademos.

Later in the summer, Chernenko made an official visit to Athens as a guest of the Greek communists, and he attended a private party thrown in his honor by Bobolas. With his Soviet support solidly confirmed, Bobolas managed to compel Yannikos to accept a buyout proposal, and simultaneously, he started to funnel the Soviet commercial projects through other companies, with which Yannikos had no involvement. Ranging from aluminum factories to arms manufacture and involving various foreign firms (one of Bobolas' trading companies, Worldtech, had a 30 percent involvement of Control Data Corporation), these deals and projects were aimed at giving the Soviets access to Greek technology and, through Greece, the West in general. One study, for example, would have involved Soviet participation in a Greek military spare parts factory.

Bobolas thus came to play a role in two major Soviet projects in Greece: acquiring Western technology and laying the groundwork for a major disinformation campaign against NATO and, primarily, the United States. Sometime in late 1979, the Russians approved a proposal for the publication of a daily newspaper. Although Yannikos had been largely squeezed out of Akademos, the newspaper project was prepared by him in tandem with a Greek journalist. In early 1980, Bobolas acquired the title "Ethnos" from a publishing company, and by October, he announced his intention to launch a daily paper.

Its staff having been assembled over the preceding year, *Ethnos* was inaugurated in September 1981. In fact, Akademos hired most of the new people during this period, even though the publication of the encyclopedia was coming to a close and the new people were experienced in newspaper work, not book publishing. It had become obvious to Yannikos that his days in this project were numbered, and he sued Bobolas in several fora for violation of their agreements; Yannikos, however, discovered that the Soviets' major interest was Bobolas and the new newspaper. Sitnikov negotiated the final arrangements between Bobolas and Yannikos, even inviting Yannikos and his son to Moscow to facilitate the deal. The dispute between the two was finally resolved only on the eve of the Anastasi libel trial, with Yannikos receiving about $650,000 in return for agreeing not to testify. In one of their meetings, Sitnikov said to Yannikos, "Don't forget that Mr. Bobolas now owns *Ethnos*. And you know how important that newspaper is to us."[4]

Ethnos was, and indeed is, a great boon to the Soviet Union. In many respects, it is a caricature of the Soviet line, so undeviating is it in its support of Soviet policies and goals. On the subject of Poland, for example, the paper not only constantly attacked Solidarity and supported Jaruzelski but also did not even bother to report the pope's trip to Poland in the summer of 1983, except for a brief piece quoting the official Polish government spokesman. The Afghan resistance was described as "bandits, paid murderers who enter from Pakistan and commit horrendous crimes against the unarmed Afghan people, crimes which even the Nazis at the Auschwitz concentration camps would be jealous of." The difficulties in Afghanistan were described as "created to serve the new strategy of the USA, that is, the strategy of preparation for a nuclear war."[5]

The paper's American "commentator," Carl Aldo Marzani, lied about his membership in the American Communist Party during the war, when he served in the O.S.S. Marzani's articles have not been friendly to the United States government; in a piece over a year ago, he wrote that "the U.S. is sinking into a unique type of totalitarianism which American sociologists describe as fascism with a human face."

The British "commentator" of *Ethnos* has similar credentials: Stanley Harrison, recently retired as chief assistant editor of *Morning Star*, the official organ of the Communist Party of Great Britain. The Cyprus correspondent for *Ethnos* is Akis Fantis, the son of the alternate secretary-general of the Cypriot Communist Party (AKEL) and editor of its official newspaper.

With such a cast of characters, it is not surprising that the Soviet Union is regarded as a model for both social and foreign policy. *Ethnos* has described the USSR as "the first peace bloc in history," and its praise for Soviet accomplishments was perhaps most dramatically illustrated by the headline, "The Soviet Woman Is Not a Feminist—She Has No Reason to Struggle Since All Her Problems Are Solved."[6] Even when *Ethnos* alludes to Soviet shortcomings, the point is made in a most friendly and fraternal way; for example, an editorial called for a continuation of Andropov's reforms, even after his death: "Without the achievement of this objective, not only will the passage to communism remain an unfeasible dream, but also the Soviet Union, and by extension the people's democracies, will be endangered. After all, daily practice proves that confronting imperialism cannot only be done with arms. Economic sufficiency at a first stage, and economic abundance at a second stage, are also necessary."[7]

The constant theme of "confronting imperialism" (primarily, the role of NATO and Greece's role in the alliance) dominates *Ethnos*'s coverage of foreign news. In an interview in May 1984, Prime Minister Papandreou stated that "our strategic aim is the disengagement of our country from NATO," and *Ethnos* fully supports him in this goal.

PROBLEMS

The Anastasi book, *Take the Nation in Your Hands* (a pun since *ethnos* means "nation" in Greek), was an instant bestseller in 1983, at least until it was banned, pending the outcome of the newspaper's libel suit. *Ethnos* sued on the basis of Anastasi's claim that *Ethnos* was the first newspaper set up by the KGB's disinformation department in a Western country. The trial was not without its melodramatic moments: Yannikos, the prime witness for the defense, was apparently bribed by Bobolas and the Soviets at the last minute; allegedly, over $600,000 were required to buy his silence at the trial. His son Christos, however, confirmed under oath that Sitnikov had told his father that the Soviets considered *Ethnos* very important to them. The court agreed with Anastasi's claim that *Ethnos* regurgitated "raw Soviet propaganda" but still found him guilty of libel and sentenced him to two years in jail. He appealed, and while waiting for a hearing on the appeal, the Supreme Court ordered his sentence overturned.

Some of the courtroom language was as scurrilous as that normally used in the pages of *Ethnos*. Foreign journalists who came to serve as character witnesses for Anastasi were labeled "foreign agents," and "members of certain circles." *Ethnos* echoed these cries by referring to "this rabble of witnesses—British, German, Dutch, one Jew from racist South Africa, one American woman and one former Greek—appeared in Greece as provocative, aggressive, impertinent advocators of the insultor and slanderer and at the same time as perfect experts as to what benefits and what damages the Greek people."

Such assaults have failed to silence Anastasi, who has now launched a new, English-language newspaper in Greece, with a more balanced editorial policy than that of *Ethnos*. In the atmosphere following Papandreou's triumphal re-election, however, *Ethnos* and similar books and newspapers (some produced by Akademos; others, by different houses) evidently have had a real effect. In the end, the ceaseless din of disinformation overcomes at least a part of the audience's resistance. *Ethnos* is, by far, the slickest, most beautiful, and most popular daily newspaper in Greece. In the past several years, it has become the lodestar of Greek television and radio coverage of the world, and one can only expect this conformity to increase in the future.

Consequently, the country that gave democracy to the world may now have given us another innovation: the first case of the political subversion of a Western country through disinformation. If this outcome is to be averted, it will require all the courage and imagination of the West; commodities that have not been in abundant supply in the past decade.

THE PEACE CAMPAIGN

From 1981 to 1983, the Soviet Union mounted an unprecedented campaign against the deployment of United States ground-launched cruise missiles (GLCMs) and Pershing IIs in Western Europe. One area of particularly intense Soviet activity was the peace movement, aimed both at preventing the deployment and at separating the United States from its European allies. The peace campaign was a historic moment, prompting a NATO foreign minister, with more than 30 years of experience in such matters, to tell the United States government that he had never seen so much Soviet money spent in his country in such a short period of time. European intelligence services obtained abundant documentation of this Soviet activity, and on at least one instance the intelligence service report was leaked to the press–first in the Netherlands, then on German television. This was particularly explosive, since earlier, in parliamentary testimony, the Dutch interior minister had denied the existence of the report.[8] An analysis of the peace movement conducted by the German security service, *Bundesnachrichtendienst* (BND), was also leaked to the press, and it evidently contained similar conclusions.

The Dutch press quite naturally picked up on the story and enumerated the general outlines of Soviet activity:

> "Stop the Neutron Bomb" was partly supported financially by Moscow. Former Minister Dr. Van Thijn denied this a half year ago in the Second Chamber. The West German security service made these accusations in

a confidential report which was leaked last month in the Federal Republic, a report entitled, "Left Extremist Influence on the Peace Demonstration of 10 October 1981 in Bonn." The Second Chamber member Dr. Aad Wagenaar (RPF) will put a question this week about the report to the new Minister of Internal Affairs, Mr. M. Rood. Dr. Wagenaar stated yesterday that he had learned from reliable sources that the information which had been leaked in Germany is based on two reports of the Dutch internal security service. According to the Parliament member, "former Minister of Internal Affairs Drs. Van Thijn was playing bluff poker when, last year in September in the Second Chamber, he declared that there was only talk of a 'slander campaign' against the Dutch peace movement," said Drs. Wagenaar. On that occasion, the minister of internal affairs called the "so-called American evidence" for the contacts between the East bloc and the Dutch peace movement "neither rock solid nor butter soft."

"This West German report goes against the assertions of ex-Minister Van Thijn," claimed the RPF Second Chamber member. In the report of the West German BND, which was compiled in November 1981, it was said, there is no doubt that the Netherlands committee "Stop the Neutron Bomb" is led in an orthodox Communist manner, with financial assistance from the Soviet Union and with the aid of Russian functionaries from the international section of the Central Committee of the Communist Party. "Stop the Neutron Bomb" organized in the Netherlands actions against atomic arms in general and against the neutron bomb in particular. Orthodox Communists are also present in a number of cells of the IKV (Inter-Church Peace Council) according to the German security report.[9]

The German government was quite well informed about Soviet activities within its own peace movement, and Defense Minister Hans Apel was quite outspoken about the conclusions they had reached (surely without providing any sensitive information):

> "I heard your remarks, general, about the communist infiltration of these protests and I agree with you," West German Defense Minister Hans Apel snapped, interrupting his commanding officer, Major General Peter Tandecki.
>
> "There's no doubt about it. The money comes from them, the infrastructure. The bus arrives on time. The soup arrives on time. All those things which can only be organized by a military or paramilitary organization."
>
> . . . German authorities believe a sizable portion of the money needed to stage what was, in effect, a gigantic public spectacle was channeled through East Germany. Most of it came from the Evangelical Church there.

Funds from East of the Elbe also helped to finance last June's dress rehearsal for the Bonn rally, a church congress in Hamburg attended by 100,000 "peace partisans."[10]

There is further evidence from Scandinavia. In Norway, a leading peace activist by the name of Bjarne Eikefjord was quoted in a leading Norwegian newspaper as having obtained United States top secret documents that indicated American targeting of parts of Norway in the event of war. Eikefjord took these documents to the American Embassy, but only after passing them to the press. When experts looked carefully at the documents, they were found to be a recent version of old Soviet forgeries that had been circulated in the 1960s. These forgeries were based on stolen army documents passed to the Soviets by U.S. Army Sergeant Lee Johnson, who was subsequently convicted of espionage. Of course, the discovery that the documents were forged came long after the public relations splash accusing America of targeting an allied country.[11]

But the biggest Scandinavian scandal came from Denmark, where Foreign Minister Kjeld Olesen announced at a press conference in November 1981 that the second secretary (V. D. Merkulov) of the Soviet Embassy in Copenhagen had been expelled when found to have been a KGB officer running Soviet agents of influence in Denmark. The details of Merkulov's activities emerged in press accounts. It turned out that he had been the case officer for Arne Petersen, a Danish author who was active in the peace movement and who specialized in Korean affairs (Petersen was a long-time member of the Danish–North Korean Friendship Association).

Petersen was the inspiration behind an appeal, signed by 150 Danish artists, for the creation of a Nordic nuclear-free zone. Thanks to the money provided by Merkulov, Petersen had the appeal placed as an advertisement in several newspapers. In addition, he seems to have acted as a recruiting officer for the KGB within the peace movement, primarily among the journalistic community. In short, at Merkulov's behest Petersen was attempting to extend KGB influence, directly and indirectly, among the Danish mass media. For this activity, Petersen received about 10,000 Danish kroner over the years . . . and was arrested on 4 November 1981. In addition to controlling Petersen, Merkulov and other members of the Soviet Embassy in Copenhagen ran lines into the Committee of Cooperation for Peace and Security, an umbrella organization of about fifty small peace groups. The committee was closely tied to the World Peace Council, the Soviets' prime conduit for KGB funding of European peace groups.[12]

Although some of the details of these particular incidents may be new to some people, the general phenomenon is well known. The use of disinformation to augment other overt political campaigns is an integral part of Soviet political strategy throughout the world. In the West European cases that I have examined, the basic thrust of the KGB's efforts was to support the massive political effort to block the deployment of United States ground-launched cruise missiles (GLCMs) and Pershing IIs in NATO member countries. Of course, a similar effort is now underway to stop the testing of the U.S. Strategic Defense Initiative (SDI); and in both cases, the KGB has worked mightily to create an image of a warlike, threatening America and a peace loving Soviet Union that was dragged reluctantly into the arms race with the United States.[13]

The aggressiveness of the Soviet disinformation campaign sounds the same bellicose and uncompromising tone of most of the public rhetoric coming from the Kremlin. I witnessed one of the more spectacular examples of the Soviet "peace" campaign in Rome, where Boris Ponomarev, the grand old man of Stalinism, came on a state visit to talk with Italian Prime Minister Francesco Cossiga. On national television, Ponomarev said that it would be a shame if his country were compelled by the Italian decision to accept GLCMs to target "all those beautiful churches and monuments" with Soviet SS-20s. And Andrei Gromyko used similar language in Madrid when speaking of the consequences of a Spanish decision to enter the NATO alliance. In public and in private, both overtly and secretly, the Soviet Union acted as if the Politburo had concluded that the Kremlin could finally impose its political will on Western Europe.

In the past, the Soviets had often shown themselves capable of considerable subtlety in their political dealing with the Europeans. The heavy-handed meddling in the national press—exemplified by the *Ethnos* operation and, subsequently, repeated in the Italian case of the Soviet-sponsored publication *Guerra e Pace,* which even some PCI leaders identified as a Soviet operation—is quite different from the more refined techniques used by the likes of Pathé in France.

One can only speculate about the reasoning for the Soviets' openly aggressive behavior toward the Europeans in the mid and late 1970s. Soviet leaders may have concluded that there had been a decisive shift in the balance of power (a "positive correlation of forces") that could be translated into political gains. Alternatively, Brezhnev and others may have judged President Jimmy Carter to be so weak that the Europeans could not possibly resist a determined onslaught from the East. On the contrary, Soviet policy was dictated by a profound concern verging on alarm over the internal structural crisis of the Soviet system, which could have led Kremlin leaders to conclude that time was short and that they had to push hard for quick triumphs: If the long and medium terms looked dismal, prudent leadership would inevitably press for short-term gains.

Whatever the basis for their decision, the aggressive policies have not produced positive results, at least in terms of the specific campaigns against SDI and NATO intermediate-range nuclear force (INF) deployments. The Soviets, particularly the ill-fated Andropov, may have unwittingly helped to forge a new sense of Western unity that would never have been possible if the NATO member states had not been repeatedly threatened by the Kremlin. Had the Soviets undertaken a more patient, soothing approach to Western Europe, they might have achieved more advantageous results.

On the other hand, there have been clear political benefits to the Soviets. In the Federal Republic of Germany, the Social Democratic Party (SPD) now sends a delegation to meet with the East German communist party to discuss "peace" issues, the aim of which is to forge a common position. The evolution of the policies of the Greek government can only be viewed with alarm from Washington, and the triumphal re-election of the Papandreou government suggests that operations like *Ethnos* may be bearing fruit. Finally, although the Kremlin has not succeeded in splitting NATO at the Atlantic fault line, the relentless campaign against SDI has made the West Europeans more cautious in their support of the United States' position on this matter. Having failed in their short-term objectives, the Soviets may find themselves stronger than anticipated in the medium term.

Discussion

John J. Dziak*

Michael Ledeen outlines two striking examples of recent Soviet political action: the *Ethnos* case, or "the Paul Anastasi Affair"; and the peace campaign in Western Europe. Although little can be profitably added to Dr. Ledeen's descriptive analysis of these two cases, I will further probe the broader operational context of the Soviet political action tradition.

The Andropov-Gorbachev era may have witnessed the elevation of political action to new heights of sophistication, though a distinct operational style and predilection for such actions undergirds it all.[14] This includes a vocabulary or argot common to clandestine, criminal-like operatives. Having attracted considerable public and professional attention, historically active measures have included diversion, provocation, penetration, fabrication, disinformation, agents of influence, and combinations. Individually or combined, such terms have described numerous Soviet political warfare initiatives from the so-called Lockhart Plot and the Trust to the Change-of-Signposts Movement and the Tukhachevskii Affair.

Presently, the operatives in this business—that is, inside the Communist Party of the Soviet Union (CPSU) and the State Security Committee (KGB)—eschew some of these terms, especially disinformation, which they attribute only to the West. Even with the term *active measures*, they use variants apparently determined by the immediacy of a given action. *Aktivnye meri* seems to denominate more immediate, short-

---

*The views expressed are those of the author and should not be construed as representing official positions of the U.S. Defense Intelligence Agency or the U.S. Department of Defense.

term actions—actions requiring creative responsiveness to take advantage of the fleeting moment. *Aktivnye meropriiatiia,* on the other hand, appears to connote broader, long-term initiatives requiring a greater degree of calculated planning. Their executors fully realize, nonetheless, that both incorporate a high degree of disinformation.

Despite decades of practice by the CPSU and the KGB, this latter term is still not fully appreciated among its Western targets. It is not misinformation, a term implying the mishandling of truth; nor is it straightforward propaganda, in which exaggeration and falsehood blatantly abound. Disinformation is, in fact, both and more, but subtly so. Its practitioners carefully conceal bias, source, and intent; and frequently lace the message with truth and factual data. The ultimate benefactor of the message itself encounters criticism to establish the bona fides of the message. But the target of the disinformant's message must be induced to harm himself either by acting against his own interests or by remaining passive when action is required.[15]

Political action also encompasses more than just active measures. Having never really been discarded by the CPSU or the KGB, direct action initiatives surpass disinformation, forgeries, and propaganda. Such actions range from foreign operations by the CPSU Central Committee (especially the International Department) in underwriting subversion and revolution through its own and the KGB's mechanisms; through support of and associations with terrorist and other so-called liberation groups; to Moscow's own assassination and sabotage operations, for which both the KGB and the Main Intelligence Directorate (GRU) maintain respectable capabilities.[16] Examples include the murder of President Hafizullah Amin in Afghanistan in 1979; the controversy over the papal assassination attempt with strong suspicions of Bulgarian (hence, Soviet) involvement; the murky business of the 1970s Henri Curiel *apparat* in France with its Soviet and terrorist connections; and the links with criminal fringe groups including the Grey Wolves and the Turkish Mafia.

For the more odious of these actions, insiders eschew the more brutal or direct nomenclature. Presently, the Eighth Department of the KGB's Illegals Directorate is the latest bureaucratic embodiment of a state-sanctioned assassination and kidnapping group. It was originally established in 1936 as the Directorate for Special Tasks and was later known as Spetsburo Number One, the Thirteenth Department, and Department V before its current incarnation. The actual operations were known as "special action tasks" or, more colloquially, "wet tasks" (*mokrye dela*); recently, however, the latter term is more representative of the argot of the true criminal class rather than government-directed hit squads. Current operations of this nature have been referred to as "direct action" or, even more innocuously as "military drill" (*boievaia podgotovka*). The state security teams that conduct terror actions were, and still may be, known as "combat groups" (*gruppa boievaia*).

Soviet political action need not, and should not, be ascribed only to the KGB. Working by itself and through satellite and surrogate communist parties, the CPSU Central Committee has respectable capabilities for prosecuting political action simultaneously on a number of disparate fronts. The mechanisms and linkages date back to the Comintern and provide opportunities not necessarily requiring KGB involvement.[17] This is especially useful in party-to-party contacts in which instructions and money can be passed through long-established channels that date, in some cases, to the early 1920s.

Similarly, it must be recalled that in keeping with Lenin's exhortation that "a good communist has the qualities of a good member of the Cheka,"[18] there is a continuing infusion of party blood into the so-called organs, that is, the KGB and the Ministry of Internal Affairs or MVD (*Ministerstvo Vnutrennikh Del*). Especially with the ascendancy of Iurii Andropov in the early 1980s, this trend accelerated and is complemented by the movement of KGB cadres into high party and government posts. Stalin initiated the process with his careful grooming of Ezhov, whom he moved from the Secretariat to the secret police (NKVD) in order to oversee the purges. Likewise, Andropov promoted his protégé Chebrikov to the KGB, after long preparation in the party apparatus. Geidar Aliev, on the other hand, traveled from the KGB to the Council of Ministers and the Politburo. Eduard Shevarnadze went from the MVD to the Georgian Communist Party to the Ministry of Foreign Affairs. At one time, General V. A. Kriuchkov, chief of the KGB's First Chief Directorate, served in Boris Ponomarev's International Department of the Central Committee.

Others in the CPSU-KGB phalanx, who ostensibly did not occupy positions involving foreign operations, have participated in such activities. When General Piotr Ivashutin (currently, the military intelligence [GRU] chief) headed the KGB's Third Chief Directorate (counterintelligence in the armed forces), he was rumored to have overseen the restructuring of the Bulgarian state security service. His *spetsnaz* (special purpose) troops were involved in the 1979 invasion of Afghanistan and the execution of President Amin. These units continue to play a key role in the fight against the Mujahideen of Afghanistan and reportedly have been involved with incursions into Swedish territorial waters.[19]

The late General Aleksei Epishev was an alumnus of Poskrebyshev's Secretariat and subsequently became a deputy minister of the Ministry of State Security or MGB (*Ministerstvo Gosudarstvennoi Bezopasnosti*) during Stalin's final years before moving to the Main Political Directorate of the Armed Forces, where he was head from 1962 until his death in September 1985. In addition, Brezhnev had him elected to full membership in the Central Committee.[20] Epishev frequently acted as a party plenipotentiary, serving writs to troublesome satellites and surrogates. A visit by Epishev frequently signaled serious trouble for a host country, as it did in the case of Afghanistan.

Michael Ledeen alluded briefly to the role of Vasilii Romanovich Sitnikov in the *Ethnos* case, an official with the Soviet Copyright Agency or VAAP (*Vsesoiuznoe agenstvo po avtorskim pravam*) and a suspected KGB officer. Sitnikov is a representative example of the genre of party-KGB-state *apparatchiki* with a long political action pedigree. He entered the state security apparatus in the early 1940s and was identified as an MGB colonel heading an Anglo-American group in Vienna during the early 1950s.[21] He reportedly served as a KGB officer in West Germany from 1958 to 1960, a deputy to General Ivan I. Agaiants at the KGB's Department D (disinformation), and an acting chief of Department D; subsequently, he was transferred to an unidentified *sektor* of the Central Committee. In the mid 1970s, he moved to the VAAP, where he is currently one of its top two officials. It is this type of background that makes Sitnikov's role in the *Ethnos* case so intriguing.

The interpenetration of experienced elites throughout the party-KGB-state apparatus, therefore, affords Moscow a reliable pool of cadres to conduct political warfare. As evident in the *Ethnos* business, the lengthy service and experience of such people are keys to the persistence and sophistication of their efforts.

The operational tradition complements this continuum of cadre experience. The *Ethnos* case does have its precedents, with due allowance for time and place. In the early 1920s a series of movements and events occurred, some connected and some not, among the Russian emigration that dealt with alleged changes within the Soviet system. Fabricated by Dzerzhinskii's state security, the Trust was a notional underground monarchist movement that beguiled emigre groups and European intelligence services with tales of a mellowing Bolshevik regime that was basically Great Russian and nationalist and that gradually had accommodated itself to the realities of governance.

Others were apparently genuine trends among the Russian diaspora, such as the Returnism (*Vozrashchenstvo*) and Change of Landmarks (*Smena vekh*) movements, which saw a similar mellowing of Bolshevism and encouragement of émigrés to return to the new Russia and participate in the construction of a new national culture and state. The *Smena vekh* movement published its own newspaper, *Nakanune* (On the Eve), in Berlin and sponsored journals in Riga, Helsinki, Sofia, and Harbin. The Soviets allowed the *Smena vekh* to operate in the USSR itself, and several of its journals were permitted to appear there. Lenin acknowledged the utility of the movement for the broader purposes of the regime, when he told the Eleventh Party Congress that *Smena vekh* was "very useful" in garnering non-Bolshevik support for the USSR while allowing Moscow to keep an eye on such "candid"enemies.[22]

Nakanune religiously parroted the party line and provided yeoman service to Moscow as an émigré instrument for converting doubters to the Soviet cause and convincing many of them to return. It was subsidized by the USSR well after it had demonstrably exhausted its appeal.[23] Moscow finally folded *Nakanune* in June 1924 but allowed *Smena vekh* inside the USSR to continue for about a year and a half before deciding to suppress it.

Another possible precursor to the *Ethnos* case is the weekly leftist newsletter, *The Week*, published by Claude Cockburn in Britain during the late 1930s. Its readership included well-placed opinion molders and politicians on both sides of the Atlantic. In January 1939, when President Franklin D. Roosevelt attempted to persuade the U.S. Senate to repeal the 1937 neutrality legislation, Secretary of State Cordell Hull was rebuffed by Senator William Borah, who claimed he had better sources of information than Department of State reports. Borah carried the Senate; his source of information was *The Week*.[24]

Similarly, in the late 1970s Pierre Charles Pathé's biweekly newsletter *Synthesis*, partially funded by the Soviet Union, served as a subtle funnel through which Moscow sought to influence French political and media establishments. Pathé, a KGB agent of influence, was tried in a French court and convicted of espionage.

There will undoubtedly be more variants of the *Ethnos* case, more peace campaigns, more USSR media events that hype new generations of glib Soviet leaders and their stylish wives. As Aleksandr Solzhenitsyn has poignantly observed, there is a credulity syndrome characterized by "wishful thinking . . . sustained by verbal incantation."[25]

Walter Jajko

Mr. Ledeen has commented on the pacifist active measures campaign in Western Europe over the past several years, a campaign that represents the most flagrant and extended example of the sophisticated skills that the Politburo revived, reorganized, and redirected more than a decade ago. Mr. Ledeen has also described the long-range Soviet active measure in Greece, which, as a tradecraft, may be exemplar. In addition, he has outlined the Anastasi Affair, pointing out the singlemindedness and tenacity of the Soviets and the self-delusion and indifference of the Americans and their allies; however, he has not explicitly drawn any policy prescriptions from it. This raises the operational issue of what should be done about Soviet active measures.

For years the West has merely observed, regretted, and occasionally protested USSR active measures—no matter how crude or successful they have been. Presently, we are, at most, archivists of this active measures effort. There are few active measures that we can neutralize permanently and still fewer that we can pre-empt or prevent. Mr. Ledeen reminds us of a well-known, but often ignored, fact: Since their ascension to power, the Soviets have sought to set the terms of conflict with adversaries in order to subvert them. Setting the terms involves gaining the strategic initiative; consequently, the primary concern of the West should be, not the finesse or failure of particular active measures, but passive acceptance of such measures as a modality of international intercourse that accepts the USSR terms of reference for the superpower conflict.

The Reagan administration is the first presidential administration in two decades to explicitly reject such acceptance and to actively oppose it. Public diplomacy is, or should be, an attempt to establish the United States' terms as the inflexible frame of reference for the conflict. The public diplomacy apparatus constructed by the Reagan administration has had some successes; particular U.S. policies on specific issues are now more widely understood and supported, both at home and abroad. Joint and single agency efforts to combat previously established Soviet active measures have been successful; that is, some measures have been countered and terminated. Despite such accomplishments, U.S. public diplomacy, by definition, can have only limited tactical success since it does not address the totality of the psychological threat. At its best, public diplomacy has been an appurtenance to our diplomatic policy in its main transient concerns; at its worst, it has been a fashionable euphemism for any assertive international public affairs activity. This hardly is harrying the Soviets to the ends of the earth, much less setting the terms for competition.

The framers of the public diplomacy charter, National Security Decision Directive 77 (NSDD-77), and subsequent policy documents on United States international information activities clearly recognized the need to wield information abroad as a weapon. They comprehended that the nation that invented the modern advertising, communications, and entertainment industries must employ information in a manner beyond mere public relations. They understood that passive portrayal of the truth, mostly to those who are open to it, is insufficient. They conceived of overseas information activities as a continuum, each of whose components is mutually supporting. They realized that a coherent world view, a long-term approach, integrated organizational efforts, and a linkage of issues—in short, a strategic direction—were all essential. However, as happens with many activities of the United States government that require sustained attention to strategic objectives and long-range applications, the concept of public diplomacy was ablated in its execution. The history of public diplomacy belies its provenance.

As requirements, activities, and practitioners have proliferated, public diplomacy has manifested its limited character. The appellation itself signifies this. Public diplomacy still suffers from a definitional deficiency: It is not clear how public diplomacy differs from traditional overseas information activities. Organizationally, public diplomacy suffers from a lapse in sustained strategic direction and from insufficient central staff to systematically orchestrate the several efforts of autonomous executive agencies. Operationally, public diplomacy lacks an offensive quality and has not targeted the hard-core, hostile audiences. On the whole, public diplomacy has been short-term, reactive, and on the strategic defensive. These deficiencies, most of which result from the style of U.S. governance, can be remedied by courage, determination, good will, and different personal preferences and institutional imperatives.

What is missing from public diplomacy is the complementary activity of psychological operations. Psychological operations (psyop) involve the overt and covert employment of selected and shaped information that is directed to manipulate the perceptions of reality by foreign governments, organizations, or individuals and are exploited to elicit behavior providing witting or unwitting support for the achievement of U.S. objectives. Together with some classified activities, public diplomacy and psychological operations are the constituents of U.S. international information activities. In the context of the current conflict, these activities—correctly conceived and expertly executed, that is, with their systematic orchestration, the pursuit of strategic objectives, and the long-term application of effort—are an indispensable instrument of statecraft. They may well be the decisive instrument; short of military superiority, they are the only instrument that could transform the terms of the conflict, placing our enemies on the defensive and giving us the initiative.

It is incomprehensible that the employment of psychological operations would be strenuously resisted by a nation that values peaceful means, particularly since the same nation applies the full panoply of these means with vigor and creativity to its domestic political competition. Resorting to such operations is both necessary and timely. In the past twenty years, national psychological operations have fallen into desuetude. Partly in response to the establishment of public diplomacy, however, the Department of Defense has begun to revitalize military psychological operations for use in peacetime, crises, and war. Although military psychological operations capabilities are still modest, genuine national strategic psychological operations—developed, planned, and executed on an interdepartmental basis—are possible with the cooperation, support, and participation of other agencies and with continuous centralized direction from the White House.

The United States should immediately establish a psychological operations organization that is subordinate to the National Security Council and similar to what existed in the 1950s. Establishing such an organization is of particular moment. A national policy and doctrine are required for the conduct of overt psychological operations in peacetime. The development of such operations policy, which does not currently exist, for crises will require direction; a policy for war and contingencies, of which the civilian parts do not currently exist, will require a similar direction. In short, a national psychological operations capability is an essential complement, which is currently lacking, of public diplomacy.

Executed on a sustained basis for strategic objectives, a revived capability could be used to render Soviet active measures ineffective by attacking their sponsors; that is, the Central Committee, the State Security Committee (KGB), press agencies, academies, and front organizations. More important, such a capability could be instrumental in transforming the source of the threat. A national psychological operations capability would provide the United States with an offensive means to manipulate information in order to exacerbate and exploit the enemy's vulnerabilities—not to discomfit him, but to undo him.

NOTES

1. There is abundant literature on the Anastasi case. The best source is Anastasi's book, *Take the Nation into Your Hands* (Athens, 1983), of which I have a

draft of an English-language translation, along with translations of all the key documents referred to in the text. See also Gordon Crovitz, "Pericles, Greece Needs You Back," *The Wall Street Journal*, 19 June 1984; Editorial, "The Anastasi Affairs," *The New York Times*, 21 January 1984; Robert D. Kaplan, "Greece's Disinformation Daily?," *Columbia Journalist Review*, November–December 1983; "Phone-tapping Charge Accepted," *Greece's Weekly for Business and Finance*, 8 October 1984. I also have a tape of a German television program, "Magazin," broadcast on Channel ZDF (unknown date), that discusses the story in considerable detail.

2. For the financing of the Italian Communist Party, see Michael Ledeen and Claire Sterling, "Italy's Russian Sugar Daddies," *The New Republic*, 12 February 1976. See also Michael Ledeen, *Italy in Crisis* (Beverly Hills, Calif.: Sage, 1977). Jan Sejna (*We Will Bury You* [London: Sidgwick & Jackson, 1982], p. 137) states that

> one way the Russians have preserved their influence in Italy is by manipulating the flow of funds from East European countries. There are two principal methods for this financing operation. The first is through the trading companies set up by Togliatti after his return to Italy from Moscow at the end of the Second World War. They have grown substantially since 1945, and Soviet policy has been to channel trade from Eastern Europe to Italy through them. The Russians have also adopted a strategy of awarding major contracts to Italian companies. The USSR bought a nitrogen fertilizer plant from Italy in 1965 or 1966, in spite of more competitive bids from Britain and the USA. In the same way, the contract for the Togliatti car plant in Russia eventually went to Fiat, rather than to British Leyland or others who tendered. Those deals were intended to strengthen the hands of pro-Soviet influence in industrial circles.
>
> The second method of financing the PCI is by direct cash subsidies passed to it through diplomatic and intelligence channels. Estimates published in the *New York Times* and the European press suggest that the PCI receives up to 35 percent of its income in the form of subsidies from Eastern Europe.

3. Yannis Dimitriades, *The Soviet Infiltration of Greece* (Athens, 1983). Both Anastasi and Dimitriades have stated that at least two KGB defectors have testified that Sitnikov was the deputy director. I have not been able to confirm Sitnikov's rank or specific responsibilities, but I have confirmed that he was a top KGB official.

4. This phrase is from courtroom testimony by the son of Yannikos; Yannikos himself confirmed the conversation to Gordon Crovitz ("Pericles, Greece Needs You Back," *The Wall Street Journal*, 19 June 1984).

5. On Afghanistan, see *Ethnos*, 12 December 1983.

6. *Ethnos*, 16 November 1982.

7. *Ethnos*, 12 February 1984.

8. A high European intelligence officer gave me the account of this story,

and several Dutch friends, including two parliament members, corroborated it. Apparently, an account of the Dutch intelligence service report on the peace movement's connection with the Soviet bloc was published in the Dutch press but subsequently denied by the Dutch government. Members of the peace movement then filed a legal suit against the journalist who had written the account. Before the trial began, however, the text of the Dutch intelligence report was produced on a popular West German television program, which was broadcast just prior to a major soccer match; this effectively put an end to legal proceedings against the Dutch journalist. Because of the deadline for publication of this article, I have not had time to obtain the names of the Dutch journalist and of the German television program, but it has been promised to me, and I will provide it to the Hoover Institution as soon as this information arrives.

9. "West German Security Service: Money from Moscow for 'Stop the Neutron Bomb.'" *De Telegraaf*, 3 June 1982.

10. John Wallach and Bernard Kaplan (Hearst Newspapers) reporting from Bonn on 1 November 1981.

11. All this information appeared in the Norwegian press. I have paraphrased an unclassified State Department cable of December 1981, sent to all European posts, that summarized the latest disinformation cases. See Michael A. Ledeen, *Grave New World* (New York: Oxford University Press, 1985), p. 224.

12. See Ledeen, *Grave New World*. The case against Petersen was announced by the Danish Foreign Ministry, which then invited Peterson to sue to libel if he felt the statements against him were false. Apparently, there was no suit. Meanwhile, Merkulov was expelled from the country, and the press was given a great quantity of damaging information about Merkulov's activities.

13. The best study of Soviet disinformation is Jean-François Revel, *Comment les démocraties finissent* (Paris: B-Grasset, 1983), especially section four, "Les cadres mentauz de la défaite démocratique." English translation published as *How Democracies Perish* (Garden City, N.Y.: Doubleday, 1984).

14. I date the Andropov-Gorbachev era to 1967 when Iurii Andropov assumed the chairmanship of the KGB, and not when he acceded to party leadership in November 1982. Chernenko's reign was too brief and inconsequential to merit inclusion with these two men.

15. I wish to acknowledge the seminal, yet unpublished, work on this subject: Natalie Grant, *Dezinformatsiya*, unpublished manuscript (1975).

16. See John J. Dziak, "The Soviet Approach to Special Operations," in Frank R. Barnett, B. Hugh Tovar, and Richard H. Shultz, eds., *Special Operations in U.S. Strategy* (Washington, D.C.: National Defense University Press in cooperation with National Strategy Information Center, Inc., 1984), pp. 95–133.

17. Boris Ponomarev, the chief of the International Department of the Central Committee, was a member of the Executive Committee of the Comintern in the early 1940s.

18. V. I. Lenin, *Collected Works*, vol. 30 (Moscow: Progress Publishers, 1965), p. 483.

19. Dziak, "The Soviet Approach to Special Operations"; Viktor Suvorov, "Spetsnaz: The Soviet Union's Special Forces," *International Defense Review* 16, no. 9 (1983): 1209–16.

20. Peter Deriabin, *Watchdogs of Terror*, 2d ed. (Frederick, Md.: University Publications of America, 1984), p. 345.

21. Peter Deriabin, *The Secret World* (New York: Doubleday, 1959), p. 249.

22. This is from Lenin's 27 March 1922 report to the Eleventh Congress (V. I. Lenin, *Selected Works*, vol. 3 [Moscow: Foreign Language Publishing House, 1961], pp. 744–46).

23. See Robert C. Williams, "'Changing Landmarks' in Russian Berlin, 1922–1924," *Slavic Review* 27, no. 4 (December 1968): 581–93.

24. D. C. Watt, "'The Week' That Was," *Encounter* 38, no. 5 (May 1972): 82–87.

25. Aleksandr I. Solzhenitsyn, *The Mortal Danger: How Misconceptions About Russia Imperil America*, 2d ed. (New York: Harper Colophon Books, 1981), p. 111.

4

U.S. Informational and Cultural Programs

Stanton H. Burnett

Having the pleasure of representing the director of the United States Information Agency (USIA) at this workshop, I include a brief description of where we are and where we hope to go. This is not, however, entirely the director's spot. I have my own set of scars from service at USIA and enigmas and questions from pondering that service: I speak of enigmas, not solutions; questions, not answers. Coming from academe and from an earlier experience as director of research at USIA, I have a dilettante's contact with, and a sharp interest in, the products of research and the current literature on public diplomacy.

To this should be added the past literature, since Thucydides and Machiavelli harbored a critical interest in the subject, along with Thucydides' fellow ancients and Machiavelli's fellow moderns. The conference program suggests that this is not the right place to explore the scholarly literature on public diplomacy and to weigh theory, although there is no real distinction between theory and practice, but faulty theory and faulty practice make it seem so. I intend to stir these strains together in order to pose some disjointed puzzles—puzzles that share a relation to the fundamental style of America's public diplomacy and that are produced by its *practice*.

USIA Programs Today

During the current director's tenure, USIA has done the following:

• Introduced WORLDNET, the first regular international satellite television network in the world, linking Washington with every continent and more than 50 foreign countries.

• Made major strides toward implementing the long-overdue modernization of the Voice of America (VOA), replacing transmitters that are so old they belong in museums and adding new studios, innovative programming, and more transmission hours that will allow us to reach more people around the globe.

• Brought the Fulbright Scholarship Program back from a slide toward extinction to the number of exchanges (about 5,200 annually) that we conducted in the mid 1960s and raised our overall exchange-of-persons programs to 8,000 annually.

• Invited about 350 midcareer professionals from developing countries to the United States through the Humphrey Fellowship Program, started in 1979, and increased the number of American experts (Amparts) sent abroad to 650 annually.

• Initiated the President's International Youth Exchange Initiative, which has enabled 12,000 more teenagers in the United States and 31 foreign countries to plant the seeds of international understanding.

• Developed new avenues of cooperation between the government and the private sector by soliciting the help of 140 American volunteers—all leaders in the film, communications, sports, and publishing industries as well as the labor movement. These volunteers have raised about $4.4 million in private donations to support our Youth Exchange Program and have obtained other important resources for us.

• Created an Artistic Ambassador Program that sends undiscovered world-class pianists on overseas cultural tours where they live with host families.

And we are about to embark on a major English teaching initiative, which will involve the use of new technology, several media, and the best current pedagogical thinking.

In the case of our relations with many countries, however, the most important thing that has been done during this period is hidden in the 74 percent budget increase that the director obtained from the Congress during the Reagan administration's first term. These resources allow us to staff libraries and cultural centers, brief journalists, forge new links with foreign groups, and be present as advocates where ideas are taking shape. This presence of USIA officers, multiplied by their level of persuasiveness, remains the core of the United States' cultural and political effort abroad.

TECHNOLOGY AND THE FUTURE

The current director's first four years have been characterized by extraordinary capital investment in the future. When the history of that period is written, it will underscore the fact that he moved us into the age of satellite television and that he brought the Voice of America (VOA) from the immediate postwar era of dependence on vacuum tubes captured from the Nazis to a condition of genuine competitiveness in the modern age of powerful international radio signals.

There were also some impressive low-technology accomplishments, in such fields as youth exchange, but one hears most about the new technology. If there was one area of agreement that was produced by all of 1984's rereading of George Orwell, it is that soothsayers do not do very well these days and that those who predict technological development do even worse. Although we cannot confidently predict the future in this area, we can probably agree on some possibilities.

Parabolic dish antennae, which are not complex machines, will probably become smaller and less expensive through the use of more powerful signals from satellites. The technical possibilities for direct broadcast in homes many miles and several political boundaries away will, therefore, become greater. As will be discussed below, all communicators, including regimes, are increasing their capacity to manipulate their respective audiences; however, the ability of such regimes to control the information flow to their citizens, and to decide who communicates with them, will decline sharply and soon. All that is likely, but not certain.

There is a lesson, here, in military affairs: With the Strategic Defense Initiative (SDI), we may be passing from a strategic era dominated by offense to one in which states have certain defensive capabilities—even against the most modern ballistic missiles. The same thing could occur in the radio or television sectors; it may be that the development of cheap interference technology will move every bit as rapidly as facilitation technology. In fact, satellite television may be highly subject to interference. A powerful radio transmitter whose signal spreads across the landscape may be far tougher for the "defense" than a satellite television transmission. Could not a blast from a single powerful transmitter overload the satellite and knock it out in the same way that hi-fi speakers blow? If that happened, would anybody know who had done it? Could we even distinguish that event from some accidental break-down? Although these questions may presently be unanswerable, the possibilities are evident.

More important, the countries that have the resources (that is, the funds, not the expertise) to broadcast aggressively over wide areas by satellite television are the same countries with the strongest interest in *not* having a chaotic, outlaw situation in international telecasting. They are the countries that will be making heavy use of satellites for many other purposes; they will be the prime users of the heavens for military communications; and they will, in some cases, have heavy commercial investments—all depending on order and international cooperation.

Although the likelihoods are becoming complicated, governments and other entities will possess, one way or another, increased power to manipulate. Preventing a person from hearing and seeing is itself a form of manipulation. Subtler and more effective production techniques also increase enormously the ability of the broadcaster, state or private, to manipulate.

Although increased capacity to manipulate is likely to be a product of the new technology, once again the opposite may be true. The result may be such multiple channels of communication that the citizen has greater choice and can be less effectively controlled. (Even if the Soviets managed to put a lid over the USSR—effectively blocking direct broadcast satellite effectiveness—would they really be able to prevent the circulation of videotapes?) The technology places into the broadcaster's hands a greater capacity to make an impression and to "zap" the viewer than previously existed. Subliminal messages were just the first egregious example of these possibilities.

We must face, therefore, an uncertain future equation that will probably contain greater opportunities and greater temptations. We appear to be acquiring an increasing capacity to deliver, with unprecedented impact, whatever it is we choose to deliver. The potential for enhancing dialogue is clear. But the new technology also offers the temptation for manipulation, frivolous simplification of issues, and drowning out of reasoned discourse.

When we reduce a complex serious issue to a slogan, we are trying to manipulate. When we choose to play on emotions rather than to respect the audience's reason, we are trying to manipulate. The question is whether we can both retain a desire to be effective advocates and resist the temptation to manipulate, to trivialize, to short-circuit reasoned discourse. The answer I have given to this question in other fora is "yes," but that may be the victory of hope over experience. It is the only answer that can keep the work going, for many of us. Civilized persuasion is a noble enterprise that benefits all who participate. It has its roots in the Platonic dialogue through which all the participants, each of whom had only a part of the truth, share those partial truths and thereby ascend to a higher level of knowledge, even wisdom, than they could have done alone. Once again, one ends with a puzzle that is also a challenge: How does one increase the odds in favor of civilized persuasion and reduce the likelihood that the new technology will simply bring more efficient manipulation? An important part of the answer lies in the way we think about advocacy.

AUDIENCES

A continuing debate within USIA has been over audiences. One hears less of this debate at the moment, probably because management is not going through one of its recurrent spasms of trying to make our target audiences broader or narrower. The debate, on the other hand, *should be* more intense now than it has ever been. We are making large new capital investments in areas that will broaden our audiences. Much of WORLDNET programming is directed toward specialized audiences that will be invited into embassies to view or participate in programs. However, USIA officials have asserted that WORLD-NET is headed toward the same kind of direct telecasting to broad audiences that has been characteristic of the Voice of America.

Yet we are doing this just a few years after a serious effort to achieve a tighter focus on our audiences. Posts abroad have gone through the agony of tough-minded appraisals of the institution-and-influence structures in their respective countries, remade their record systems in order to target the small group of leaders that seem to matter—often ignoring, or even actively discouraging some of the self-selected interested audience members from previous years.

The current change appears to be driven, not by a fresh appraisal of our appropriate audiences, but by the available technology. This is not, incidentally, grounds for disagreement with current initiatives. However you slice audiences, they are watching more television, so we would be derelict if we were *not* exploring the ways in which we can utilize satellite television.

The relation between the medium and the target can be miscalculated. In one country of Western Europe, we sought to communicate specifically with university students. The country's campuses had several student newspapers. Since almost 100 percent of the readers of these newspapers were students, they would appear to be an important target for us. That calculation, however, can be misleading: A major national daily in the same country, popular with young people, had university students comprising only about 15 percent of its readership. It was still our best vehicle, because, although 100 percent of the readers of the student papers were students, only 25 percent of the students read the student newspapers. According to our media survey, however, more than 50 percent read the national daily. We concluded that the general interest newspaper with a large circulation was the best way to communicate with the students, even if thousands of nonstudents were listening in. Consequently, the broader medium was more effective in reaching a narrow audience than was the narrow medium. This is an important vignette to consider in light of USIA's new television and radio initiatives.

We do know something about our audience alternatives worldwide. John Merrill has described an international informational elite that is similar to the chief target audiences identified by most of our posts.[1] We choose them because they are influential, but according to our research, influence goes together with other characteristics, especially education. In most countries, the educational elite and the influence elite are so similar that focusing on the former approximates an easy way to find the influential ones.

The question of which people and which institutions are most influential depends on the topic; it is different for each set of issues. In Europe, for example, the influence elite on military issues is not the same as that on economic issues, although there is some overlap. The point about education, however, generally holds when one places adjectives, such as "military" or "economic," into the mix. Education is a force for convergence: The elite's education has given them some characteristics that converge with those of other educated people. One of those characteristics, incidentally, is an understanding of the English language.

Recent literature and research says something else about this audience: We may be witnessing an information explosion, although it brings with it an implosion of ideas (that is, more people sharing common funds of information). Peter Janicki, who has done some excellent studies for the USIA's Office of Research, reports that at least 15 percent of the people in professional occupation categories regularly read *Time* in the following countries: Thailand, Indonesia, Turkey, Kenya, Lebanon, Kuwait, Saudi Arabia.[2] The figure rises to 40 percent in the major cities of Korea, Nigeria, and Ethiopia.

As we head into this extraordinary expansion of the Voice of America's ability to reach audiences and into an era of heavy investment in satellite television—with the expectation that we will soon be focusing on direct broadcast satellite television—it is important to grasp what this means in terms of audience. USIA's Office of Research has been doing a systematic analysis of the international radio audience for some time, and the high educational level of VOA audiences in the developing world is regularly noted.

In his previously mentioned paper, Janicki describes "a sharp and consistent pattern among VOA listeners." Here are examples in the Third World: In Kenya, where 5 percent of the adults had a secondary education, they comprised 32 percent of VOA's regular (that is, at least once a week) audience; in urban Tunisia, 15 percent and 37 percent; in Argentina, 19 percent and 66 percent; and in Brazil, 24 percent and 59 percent. The proportion of adults listening to VOA in such countries is higher among those with a secondary education than those with less schooling, the listening rate often reaching as much as seven times higher. Levels of listening in the developing world are usually highest among those with a university education.[3] As shown in the analysis of student newspapers, expanding our mass media operations need not mean abandoning a tight focus on the definition of our target audiences for certain important objectives; it just means that more people might be listening.

This is significant for the concern expressed below about the quality of advocacy, that is, reasoned discourse versus slogans and manipulation. Risking attack for being an undemocratic elitist, I would suggest that our message can be directed to the knowledge and reasoning abilities of a narrow part of our audience. Our style and our insistence on a certain quality of advocacy need not be corrupted by the technology; if it is, that will be our fault.

USIA made a leap in sophistication when it judged that it might be cost-effective in terms of overall policy objectives to bring a speaker across the seas at considerable expense and then arrange a long working lunch with six editors as the speaker's main program in an important country. If the cost-effectiveness has been honestly calculated, are we courageous enough to defend frequent use of radio and television for pinpoint communication with only a small segment of the potential audience? If we are not, then USIA's best-reasoned advocacy will be a victim of, rather than a user of, our new electronic muscle.

ADVOCACY

The recent history of advocacy in public diplomacy is something less than a contest of champions. Although we have not performed effectively in some areas, this has been less costly than it might have been, since the Soviets have been more inept in some of the same areas. The Gorbachev era may bring some improvement in Soviet capabilities, so some of our improvements are timely. From my experience, the United States has often not done well because we have tortured ourselves in trying to decide what it is we are doing. Some of our better instincts have set in motion a pendulum that keeps swinging through a proper definition of our role on its way from one unfortunate extreme to the other.

In the past we have occasionally engaged in activities close to the American understanding of "propaganda." I know how the dictionary defines this word and how the word feels to a European. The Catholic church has offices for the propagation of the faith in Rome on Via della Propaganda. To an American, however, propaganda suggests manipulation, slogans, borderline lying, something less than reasoned debate. One does not propagandize one's friends, although one might debate with them.

These rare examples of propaganda—or more frequent instances of concern that a slide into "hard" propaganda was just around the corner—have triggered periodically a strong reaction in the other direction. At times, we have been told that we were not advocates and that we were mere impresarios providing the public platform abroad for an indiscriminate range of views. At the height of this doctrine's influence, during the Carter administration, when USIA officials wanted to send telegrams to posts in the field to hint at the significant issues and policy concerns in Washington, they often found it impossible to receive approval for their telegrams. The logic behind this was that, to avoid becoming handmaidens of the current administration's ephemeral policies, public affairs officers abroad should not have their planning corrupted by such knowledge. Because we have many sensible people, the result was an increase in telephone bills.

Civilized advocacy is not neutral: It *is* advocacy. However, it requires respect for the reasoning capacity of your interlocutor. If you deliver the right information to him and reason through with him about your understanding of its significance, one of three things will happen. He may be persuaded, and you can cash your paycheck with a clear conscience. Or he may offer some information and reasoning of his own, which sends you back to your base for consultations. Or most likely, the dialogue will be pursued—and will ascend, in the Platonic sense—and everybody will eventually benefit. It is never that tidy, but civilized advocacy involving serious people must take place in such a framework.

This is, of course, applicable only to a relatively small part of the world's population: the citizens of the genuine democracies, plus the people who count (whatever their number) in relatively free and open societies that are not fully democratic. When dealing with "unfree" societies, we must rest satisfied if we can find a way to let in occasional shafts of light for the support and encouragement of the brave people who thirst for something better and who are seldom able to let us know that we are in contact.

CULTURAL AND EDUCATIONAL PROGRAMS

This civilized and civilizing relationship with the foreign public works best when we share with our interlocutors at least some elements of the common base of education and culture that permits us to live in the same world of thought with them. To anyone who generally believes that opening human minds is good, these programs do not appear to need any external justification. Although many have tried to separate them, they should not be viewed as distinct and different from the USIA's advocacy role. I am referring only to the intellectual relationship—not the organizational, which is discussed by Gifford Malone.

USIA's efforts in the five European countries that were due to receive deployments of American intermediate-range nuclear (INF) missiles under NATO's two-track decision exemplify the advocacy role being performed at its best. For USIA, that situation was an appropriate chore: The issue was "hot" in the public arena; the objective was clear and finite; and our success and failure were easy to gauge. Most of us believed that the policy was so sound that the delivery of good information and strict logic really *would* be highly persuasive. Our backup was excellent: if a mayor did not believe that missile emplacement would really work, we would provide the necessary technical data to convince him; if an editor did not believe we were negotiating seriously in Geneva, we would arrange a meeting with Ambassador Paul Nitze.

The situation and resources were perfect, and our performance—now being analyzed by two scholars—will probably receive high marks for accomplishing the immediate task, with differences among countries in the political price paid, if any, for our success. But if we were honest concerning our conversations about INF with the Europeans who mattered on that issue, we would have to say that we were just applying a little touch-up to the European view on INF deployment—that is, a final 5 percent to that view, 95 percent of which had already been determined many years earlier. Most of the eventual European attitude on the subject was a product of how they felt about the United States, the Soviet

Union, and the new Europe's role in the world. It was a product of which languages they had learned to read and where they had traveled. And then we came along at the last minute to make a small difference in the context of these predispositions. Their language teachers, their American studies instructors, the Fulbright Commissions or the cultural attachés who chose them for an educational exchange or an international visitor program, and the Americans they met while visiting the United States—all of these people probably counted for more than we did on the specific issue of INF deployment.

As USIA launched its work on INF, one of our embassies in Europe submitted an artfully written and uncommonly persuasive analysis of the situation we faced in Western Europe. The ambassador who drafted it was intelligent, experienced, and accustomed to serious analysis of political situations. He said the problem was a simple one: fear. The West Europeans who did not want the missiles deployed in their country feared the Soviets: They feared becoming a more likely target. It all sounded so right, so plausible, so in tune with what we had been reading in the European press that most of us accepted it. The problem appeared tough, yet simple.

Extensive recent survey research on these questions had been conducted, however. If the ambassador were correct, then it would surely show up there. We had good poll data on opinions about INF from the basing countries, which included questions on the likelihood of war and perceptions of the Soviet threat. We would merely run a cross-tabulation and note the strong statistical correlation between fear and opposition to INF deployment. But our tabulation came up empty; there was almost no correlation. I asked for a few other attempts at secondary analysis of the data—still nothing. At the time, I was research director and assigned several analysts to run cross-tabulations on everything except demographic data. Finally, against absolutely flat fields of nothing (that is, no statistical correlation with opinions on INF), five questions stood out, and in all countries these questions had a high correlation to opinions on INF deployment. These five questions measured fundamental attitudes toward the United States and the Reagan administration: perceptions of American leadership in world affairs and of the United States' wisdom in coping with the problems of modern society. The ambassador, I believe, had been wrong.

The point is that most of the opinions on the INF issue were not the product of calculations about the issue itself; they came from deep within that first 95 percent, in experiences that had been untouched by information officers but in which cultural attachés may have been heavily involved. Anyone who believes that, when we operate effective educational and cultural programs, we are not doing hard mainstream overseas work on the United States' fundamental national interests would be quickly disabused of that view, not by greeting some wide-eyed high school exchangees, but by debating United States policy with the tough editor of a European daily newspaper.

INFORMATION AND UNDERSTANDING

There is a common assumption running through both our cultural and our information (that is, political advocacy) programming: Information and understanding move together; enhance information, and you are bound to enhance understanding. So, for a long time we have trumpeted USIA's primary objective—to tell America's story, warts and all. There are two difficulties with this seemingly unassailable bedrock of the USIA's work.

First, there may be issues and areas where the warts are so large that, where a change of style is indicated, the investment to tell the story is questionable. Where, e.g., American abundance has not brought enlightenment, there may be more to our job than advertising the abundance and the machine that produced it. In these cases, the major public diplomacy role may be more properly one of stirring international enthusiasm for joining the United States in a common search for solutions. We have done this with some success, for example, in the case of narcotics. The work of the United States Information Agency has made it easier for governments in Italy and Colombia, among others, to work with us. That is a change in the old description that USIA seems to be handling de facto.

The other difficulty is more complicated and interesting. While it relates to all of USIA's work, it has a special meaning for communication with closed societies where only certain communications get through and, more important, only a certain segment of the population has any considerable access to serious materials about America. About five years ago, USIA's Office of Research undertook a daring (and, therefore, initially unpopular with management) project of surrogate research about the Soviet Union. Recognizing that survey research in the USSR is impossible, but dissatisfied with the content analysis and anecdote-recounting that passed for research on the Soviet Union, USIA carefully ventured into surrogate interviewing.

One finding was particularly striking: Since 1966, information about the United States flowing to Soviet elites increased vastly, but this increased information did not seem to have brought with it a commensurate understanding of the fabric of America. Some even spoke of a decline on that score.[4] Critics of the USIA study drew particular attention to its description of egregious failures to comprehend the United States on the part of the top Soviet political and economic elites: "Many search with great intensity for the 'key' which will explain how such a complex and apparently unregulated society can maintain such a high level of production and technological innovation. They are baffled by the system. Even the experts are convinced that there must be a private-sector planning apparatus, hidden from their view, which ultimately controls the economy."[5]

For some commentators, that finding cast doubt on the methodology and results of the entire study. You can imagine my interest, therefore, in reading the following passage from Arkadyi Shevchenko's *Breaking with Moscow:* "the Soviet leadership is . . . simply baffled by the American system. It puzzles them how a complex and little-regulated society can maintain such a high level of production, efficiency, and technological innovation. Many are inclined toward the fantastic notion that there must be a secret control center somewhere in the United States."[6]

The least one can say is that the relation between information and understanding is tricky and that, to return to the first point, even a simple search for understanding as a good in itself is probably insufficient to justify the USIA's work. We are at our best as stewards of the public funds when we speak clearly about the policy objectives of that understanding.

Conclusion

If a future historian could peer inside the heads of foreign audiences some years hence, it would be interesting to know which of the initiatives of the incumbent director, the Honorable Charles Z. Wick, had counted most in rallying world support for Washington's policies. Will it be WORLDNET, the doubling of the youth exchange program, the revamping of the teaching of English, or the maintenance of sufficient well-qualified USIS officers in the field? The apparently-obvious answer may not be the right one. But the questions suggest what is needed: sound scholarship on public diplomacy. We need more serious events, such as this workshop at the Hoover Institution, that scrutinize how America is fulfilling this task. We also need a precise definition of our work, at least in relation to free and open societies, and then we need to live precisely by this definition.

Public diplomatists are, first of all, diplomatists. I use that old-fashioned word to emphasize that, at our best, we are no different from the diplomatists described by Harold Nicolson and that we should try to meet his explicit standards. The adjective *public* is not so much a description of style as a rough description of the audience; it indicates that we are not confined to our opposite number in the foreign ministry. This aspect of diplomacy has become so prominent in the daily work of most embassies that it has been years since I have heard the traditional fretting about whether USIS officers were second-class citizens in the embassy context. I do hear many political counselors complaining that they cannot see the ambassador in the morning, because he is always meeting with the public affairs officer. When the two words are placed together, it becomes evident that our role—our noble and significant role but our *only* role—is that of the civilized advocate. Edward R. Murrow did not believe that new technology would change that. I know that Charles Wick does not believe that the new technology has changed it, or will change it.

Discussion

Sig Mickelson

I intend to comment more fully on some of the issues raised by Stanton Burnett, but first let me respond to his suggestion that, as time passes, satellites may play an increasingly more significant role in public diplomacy. I cannot be as sanguine about the future of satellites in American public diplomacy as, apparently, Stan Burnett and some of his colleagues are. Undoubtedly, satellites will continue to increase the load that they carry in point-to-point transmission. WORLD-NET and teleconferencing ventures have proven that the satellite is a powerful and cost-effective tool in moving material to distant sites where it is redistributed by conventional processes.

Direct broadcast from satellites is something entirely different. The technology to reach directly into the home is available; it has been for some years. But there is a big difference between having the technology and putting it to use. There are simply too many obstacles, particularly if we are thinking of Eastern Europe and the Soviet Union as primary targets. This applies to both radio and television, although, if Direct Broadcast Satellite (DBS) technology ever does become a tool for international transmissions, radio seems the more likely because it requires less power and smaller receiving dishes.

Unfortunately, transmissions from satellites can only reach geographical areas the satellite can "see." Parts of Eastern Europe are within the line of sight of satellites serving Western Europe, but most of the Soviet Union would have to be reached from parking space over the Indian Ocean. Authorization for parking space and frequencies would have to be obtained from the International Telecommunications Union, where the Soviets have the power to block a grant. Even though West European satellites have "foot prints" that extend as far east as Moscow, putting a signal into Eastern Europe would be more difficult than it may sound. One of the major points of contention at meetings of various international bodies considering problems of space communications has related to "spillover." Consider, for example, the uproar one would hear from East Germany if a West German satellite were to transmit Voice of America (VOA) or Radio Free Europe (RFE) signals that could directly penetrate East German homes.

It is not totally inconceivable that an Indian satellite might be used by Radio Liberty (RL) to reach into Soviet Central Asia and Siberia. But the Indian government would certainly be subjected to the harshest pressures to reject an Indian-American agreement to make this possible. Furthermore, it is unlikely that the Indian satellite's antenna could be reconfigured to throw a strong enough beam into the contiguous areas of the Soviet Union to provide a legible signal for reception by a home set, either radio or television.

However, let us assume for a moment that licenses were granted, parking space obtained, and friendly countries leased transponders to VOA, RFE, or RL permitting them to transmit signals directly into East European or Soviet homes. In order to receive the transmitted program material, the potential viewer or listener would have to visit his local hardware store or electronics shop to buy a receiving dish and a converter. Without them, it would be impossible to capture the satellite signal and convert it to a frequency acceptable to his radio or television receiver. He could make his purchase only if the Soviet government were to permit such equipment to be manufactured and distributed.

It all sounds a bit implausible. For the time being, it seems more sensible to concentrate on more effective use of the available technology, primarily shortwave radio. It makes a beautiful dream to visualize millions of Poles, Czechs, Romanians, and Russians riveted to their receiving sets enthralled by programs from Television Free Europe, Television Liberty, or Picture of America. Perhaps it may happen in the future, but for now, shortwave radio is the only practical delivery system.

Apart from Stan Burnett's preoccupation with satellite transmissions, I should like to comment on his efforts to determine the proper role of advocacy in the operations of USIA; particularly, his concern that "we have tortured ourselves in trying to decide what it is that we are doing." It is probably foolhardy and certainly presumptuous for an outsider to lecture the USIA on its proper role in the practice of public diplomacy, but perhaps a few random thoughts might furnish a useful perspective. To do so, from my vantage point, it is necessary to position USIA in the spectrum of American public diplomacy. This is important because USIA's mission is complicated by distinct differences between its general informational and cultural activities and its Voice of America, differences that call for different policies and different approaches.

Virtually every executive in the United States government, particularly those engaged in any way in foreign relations, is a "public diplomatist" and should recognize that he has public diplomatic responsibilities. Some international negotiations clearly must take place behind closed doors, but this does not negate the obligations of those who serve in the international arena from recognizing that their public words, deeds, and actions reflect directly on the national image and are a part of the nation's effort to gain support for its policies and programs.

The position of the USIA is central to the practice of public diplomacy; the agency's (almost) sole concern is to obtain a favorable hearing for American policies and to serve as an advocate of United States positions. In many respects, it is comparable to the public relations department of an American corporation or, even, an outside public relations counsel. It specializes in obtaining a favorable hearing not only for American programs and policies but also for its culture, institutions, and traditions. Like the public relations counsel, its function is, in part, to build image.

The point at which USIA's role becomes contradictory involves the inclusion within its domain of the Voice of America. Within VOA, there are inherent contradictions. The straight news broadcasts will suffer if they are not clearly divorced from advocacy. On the other hand, VOA's cultural programming must call attention to the cultural diversity and strength of American institutions and, thus, become an advocate of the American way of life.

News broadcasts, however, are a different story. To build an audience, news broadcasters must build confidence; to build confidence they must establish a record for credibility. Any deviation from credibility, any distortion, any omission of embarrassing facts will inevitably diminish confidence. An erosion of confidence and, consequently, of audience size will almost certainly follow.

This is not to say that editors must be so devoted to a warts-and-all policy that they must constantly search for warts and fall over backward to broadcast them. On the other hand, their confidence ratings will suffer if they seek to avoid potentially embarrassing information that is given prominent display by other news media. If VOA were the only agency distributing news internationally, it might be possible to gloss over blunders and misstatements, but since so many other news sources are available, omission inevitably endangers credibility.

It is also tempting to criticize U.S. broadcasts for being too soft, too disinclined, for example, to strike back at communist radio. There are those who recommend that VOA remove its gloves and slug it out blow for blow—give an eye for an eye. It is a tempting suggestion; retaliation on a program-by-program basis would furnish emotional satisfaction. Although it would serve as a catharsis for those who resent attacks from foreign radio, it would almost certainly create a negative response from those who count most, the regular listeners. In doing so, it would set in motion an erosion of credibility. Antagonizing listeners by belittling their institutions can offend, or even anger, them and further destroys the base of confidence. It is a mistake to assume that all listeners are sympathetic to the West and indifferent to their own histories and cultures, or even their leaderships.

We must remember that American international broadcasters (VOA, RFE-RL, and Radio Marti) broadcast into an environment that is saturated with bombast and propaganda. The domestic media proudly affirm their propagandistic role, and the citizen has propaganda coming out of his ears. He is, understandably and properly, sick and tired of it.

If VOA, RFE-RL, and Radio Marti use the same tactics—that is, if they try to slug it out with the same stridency and bombast that characterizes the media in Eastern Europe and the Soviet Union—they risk dealing a damaging blow to their own credibility. A heavy-handed approach might appeal to those in the audience who are already convinced. Among others, the most charitable judgment would probably be that the truth lies somewhere between the official propaganda and the American version of it; that would be a damning judgment. It would reduce the level of the American message nearly to that of the opposition.

Insofar as VOA is a news agency, it would be far better advised to follow the standards prescribed for good journalism: accuracy, reasonable objectivity, and avoidance of the inflammatory, the hortatory, and the pejorative. This does not completely rule out advocacy. Simply elaborating on the actions of the American government to fill in details omitted by editors in paring stories for international transmission constitutes advocacy of a sort in that it furnishes additional information to enhance understanding. Furnishing an opportunity for government officials to explain reasons for action or for the adoption of policies serves the national interest without damaging credibility or undermining confidence. In a sense it is advocacy.

Officials of BBC's External Services, the most prestigious of international broadcasters, have told me that they regard their function as presenting to the world a view of the news as seen from London, and they do it in a low-key, objective, and nonpejorative fashion. The success of BBC over the years suggests that it might have discovered the key to gaining attention and winning listener confidence years ago.

Radio Free Europe and Radio Liberty are also cogs in the nation's public diplomatic machinery but in quite a different way. Whereas VOA can aim at short-range objectives, RFE and RL must look to the long-term. Whereas VOA's mandate is to concentrate on representing American institutions, culture, and points of view, RFE and RL serve as surrogate domestic radio in the countries into which they broadcast. VOA is clearly an American institution; it is, in fact, the voice of America. RFE and RL do not try to conceal the fact that they are American-supported and managed; however, in Warsaw, Prague, Budapest, Kiev, and Leningrad, programs are built as if they were local radio. RFE and RL cater to the backgrounds and interests of their local listeners and fill the information gap created by censorship, with information of special interest to their local audiences.

As spelled out in the 1974 legislation that provides for their financing, the only obligation of RFE and RL to American governmental policy is "to operate in a manner not inconsistent with broad United States foreign policy." This is a function quite different from that performed by VOA. It is public diplomacy only in that its long-term objective is to bring the level of understanding of international affairs in the countries in which censorship is a way of life up to that of the free democracies. This is not to say that RFE and RL do not or should not devote a good deal of attention to arms control negotiations or to the Strategic Defense Initiative. But their aim must be to satisfy the curiosity of their regular listeners about these activities—not to plead the American case.

Supporting this long-range approach demands patience. Prior to the 1956 Hungarian Revolution, some persons in positions of influence had hoped that RFE staff members who were East European refugees might form cadres to lead the march back into their homelands should their communist governments begin to crumble; Hungary ended that. One of the early objectives of the two radios (RFE and RL), however, is still valid: to keep the spirit of freedom alive. Another specific objective is more rarely mentioned, but it is of critical importance: As the information level rises, we can confidently expect that international understanding will similarly improve and that communist leaders will be forced to listen in greater measure to public opinion.

If Western radio incessantly bombards the censored nations with information that is denied to them, leaderships are faced with a dilemma: Either continue to wield indiscriminately the blue pencil or relax a little and avoid suffering a damaging loss of confidence. The Soviet

Union, for example, could not pretend forever that its air force had not shot down Korea Air Lines (KAL) flight 007 over the China Sea. It eventually had to admit the event had occurred; the admission came, at least in part, because the event became common knowledge in the Soviet Union as a result of Western broadcasts. The case of KAL 007 is one among scores that can be told regarding the capitulation of Soviet and East European censors in the face of a barrage of accurate information from the West.

As a result, censorship rules are not as harsh as they once were. Leaderships have discovered that they cannot permit their censors to hold to rigid positions in the face of a torrent of accurate information from the West and from Kol Israel and Radio Peking. Jamming is one method available to communist leaders for fighting back; however, although the effect of jamming is maddening to the listener, it is not wholly effective.

These comments may seem somewhat remote from the aspects of public diplomacy that we are discussing here and, particularly, as it is practiced by the USIA (from a short-term viewpoint, it probably is). No RFE or RL broadcast is likely to have a direct and immediate effect on the current arms control negotiations, but in the long run the impact may conceivably be more impressive.

Each step a communist leader takes to weaken censorship furnishes his citizens with more basis for questioning policies. Obviously, this is more than a nuisance; it means he has to pay some regard to public opinion before making an important move. To a limited extent, he must consider the reaction of citizens before he acts. We are not speaking of a democracy, but such a consideration is a small step in that direction. If we can maintain that pressure and not become impatient, we may eventually see significant results.

This places a heavy burden on the broadcasters. If they are guilty of serious errors, they lose their credibility. If they become too bombastic, they lower themselves to the level of the propagandists of the local regime. If they are critical of institutions or the culture of the country into which they are broadcasting, they risk alienating their listeners. And, finally, if they encourage their listeners to take retaliatory action or use force, they risk the imposition by the regime of greater power, possibly involving bloodshed or death.

The potential power of information is so great as to be incalculable—for good or for harm. Discretion is required in its use—and patience. Most important, from the viewpoint of this workshop, the dissemination of news is one facet of public diplomacy, even though it is only distantly related to the more overt forms with which this conference is primarily concerned. Nevertheless, it is a part of the spectrum and should be seen as such.

Elie Abel

Mr. Burnett reminds us that the United States Information Agency (USIA), under the leadership of Charles Wick, has taken significant forward strides over the past four and a half years. I believe that generally this is good, though some of the Wick innovations are more controversial than others.

I would like to focus initially on my impressions of the changes wrought, as they affect the Voice of America (VOA). Just a few weeks ago, my wife and I were traveling in the People's Republic of China. Thanks to our habit of carrying a small Japanese shortwave radio in our luggage, we listened to VOA almost every morning, as large numbers of the Chinese do, or so we discovered. The Chinese will tell you that they listen primarily to improve their English. We wanted nothing more than a capsulized version of uncontrolled overnight news because, except for Peking and Shanghai, it was virtually impossible to buy even the highly controlled English language newspaper, *The China Daily*, on the day of publication.

The habit of listening to overseas broadcasts is not strong in America. My wife and I adopted it many years ago when I was a foreign correspondent assigned to various countries in Central and Eastern Europe. In short, we were "old hands" at tuning in VOA and the British Broadcasting Corporation (BBC) on shortwave. On most days, the Voice boomed in loud and clear. For technical reasons because of the proximity of the transmitter, we found that it took less "dial twiddling" than tuning to the BBC, at least in that part of Asia. Thanks to VOA, we learned that Richard Nixon was in Peking while we were in Canton. It is a vast country, and we never did make connections. Nevertheless, we continued to listen, but it seemed to us that we were not listening to the same old VOA.

The news bulletins had a commendably professional touch: no heavy-handed propaganda, at least no more than I remembered from the 1950s and 1960s. But bells and whistles had been added, as if VOA producers had gone to school at ABC: Perky little tunes and the beep-beep-beep (suggestive of the modernity all too familiar from home) sounded between segments of the program. Only the commercials were missing—admittedly a welcome break—but somehow, we kept waiting for them. The format struck us as less dignified than, for instance, the overseas service of the BBC and, to a certain extent, more superficial. This is not meant to denigrate VOA correspondents; they certainly sounded professional and appeared to be broadcasting from most of the trouble spots around the world. The format, however, struck us as cheap and jangly, not wholly appropriate for a government broadcasting service that is supposed to reflect the majesty of these United States; in short, too much Hollywood twinkle.

One of the reasons VOA has never caught up to the BBC in public acceptance around the world is that, although the BBC ("The Beeb") is government financed like VOA, the BBC has refused to preach administration gospel. Despite recent attacks from Downing Street, the BBC, to its credit, does not broadcast Thatcherite editorials. Two examples illustrate this fact: Prime Minister Thatcher's rage at the time of the Falklands campaign and, more recently, the fuss raised by her home secretary over the showing (now delayed) of a BBC documentary profiling two Northern Ireland firebrands (one a Protestant loyalist, the other a Catholic militant, allegedly high-ranking in the Irish Republic Army, and both preaching the gospel of the gun).

As we listened to the Voice of America in China, we caught what may, or may not, be a Wick innovation; that is, broadcast commentaries that analyze events from a Reaganite perspective. These commentaries were separated from the daily news and labeled as official, but they bothered me. Of course, Radio Moscow does the same thing, but I can think of more appropriate models for VOA. The Soviets do many things that I would rather we did not emulate because they are un-American. They will undoubtedly continue censoring all media, including literature, and publishing nothing but party-line opinion in the press. We emulate them, however, at a cost we do not have to bear. I see no conflict between that kind of self-restraint and Mr. Burnett's goal of letting occasional shafts of light into dark corners of the world; restraint would help our credibility.

With that small, highly personalized caveat, let me tip my hat to Charles Wick for somehow persuading the Congress that the Voice of America desperately needed state-of-the-art transmitters, even at a cost of many millions of dollars. He has also found more money for Fulbright Scholarships and Humphrey Fellowships and greatly expanded other exchange programs. A budget increase of 74 percent over four years is a great achievement, even after allowing for inflation.

Mr. Burnett is a cautious prophet, and I find that commendable; however, some aspects of his projection strike me as more cautious than they need to be. The advent of a new generation of more powerful and bigger communication satellites will mean that dish antennas on earth will become smaller, cheaper, and less obtrusive. But does that mean that the ability of authoritarian or totalitarian regimes to control the flow of information into their countries will increase? According to Burnett, this is likely but not certain; I share his diffidence. Some of those regimes (for example, Romania) manage to license and thus control private ownership of typewriters, not to mention photocopying equipment. Beaming uncontrolled, uncensored signals into Romanian homes via direct broadcast satellites (DBS) may have a less-than-brilliant future. This even includes smaller parabolic dishes, which technologists keep promising, but will be difficult to hide in any country where the secret police are on the prowl (tapping telephones, opening mail, watching and listening around the clock).

The personal computer may do far more than DBS to penetrate the information-control systems of these countries. The Soviet leaders are now aware that they have been lagging far behind the West in computer technology. They have targeted a substantial increase in computer power over the next several years. I cannot predict how far, or how fast, the computerization of the Soviet Union will go. I would guess that they will attempt to restrict access to their newly acquired computers in various governmental, educational, and scientific institutions, possibly prohibiting or licensing private ownership of these potentially subversive instruments. However, thousands of Soviet citizens will necessarily have access to them, and software is comparatively easy to smuggle. It would not be surprising if *samizdat*, still utilizing the method of typing and carbon-copying of forbidden texts, were to be supplanted over the next ten years by a form of electronic publishing (that is, bootleg publishing) that would be capable of reaching vastly larger audiences with less human effort than it currently does.

Finally, as one who has frequented American diplomatic establishments in many parts of the world over the years, I am delighted to hear from Mr. Burnett that public affairs officers are receiving more attention from their chiefs of mission. That is, indeed, a change; and, if the Wick administration is responsible for that, I salute Mr. Wick. I go back to the days when public affairs officers were generally treated as second-class citizens, and sometimes as public nuisances, in many American embassies. There were, of course, occasional "duds" among them, as there have been "duds" among our diplomatists. In my experience overseas, however, the high-and-mighty who had no time for public diplomacy were depriving themselves, and the United States government, of information and insights that could have made a difference. Some of the wisest and best-informed Americans I met in various countries were, in fact, USIA people. May their tribe increase.

Alfred H. Paddock, Jr.

Stanton Burnett's excellent paper deals principally with the activities of the U.S. Information Agency (USIA), his parent organization. In my remarks, I would like to broaden slightly the scope of the panel by examining the Reagan administration's philosophical, conceptual, and organizational approach to public diplomacy—or, as I prefer to call it, the psychological dimension of national security. I will also assess some of the strengths and weaknesses of this approach.[7]

There are at least three hallmarks of the current administration's approach to public diplomacy. The first was a major review of U.S. national security strategy completed early during the administration's first term. The result was the president's announcement in the summer of 1982 that his national security strategy would have four basic components: diplomatic, economic, military, and *informational* (emphasis added). The president's overt expression of the importance of the psychological dimension is a phenomenon that had not been witnessed in Washington for some time.

Next, there was President Reagan's address to the British Parliament on 8 June 1982, in which he announced the United States' intention to make a major effort to help "foster the infrastructure of democracy . . . which allows a people to choose their own way, to develop their own culture, to reconcile their own differences through peaceful means." In addition, the president exhorted the Western allies to engage more vigorously in a peaceful "competition of ideas and values" with the Soviet Union and its allies. A number of public and private sector initiatives have their philosophical genesis in this oft-quoted speech.

Finally, there was the president's signing of National Security Decision Directive 77 (NSDD-77) in January 1983, entitled "Management of Public Diplomacy Relative to National Security" (for the full unclassified text of this document, see appendix). This directive defined public diplomacy rather broadly, stating that it "is comprised of those actions of the U.S. Government designed to generate support for our national security objectives." The decision also established a Special Planning

Group (SPG) under the chairmanship of the assistant to the president for national security affairs. Membership consists of the secretary of state, the secretary of defense, the administrator of the Agency for International Development (AID), and the USIA director. Four interagency committees report to the SPG: public affairs, chaired by the National Security Council (NSC); international information, chaired by USIA; international political, chaired by the Department of State; and international broadcasting, chaired by the NSC. Most of the actual work is done in these four committees and the working groups or ad hoc task forces that they establish to deal with specific issues or programs.

How effectively has this interagency organizational mechanism worked to conduct the president's intuitive understanding of, and emphasis on, the psychological dimension? Not all the reviews are in, but so far the results have been mixed. Government agencies not only have become increasingly aware of the importance of public diplomacy but also have made some useful efforts to address specific issues and problem areas (most notably, as Stanton Burnett has pointed out, those involving INF deployments). The USIA budget has expanded to its highest level since the height of the Vietnam War, and a vigorous equipment modernization program is underway, particularly for the Voice of America (VOA). Our analytical capability has improved and, at times, has been most impressive, particularly with regard to uncovering evidence of Soviet active measures and disinformation. A small core of dedicated people on the NSC staff and among the agencies have worked hard to effectuate the mechanism.

But there is an ad hoc quality to the overall effort that is reactive in nature and lacking in the strategic coherence that the subject deserves. This kind of effect deserves planning conducted on an integrated, worldwide basis and in response to national policy. Ad hoc committees and working groups created in reaction to regional crises are not a satisfactory long-term solution to this requirement. Why then does this ad hoc approach prevail?

In part, it prevails because of the difficulty in getting the policy and public diplomacy communities to communicate effectively with each other. Despite the heightened awareness mentioned earlier, public diplomacy is still not a consistent, integral aspect of the policy process in terms of the major decisions made by the principal actors. This has been exacerbated by the sheer inertia of the massive interagency bureaucracy and by the lack of timely action among agencies (unless principals apply "top-down" pressure and emphasis). Since the Senior Planning Group of the NSDD-77 mechanism convenes infrequently, lower-level officials of the SPG Executive Committee (Excom) are left to actuate matters. The linchpin of this whole operation is a two-person office on the NSC staff, the head of which chairs the Excom. The operation is thus aggravated, not only by this woefully understaffed office but also by the president's preferences for cabinet-style government (hence, the NSC staff's relatively weak role in centralized direction). Consequently, there is inadequate strategic, coherent, and long-term focus, as well as insufficient discipline and follow-up on actions, to make the NSDD-77 mechanism effective.

The fragmented public diplomacy community, even among the key agencies, also contributes to this ad hoc quality. The Department of State, for example, has at least three identifiable public diplomacy fragments with no strong central focus or direction, and these do not include the public affairs organizations. As Stanton Burnett and Walter Hahn have indicated, the ongoing internal "tortured debate" on terminology is another contributory cause to the relative disarray. This not only impedes the progress of integrating the government's resources in a coherent approach but also results in a more defensive, reactive interagency effort and a diminished willingness to undertake an aggressive, offensive pursuance of U.S. national security objectives.

Although the Reagan administration has made some positive strides in emphasizing the importance of public diplomacy, the U.S. government can, and should, harness more effectively its resources in order to compete more effectively with American adversaries in the psychological sphere. This can be achieved, not only without sacrificing U.S. democratic values and attempting to emulate totalitarian political systems but also without a massive overhaul of the existing public diplomacy machinery. One requirement is to upgrade the staff of the NSC office, mentioned previously. Certainly, more frequent SPG meetings would encourage senior policy officials to become increasingly involved in public diplomacy matters. Some reorganization of the public diplomacy community within the various agencies would help to provide a more cohesive approach, particularly within the Department of State, which should be playing a strong leadership role in this area. Resolving the internal "tortured debate" on terminology would provide a clearer understanding of common purpose among the differing agencies; this consensus on common purpose, however, must be effectively articulated to the U.S. Congress and the American public. Finally, the United States needs to approach the psychological competition in a more strategic, coherent, and offensive long-term manner.

5

Public Diplomacy
and the Private Sector

Mark Blitz

Public diplomacy is increasingly effected through private institutions and individuals. To discuss this topic intelligently, we must first examine the meaning of *public diplomacy*. The term is seemingly a euphemism for *propaganda*, which is itself a variation of what the earliest political thinkers understood as *rhetoric*. Indeed, public diplomacy displays the art of euphemism and embellishment thought to be a chief tool of its trade.

Defining Public Diplomacy

Although its promulgators do not believe propaganda is false (in fact, it is normally true), the term *propaganda* strikes us as somehow unsavory—a fancy species of lying, perhaps minor lying in the best of causes, but lying nonetheless. However much twentieth-century social scientists once expected that it might be, *propaganda* has never been a value-free term.

A better term, normally used in place of propaganda, is *information*. We do not propagandize, but inform. Today, however, *information* suggests a mindless generating of passively accepted facts; it has lost the sense of shaping interest in its original meaning. It strikes the diplomatic ear as a bit too one-sided or imperialistic a term. Hence, we have the occasional use of *communication* as the euphemism for propaganda. Embracing almost any activity, however, communication is too vacuous a concept to have much meaning; it is especially vacuous when it shades into sharing, relating, and "being open" (its meaning when used synonymously with informing and persuading).

Public diplomacy is, therefore, a substitute for *public information* or *public communication* as the decent term for what would otherwise be called propaganda. Beyond this, if we consider the root sense of information and some of the senses of propaganda, we notice that public diplomacy is primarily the active shaping of public opinion by telling or displaying the truth—not merely the injection of undigested material into an opinion that has already been formed.

The traditional term for this practice is *civic* (or public) *persuasion*, or, better, *civic education* because persuasion carries too artful and sly a connotation. The publics in question, however, are foreign, so the term *civic education* fails to differentiate our subject clearly enough. Although it is altogether proper for citizens to give themselves and their children continuing civic education, to educate foreigners seems a bit meddlesome and may be interpreted as unwarranted interference in someone else's affairs. Therefore, public diplomacy is a useful and diplomatic way of conceptually differentiating the civic education of foreigners from the civic education of fellow citizens.

Public diplomacy also refers to the kind of civic education that occurs in public, not secretly or in private. Governments usually talk to other governments secretly or, at least, behind doors that initially are closed. Their persuasion can exercise skills and use facts that cannot always be displayed publicly to advantage. In contrast, public diplomacy refers to the open education of foreigners, most of whom are private citizens and not government officials.

To summarize, public diplomacy is the open civic education of citizens of other countries using means that are not deliberately false. The point of public diplomacy is primarily political (although it often uses nonpolitical methods), and there is nothing knowingly false in what it does (although which facts should be emphasized, when, and where is a matter of judgment).[1]

The Goals of Public Diplomacy

Using this definition, American public diplomacy has two goals. One is to inform foreign citizens about U.S. policies and the facts that produce them and, consequently, to inspire public trust and understanding. The second is to inform them of the American way of life, primarily as this is shaped by the U.S. form of government. We hope that once they have been properly informed, foreign citizens will appreciate our policies; or, ultimately, support them actively and appreciate our way of life; or, better yet, seek to imitate us.

The purpose of public diplomacy is, first, to enable others to respect our policies and then to become as much like us as they can (this purpose is pursued more haltingly and less confidently). These two purposes belong to the two ends that motivate our foreign policy. One end is to protect our interests and resources, secure our borders and independence, and permit the open markets necessary for economic growth.

This requires a series of actions that involve the panoply of alliance, security, and trade relations. These policies are intended to permit tangible outcomes and often involve tangible assets. They also involve, however, creating or changing attitudes, instilling trust and confidence, and convincing others that a course of action is just or unjust. Obvious examples are the issues surrounding deployment of intermediate-range nuclear force (INF) missiles in Europe and the Strategic Defense Initiative (SDI). Public trust and perception were and are no less important to achieving the short-range ends of INF deployment and SDI development than are the hardware itself and the economic inducements involved in its development. To ignore the technological realities and the public opinion these realities help to create is a fantasy; but it is also a fantasy to ignore public opinion and its molding.

Public democracy helps to explain the policies directed to securing these concrete ends and helps these measures succeed by allowing them to be accepted. It also helps to create the trust and beliefs that are themselves a central aspect of what other policies are also trying to achieve. In this sense, public diplomacy is not merely a means to secure other ends but rather a central means to create the kind of public opinion that is part of what successful policy tries to achieve. Public diplomacy concerning SDI, for example, must do more than defend strategic defense systems. It must re-educate the public about the necessity for defense, the possibilities of deterrence, and the importance of alliance.

Healthy public opinion is a goal of policy, not just a framework for the acceptance of still other policies. Public confidence is not merely something that allows this or that economic or military adjustment to be understood; it is part of a healthy economic and security situation. Successful public diplomacy, therefore, does not merely explain policy: It contributes to public trust, public confidence, and the foreign public's view that its participation or acquiescence in American actions is proper and worthwhile. Churchill's exercise in public diplomacy and private persuasion directed toward the United States, for example, was a central element in Great Britain's war effort, which was aimed at reminding Americans of shared values with Great Britain and of what was at stake in Britain's battle with tyranny. These principles were the wellsprings that nourished full U.S. engagement in a mutual effort; to be reminded of them constantly was as important as, or more important than, any particular decision concerning credit and weapons.

The second goal of public diplomacy is to inform others about our way of life so that they will admire and, perhaps, imitate it. This goal is obviously less concrete than is the first, but it is coherent with the idea running through American history that a government based on natural rights is a blessing meant for all mankind and that we are its first true example if not its historic promoters. This theme inspired Lincoln, as is evident in the unmatched eloquence of his Gettysburg address; the authors of the *Federalist Papers* know themselves to be describing a government based more on timeless principle than on accident or exigency; Roosevelt used American resources in World War Two not so much to defend interests as to defend a way of life.

Public diplomacy is meant to display and describe this way of life; more concretely, at its best it brings to the fore the implicit vitality and the political structure that forms and organizes the American community. As Aristotle shows in *Politics,* a country is defined primarily in terms of the virtues it favors and elevates, how these virtues are understood, and the human character that sums up these qualities. This character and this human type can be grasped most completely through an understanding of how and why the country is organized constitutionally to produce and replicate it.

To display our way of life to foreigners, therefore, is the foundation of public diplomacy or *civic* education, because the connection of all our activities to representative democracy and liberal individualism is an implicit or explicit theme when we display these activities. One purpose of this broader effort is to create a backdrop of sympathy and understanding against which particular issues or crises may be played. Another is to overcome distortions—for instance, the allegation that the American way of life is so materialistic that it can support only vulgar entertainment. The purpose is to create understanding and appreciation that, along with other factors and under the proper circumstances, would help foreign nations achieve a government based on individual rights. In this fashion, public diplomacy strives to create the deepest kind of friends and allies.[2]

THE ROLE OF THE
PRIVATE INSTITUTION

Obviously, private individuals and institutions can contribute to American public diplomacy as it has been defined here. Our way of life is dedicated to and built upon liberating the spirit of individuals who are equal in their rights. Its genius lies in permitting individual talent to blossom and in rewarding, and thus encouraging, individual energy. It would be impossible, therefore, to adequately display our way of life without featuring the private individual, because such a display focuses on individual talents and the community that allows them to flourish. Moreover, this liberation of the individual has produced a cornucopia of knowledge, understanding, and skill in the private sector—a resource that government allows to express itself but does not simply direct. An effective program of public diplomacy would be foolish to ignore such a resource; effective efforts must work together with the private sector to display this way of life and to utilize this liberated resource.

Displaying our life-style for appreciation and emulation is the first clear way in which the private sector can contribute to the deeper goal of public diplomacy. Private action is at the core of the way of life we wish to exhibit. Private citizens are the vortex of all exchange programs; visits and studies in the United States, even when government-sponsored, primarily involve private citizens. Manifested in the daily lives of private citizens are the vitality of our economy; the expression of our freedoms of religion, speech, and association; and the energy of our participation in politics. To become familiarized with the United States is to observe its citizens in action.

It is important to draw explicitly the connection among private action, freedom, and constitutional guarantees—or, at least, to make the connection obvious, even if it is not drawn didactically. Our interest is not simply to have others know and like us as people, or to appreciate us because of the benefits (teaching, advice, resources) they receive from us; rather, we must make evident the constitution (in a broad sense) that nurtures our private talents. Otherwise, we have not told the truth about our country and will leave others unnecessarily and unfairly in the dark. Clearly, it is easy to fall on the wrong side of the line between useful understanding and unattractive preaching, but this is no excuse for pretending that our politics, wealth, and freedom are unconnected.

Even if it appears to be an embarrassing exhibit of pride, public diplomacy should not be afraid to display the truth. When Tocqueville came to America, he primarily uncovered the connection between the democratic spirit and the separate elements of religious and economic life, voluntarism, and self-government. He was thus able to grasp the deep and long-range dangers to which the American public is prey. Tocqueville provides the model through which foreign citizens seek to understand us and to which those engaged in helping them to understand should aspire.

The effect of our form of government is most visible among private citizens; hence, they are at the core of successful public diplomacy. Private citizens and institutions also are useful when public diplomacy is pursued more explicitly, because they often have expertise and credibility that the government lacks. When the U.S. government is explicitly promoting appreciation or emulation of the American way of life, private institutions can be vital. If voluntary organizations, free labor unions, business associations, free elections, or fair judicial systems are to be described or instituted, who can train more professionally and credibly than the members of the institutions themselves? If American political institutions and principles are to be taught successfully, who is more qualified than scholars from private or local institutions? Private institutions have a freedom of action that displays what government can only discuss. Indeed, the explicit public diplomacy of our citizens demonstrates their vitality to foreigners and contributes domestically to our own civic education.

There are, however, areas of tension between public diplomacy and the private sector. From the government's standpoint, a private institution is most useful when it emphasizes the country's or institution's desirable, rather than undesirable, features; does just what the government would have done without the stigma of government; advances the broader understanding of our way of life, promoting more than friendship and good feeling; and does all this without negating the more narrow explanation of particular policies that an administration is offering. Naturally, private institutions engaged in public diplomacy are unlikely to meet these criteria perfectly.

If an institution is not supported by the government but is simply being itself (for example, a university with foreign students, a U.S.-based multinational corporation, a private exchange group), it has its own interest. Its own interest will be to further its narrow and immediate aims, not usually in conscious opposition to the government, but usually disregarding it. If a private group is supported by the government, it will have the same motivation as other private groups, but with less justification for pursuing this motivation. For the government to usefully engage private institutions in its public diplomacy efforts, private institutions must allow the public interest to moderate self-interest, but the government must understand the independent status of private groups.

Although private institutions and individuals normally will think of their own interests first, and not adjust their programs and activities to serve a public diplomatic interest not identical to their own, we should also recognize that they often find themselves serving the country, especially when they notice that by dealing with foreign citizens they have placed themselves within a public situation. Private exchanges often immediately and directly display the quality of American patriotism and the unique strength of devotion to the common good visible among citizens whose individual rights have been secured. In fact, the public activity of private citizens—their voting, judging, and deliberating—is probably the most characteristic American phenomenon and the most instructive theme of public diplomacy. The work of elected representatives is similar to the public activity of private citizens. Displaying this activity is crucial to properly presenting our way of life.

The credibility and expertise of private individuals also serve the more narrow public diplomatic task of clarifying U.S. policies, which is ordinarily best left to officials. Private citizens, however, can be helpful in informal discussions with other private citizens or, even, in unofficial discussions with other governments; private citizens are independent and, therefore, especially believable to some.[3] Few things are as convincing as an intelligent scholar's or journalist's independent conclusions. Moreover, private citizens are often able to explore the grounds and direction of policy more freely than officials can and, thus, frame the terms of debate in which immediate issues are discussed. The Strategic Defense Initiative (SDI) debate, for example, has largely been conducted by private individuals who can offer evidence and argument that stray from approved positions but are, nonetheless, convincing.

Obviously, a government that makes explicit use of private individuals to explain policy must be especially careful. Although the free flow of debate and discussion is so central to American life that it is always useful and proper to display it, the explicit defense of current policy must sometimes be clarified, without hesitation and opposition. The same effort cannot always serve the dual purpose of public diplomacy.

Guidelines for the Future

Our discussion of the use of private individuals and institutions to serve public diplomacy points to guidelines for government in dealing with these institutions. I will frame these guidelines generally rather than in terms of specific subjects. The government's financial support for the public diplomatic efforts of private institutions and individuals should be commensurate with the strengths of private institutions. Because these strengths are independence, credibility, and expertise, support should not be so great that it fosters dependence and saps vitality, so intrusive that it weakens credibility, or so restrictive that it causes excessively hesitant judgment. What support exists should be directed toward and conditioned upon the manner in which recipients serve the goals of public diplomacy, and not merely their other aims.

A government has no particular requirement to subsidize the promulgation of private informational efforts abroad whose policy views it disputes. The deeper goal of public diplomacy, however, does require that the self-criticism and openness, which are as much a part of our policy debate as they are a part of other areas of our life, be displayed adequately. But this self-criticism is not the only factor defining us. From the government's point of view, the crucial factor in judging the utility of a private effort is its contribution in displaying a broad, unashamed, and realistic understanding of our way of life and its central institutions. To be more precise than this would be to suggest falsely that good government can be reduced to exact calculation, when at best it is the exercise of prudent judgment.

This may seem unfortunately imprecise to those who desire a fully coordinated public diplomacy strategy. But the very existence of private efforts makes evident the limits to simply controlled and coordinated policies. Rather than attempting to ape the structures of complete control, practitioners of U.S. public diplomacy should recognize and enhance the spirit of independence.

DISCUSSION

John D. Sullivan*

Mark Blitz's paper provides an excellent guide for examining, not only the role of the private sector in public diplomacy, but also the appropriate circumstances under which the U.S. government and the American people should support private institutional and individual involvement in public diplomatic activities. To illustrate the conduct of public diplomacy through private sector activity, I will briefly describe the Center for International Private Enterprise (CIPE). From the perspective of a private sector participant, I will then offer some additional remarks on Dr. Blitz's concept of the tension between the goals of public diplomacy and the related concept of credibility.

In 1983 the U.S. Chamber of Commerce established CIPE in response to President Reagan's democracy initiative, presented in his address to members of the British Parliament. The president's speech exhorted the American private sector to provide assistance to their counterparts abroad in order to strengthen the infrastructure of democracy by fostering the development of pluralist private sector institutions. After extensive study, representatives of the Chamber of Commerce, the AFL-CIO, the democratic and republican parties, and other private individuals proposed establishment of the National Endowment for Democracy (NED). Thanks to the efforts of a bipartisan group of congressional sponsors, in late 1983 the NED concept was approved by

*John D. Sullivan is director of public and congressional affairs at the Center for International Private Enterprise, a nonprofit affiliate of the U.S. Chamber of Commerce. His remarks are his own views and not necessarily the policy of the CIPE or the U.S. Chamber of Commerce.

Congress as a funding mechanism to support the efforts of various private sector organizations.

CIPE's objectives are to support the development of open market, private enterprise systems and independent business institutions abroad as a means of fostering the growth of democratic pluralism. In this respect, CIPE is partly an example of the broader conception of public diplomacy described by Dr. Blitz. He notes that the second goal of public diplomacy is to inform others about the American way of life so that they might admire and, perhaps, imitate it; such an objective highlights the implicit connection between our economic and cultural vitality and the political structure that forms and organizes the American community.

In part, however, CIPE's goals transcend the traditional definition of public diplomacy. As President Reagan remarked in a White House ceremony celebrating the creation of the NED:

> Now, we're not naive. We're not trying to create imitations of the American system around the world. There's no simple cookbook recipe for political development that is right for all people, and there's no timetable. While democratic principles and basic institutions are universal, democratic development must take into account historic, cultural, and social conditions. Each nation, each movement will find its own route.[4]

In the sense described by the president, CIPE and the other private sector institutions that shape the NED contribute to the broad conception of the national interest; that is, to aid U.S. friends and to encourage the development of democratic forms of governance throughout the world. In terms of the war of ideas, it is the ideas and ideals of democracy that are being counterposed to those of the Soviets, other Marxist movements, and authoritarian regimes.

A few summary descriptions of a cross section of CIPE programs will illustrate these thoughts. Our assistance is enabling the Center for Economic and Educational Studies (CEES) of Monterey, Mexico, to train 39 journalists in economics and to prepare editorials on open market issues to reach a combined daily readership of more than 3 million Mexicans. Since economics is frequently misunderstood in Mexico, the CEES program is a vehicle to create an awareness, directly through editorials and indirectly through the journalists who participate in the economic education program, of the essential role that private enterprise plays in a democratic society.

Through a grant to the Pan American Development Foundation,

CIPE has supported efforts of the Nicaraguan Development Foundation to document the small or informal business sector's determination to resist the collectivization campaign launched by the Sandinista government. CIPE funds have enabled the Nicaraguan entrepreneurs to warn their counterparts in other Central American republics of the dangers that will befall those business communities that fail to implement open markets and democratic institutions.

Similarly, the Institute for Liberty and Democracy (ILD) in Lima, Peru, is using CIPE funds to advocate open markets and open political institutions. ILD has found that nearly 60 percent of the entrepreneurs in Lima have been forced to operate outside of the legal economy through a system of government by decree. These "informal" entrepreneurs find their path to credit, property rights, insurance, and market entry blocked by a complex web of regulation and bureaucracy inherited from the traditional Spanish mercantile system and by the dearth of democratic institutions for redress of grievances. ILD's efforts to reform this system have resulted in extensive media attention to the open market approach and to the need for greater participation in the public policy process.

In a different type of program, CIPE support is enabling the Zimbabwe National Chamber of Commerce to strengthen its position as a national business voice on policy issues through a program designed to expand membership and chamber programs throughout the country. Establishing a broad membership base outside the large metropolitan areas, and introducing chamber programs directly benefiting small businesses and entrepreneurs, greatly enhances the business community's strength and influence.

The common theme of all these programs is the notion of enabling indigenous organizations to fortify their strength and their role in the democratic process. Although some of CIPE's training programs are conducted in the United States to the benefit of foreign association executives, many are not. All of the programs, however, expose the participants to the fundamentals of democratic processes and the implicit relationship between open markets and open political systems.

Given Dr. Blitz's intriguing concept of the tension between the goals of public diplomacy, it is difficult to understand how programs such as those described above will always promote an administration's specific policy initiatives. Indeed, should it be maintained that a foreign business association had to subscribe to the specific policy positions of the U.S. government to participate in a CIPE-funded program, the very success of such programs would be undermined.

Perhaps a more minimalist construction is appropriate, that is, requiring privately operated public diplomacy programs not to conflict with official policy. If the understood purpose is not always to support every policy position but rather to support the general conduct of foreign policy, then coordination is not a difficult task. This is the sense of what President Reagan exhorted in his remarks about NED.

In discussing the relationship between debate and credibility, Mark Blitz makes an excellent case for private involvement. I would add that credibility is the product of the creative tension between short- and long-term goals. The Soviets do not understand these points, and their programs are, consequently, often heavy-handed and counterproductive. Their communist international front organizations lack the effectiveness of privately conducted public diplomacy precisely because they require subservient adherence to specific policy initiatives without freedom of expression.

In his conclusion, Dr. Blitz advances general guidelines that are worthy of careful consideration. Private efforts should not simply be extensions of the interests of their respective parent organizations; for such programs to be effective, they cannot simply be self-serving. The genius of America's global role has always been, and should remain, to further broad principles—even if that role is purely public, as in the case of government or publicly supported private efforts. I would add an additional criterion: effectiveness. Greater efforts to measure effectiveness would benefit the public diplomacy community; given the meager resources available in contrast to the magnitude of the task, we cannot ignore the question of what works.

Michael Joyce

As a representative of a private foundation that makes grants in the area of what loosely might be called public diplomacy, my associates and I are guided by our own insight and act in our own peculiar, idiosyncratic manner. In this sense, we are a private sector within the American private sector. Many critics are quick to note that such behavior only highlights the need for effective coordination, that is, a centralization of programs and purposes, perhaps orchestrated by agencies in Washington, D.C.

By serving strong and vigorous purposes, however, private institutions can contribute to the vitality of our national ethos. Those who care most about private sector institutions are likely to care most about our nation's welfare. The resultant federalizing spirit draws from the energy of citizens in different ways and through the mediation of different institutions. This spirit does not pit local institutions and sentiments against national concerns but, instead, harnesses them for purposes varying yet complementary.

I would like to discuss three points from Mark Blitz's admirable paper. First, I commend his effort to define, precisely, the term *public diplomacy*—a term that has different, often incompatible, meanings to different people. Someone once remarked that although Americans never invent new political ideas, they endlessly invent new applications for the old ones. As Mark Blitz has demonstrated, this assessment of public diplomacy represents a new application of an old political idea.

Second, his paper openly discusses the tensions between public diplomacy's requirements and the private sector's character. Public diplomacy is concerned with the larger aims of the regime and is, therefore, mostly the responsibility of the U.S. government; however, the government often inspires, sponsors, or even directs a private sector component. Such an arrangement is fraught with problems and tensions, since Americans do not like to be directed by the national government, particularly when the directives concern the central ideas of the republic, ideas that the American people believe specially identify them. This sensitivity to governmental coordination is more exaggerated among academics and journalists.

Mark Blitz has aptly avoided a digression about the so-called public-private partnership; in fact, his paper might just have a historic significance. Has any public official in the last decade discussed private sector roles without pushing for a partnership? Too often such discussions of public-private partnerships focus on fund-raising, arranging for others to pay for a particular agenda, or even organizing private groups to press their special interests on the federal government.

There is an older sense of real partnership in America, one that transcends the private-public sector distinction and that restores a view of citizenship that has gradually eroded. We often interpret this notion too narrowly by becoming overly absorbed in various technical questions: how partnerships will be implemented, who will be the managing partner, and who will pay for what. Before real partnerships can exist, there must be common purposes, at the core of which is the character of our social compact itself. Perhaps the greatest strength in the U.S. private sector is the healthy competition of ideas, with many different centers of authority and opinion vigorously debating American purposes. In connection with the implementation of public diplomacy programs, allegations about blacklisting inquisitions partly reflect an unwillingness to consider seriously these questions of purpose. This should, however, not surprise anyone.

In the early part of this century, the Englishman G. K. Chesterton visited the United States and recorded his impressions:

> The American Constitution does resemble the Spanish Inquisition in this: that it is founded on a creed. America is the only nation in the world that is founded on a creed. That creed is set forth with dogmatic and even theological lucidity in the Declaration of Independence; perhaps the only piece of practical politics that is also theoretical politics and also great literature. It enunciates that all men are equal in their claim to justice, that their governments exist to give them that justice, and that their authority is for that reason just.[5]

The most profound observation in Mark Blitz's paper is that healthy public opinion is a goal of policy and not just a framework for the acceptance of still other policies. Although I would have liked him to explicate more fully on this point, it accentuated the essential and defining characteristic of successful public diplomacy efforts: leadership. Good or bad leaders will always be with us. Democratic governments become a menace to civilization when they evade this truth by appeals to effective management, partnership, and reorganization; or, in particular, by the conceit that a substitute for leadership can be found in numerical majorities reflecting a vague notion of the general will. American public diplomacy efforts will be judged, no less than those of other nations, by the quality of U.S. leaders; they, in turn, by the quality of their ideas and vision.

Alan A. Rubin

I wish to address the subject of public diplomacy exclusively from a "people" perspective, which has been neglected at this workshop. I feel a bit like Rodney Dangerfield exclaiming emphatically that "we ain't got much respect": I represent probably the most powerful group of public diplomats currently in the business. I am referring to the private sector, nongovernmental public diplomacy efforts not only of my organization, Partners of the Americas but also of dozens of other people-to-people nongovernmental organizations throughout the United States, Latin America, and other parts of the world.

I am convinced that it is the person-to-person contacts across national boundaries that play an increasingly significant role in overcoming areas of misunderstanding and in opening and maintaining channels of communication—be it the Peace Corps and its third mandate (to bring the world back home through its 100,000 returned volunteers); the thousands of incredibly creative high school youth exchanges that annually take place; a Sister City relationship; a Friendship Force flight of private citizens to the Soviet Union; a local council for international visitors in Salt Lake City, Des Moines, or Denver to host an important foreign visitor; or a partnership between a U.S. state and a country in Central America that has endured twenty years of good and bad times. These person-to-person contacts facilitate the appreciation of human values and of cultural differences and, thereby, improve the climate for coping with the problems of an interdependent and rapidly changing world.

America's two-way involvement with the rest of the world is so diverse and so rich that it is virtually impossible to keep track of it all, or to measure accurately its impact. One must, however, recognize its magnitude and potential.

Private Sector Public Diplomacy

Private sector personal contacts across national boundaries serve as channels of communication that are basic to international understanding and cooperation, and maintenance of the realities of an increasingly interdependent world. The nongovernmental sector in the United States and other parts of the world provides a copious resource for fruitful personal interaction. Academic institutions, corporations, philanthropic groups, state and local governments, labor unions, professional associations, libraries, museums, hospitals, and community organizations hold great potential to communicate with other societies and involve them with the United States.

Person-to-Person Communication in Perspective

International personal interactions form vast networks based on common interests cutting across national boundaries. More than any other form of communication, these face-to-face interactions enable people to truly know and understand one another. They provide the opportunity for two-way dialogue and give-and-take communication.

Person-to-person contacts contribute to international cooperation in several ways. They strengthen the individual's vested interest in a pluralistic and stable international system and contribute to a reduction of tensions by breaking down polarization along purely national lines. Nations whose citizens have many contacts in areas of similar interests can communicate more readily and accommodate on particular conflict issues. Such contacts lead not only to global perspective on issues that might otherwise be seen only in national terms but also to a stronger commitment to international institutions and organizations. They can foster peace and stability.

Each year many hundreds of thousands of individuals contribute to this intersocietal understanding; they do so through their normal pursuits in all walks of life. Citizens in the business, professional, arts, sports, science, labor, and education sectors and in humanitarian, civic, and private endeavors encounter with international counterparts. Such contacts usually are byproducts of individual or organizational activities and are not undertaken with the specific objective of increased understanding. In addition, many private exchange organizations have the clearly defined objective to promote understanding through personal contact.

Recommendations

The private sector could and should do much more to further international understanding through person-to-person contact.

1. *Increase public awareness and recognition of transnational personal contact.* There should be a more conscious effort to heighten awareness of the contribution of meaningful two-way person-to-person contact. It should focus on the imperative created by growing interdependence. Such an effort would lead to greater commitment by individuals and organizations to involve themselves in purposeful activities both in the United States and abroad.

In developing this informed public concern, many separate publics will have to be motivated through opinion molders and group leaders. They include journalists, scholars, professionals, scientists, and state and local government officials as well as leaders of businesses, foundations, labor organizations, and voluntary groups.

2. *Enhance the contribution of existing private American person-to-person exchange organizations by reorienting programs to cope with interdependence, promoting democracy, strengthening management capabilities, and increasing financial support.* Ironically, despite the increasing awareness and impact of interdependence, American nongovern-

mental organizations that have promoted international understanding through exchange-of-persons programs often find themselves in great difficulty. Inflation has reduced their financial powers; global recession with rising unemployment has increased pressure on these programs to become more economical and vocationally relevant.

Private agencies currently active in person-to-person exchanges should re-examine their purposes and their goals. They should more aggressively seek support and assistance to undertake such reviews. They must find ways to attract volunteers, to raise funds, and to improve their programs. These organizations must consider more deliberately how they can become more responsive to the needs of an interdependent world.

3. *Develop new approaches and organizational arrangements at the national, state, and local levels to reciprocate exemplary initiatives of the many non-exchange-oriented organizations and institutions involved internationally.* Many private sector groups involved in international person-to-person activities provide an abundance of program ideas that should be conducted more broadly. Some of the areas in which there is a need for identification and replication of outstanding programs are the following:

- Providing hospitality and programming to foreign students, scholars, and other visitors (under both government and private sponsorship)
- Strengthening ties with international alumni of American colleges and universities who have returned to their home countries
- Programming for visiting business, labor, diplomatic, sports, cultural, and professional groups
- Providing common interest opportunities to foreign scholars in the United States and to Americans studying abroad
- Engaging retired U.S. diplomats in voluntary organizations
- Involving American business persons and their families living abroad in worthwhile cross-cultural activities

There are many more possible programs. To achieve maximum national and international impact, such programs and opportunities must be identified on a continuing basis. Essential to the success of such endeavors is its implementation by the private sector. The government should support such high-quality private sector initiatives because of their multiplier potential.

4. *Increased recognition by the transnational business community that it has much to gain by investing more in person-to-person relations.* Personal interaction between American companies and their counterparts abroad occurs (both abroad and in the U.S.) while conducting their normal business and fulfilling their international corporate social responsibilities. Although substantial progress has been made in this area by a number of companies, there still remains a great deal to do. As multinational enterprises expand their operations, such responsible corporate behavior is not only in their own interest but can also be designed to meet host country development and education priorities. The potential for greater contribution is thus unlimited.

There should be an ongoing effort to stimulate wider adoption of proven program ideas. Although government helps to provide recognition, business is most responsive to private sector encouragement. Worthy proposals receive full attention, many specific program ideas have been developed and tested. There is enormous potential for business to contribute through more creative and purposeful leadership in this area.

5. *Strengthen the commitment of America's foundation community to this important aspect of international affairs.* America's foundations, both private and corporate, currently support person-to-person activities. There is, however, a need for greater commitment to reflect the increased international involvement and responsibilities of Americans to cope with interdependence. Joint programming by foundations can play a significant role in sponsoring re-evaluation of purposes and operations and can help instill increased national acceptance of the importance of person-to-person communication on a global scale.

6. *Expand scholarly research in this field and improve its utilization and quality.* Both abroad and in the United States, there is considerable worthwhile scholarly research available in academic institutions that bears on the question of promoting mutual understanding. New research needs to be undertaken that can, subsequently, be disseminated widely, especially research related to geographic regions and the nature of person-to-person communication.

The Government's Support of Private Sector Efforts

The United States has a large stake in the strength and adaptability to change world conditions of nongovernmental person-to-person programs that delve directly into American communities. Governments everywhere, therefore, need to nourish and reinforce the private sector's efforts—as I have outlined them above—as a matter of conscious public policy. There are two priority tasks.

First, the scattered elements of the executive branch of the government need to be coherently mobilized to encourage private sector support and participation. These elements include the educational and cultural programs of the U.S. Department of State, USIA, AID, the Peace Corps; and the international activities of the U.S. departments of education and commerce and other executive agencies.

Second, presidential leadership and appropriate congressional support along these lines will have an enormous multiplier effect in galvanizing person-to-person international activities by local communities and national organizations. Launched in 1982, President Reagan's International Youth Exchange Initiative was a historic first with an enormous yield in the quantity and quality of exchanges. Recognizing the need to expand youth activities—our future leaders—is absolutely essential for the future.

A Next Step

A nongovernmental mechanism has long been needed to draw together the private sector's power and potential in the public diplomacy field. An organization outside of government should be established to ensure cooperation of the nation's diverse private sector elements and the various governmental units concerned. As its purpose, the national body should develop an international activity council in each state. Under the leadership and guidance of state governors, the state councils could stimulate and foster the purposeful international involvement of concerned groups and persons in their respective states. Ultimately, these state councils could form the basis to establish a National Endowment for International Activity.

Given leadership and commitment, within a year we can create a national network—drawing together the copious resources and energies of the American people and their organizations—to conduct more significant international programs of public diplomacy. We have the opportunity to tap the American people's contributions to an expanded person-to-person public diplomacy that will ultimately lead to a more peaceful and predictable world order.

NOTES

1. Because domestic and foreign civic education are not identical, it would be useful if *public diplomacy,* as a term, were reserved for international activities. The euphemistic imperative, however, sometimes suggests *public diplomacy* as a useful term to describe a major effort to defend a foreign policy domestically.

2. On this basis, we can see how public diplomacy often shades into more concrete efforts to promote political development.

3. This accounts for governments with no true individual freedom occasionally establishing or supporting front organizations that mimic the genuine private sector.

4. President Ronald Reagan, "National Endowment for Democracy," *Weekly Compilation of Presidential Documents,* vol. 19, 19 December 1984, pp. 1702–4.

5. G. K. Chesterton, *What I Saw in America* (New York: Dodd, Mead and Co., 1922), p. 7.

PART TWO

PROSPECTS AND OPPORTUNITIES

6

Some Issues in Public Diplomacy

*Edwin J. Feulner, Jr.**

When the annual report of the U.S. Advisory Commission on Public Diplomacy came out, my wife looked at my picture on page four and said, "I note your characteristic modesty." As a senator once said about a colleague, I have much to be modest about: The advisory committee's report was predominantly the work of our extraordinarily fine staff at the commission. Our staff director, Bruce Gregory, and his colleague, Mike Morgan—both career officers at the United States Information Agency (USIA)—have been extremely helpful to my six colleagues and myself, interested citizen volunteers, in grappling with public diplomacy issues.

Our definition of public diplomacy is articulated on the inside cover of the annual report:

> Public Diplomacy supplements and reinforces traditional diplomacy by explaining U.S. policies to foreign publics, by providing them with information about American society and culture, by enabling many to experience the diversity of our country personally, and by assessing foreign public opinion for American ambassadors and foreign policy decisionmakers in the United States. The organization principally responsible for carrying out our country's public diplomacy is the United States Information Agency.

*The author would like to thank Martha Muse and her colleagues at the Tinker Foundation as well as Glenn Campbell and others at the Hoover Institution for their hospitality.

It is not one-shot dramatic efforts that make public diplomacy succeed. Rather, it is the steady, wise use of all of the resources of public diplomacy over time. It is recognition by those who seek disproportionately to enhance educational and cultural exchange that the articulation of U.S. policies is also necessary to mutual understanding and rational international dialogue. It is understanding by those who support the vigorous expression of U.S. policies that the Fulbright and International Visitors programs provide foreign audiences with the background and knowledge of our culture that put those policies in perspective. And it is appreciation by our elected and appointed officials of the importance of foreign public opinion and the power of ideas in international political discourse.[1]

As chairman of the commission, I am pleased that during the course of this workshop many participants have referred to our slender report as the most definitive work on public diplomacy available. I particularly commend Ambassador Staar and his Hoover colleagues for convening this conference and providing the opportunity for so many people from so many diverse perspectives to gather and discuss various aspects of public diplomacy. Although governments and the media are paying increasing attention to public diplomacy, it does not receive adequate attention as a subject of research and serious academic inquiry at universities and think tanks. This workshop is a welcome exception and certainly a start toward meeting this need.

I would like to address some of the views that we, as citizen volunteers, have as members of the advisory commission. Particularly those of us who have been involved in the Washington public policy process (Herb Schmertz, Tom Korologos, bob wallach, and others) have found that the urgent overwhelms the important in our nation's capital. For those involved in the management of a government program, the daily problems do tend to overwhelm the underlying themes—in this case public diplomacy, largely a USIA task but also that of other U.S. government agencies.

Those of us on the advisory commission who are not responsible for daily management have a more detached perspective. We have worked together for several years in attempting to classify some of these important underlying issues. As Mark Blitz has discussed in his paper, one of these issues is the tension between the two separate roles of USIA: advocacy, on the one hand; education, on the other. Authorized by the Smith-Mundt and Fulbright-Hays acts, both roles are important aspects of the agency's mandate.

A new set of tensions can be characterized as the conflict between security for American diplomats and access by foreign publics to USIA's libraries and information centers. Those involved in this conflict on a daily basis are cognizant of the Advisory Panel on Overseas Security, known as the Inman Panel. Frankly, if the report of the Inman Panel is enacted to the letter at every USIA post, a great deal of our nation's public diplomacy programs will no longer be possible in many countries. The panel's recommendations involve 100-foot setbacks for buildings and very tight security for operations and facilities that fundamentally require an openness to the broad public.

People who stand in lines at U.S. embassies waiting for a visa probably have the initiative to travel ten miles outside a city center at 5:00 A.M. so that a consular official can process their application in a remote, secure building that meets all of the Inman Panel's standards. But if one is trying to encourage journalists to come to a United States Information Service (USIS) center or audiences to attend a lecture by an American speaker or students to visit a USIS library, one will probably not encounter that kind of motivation. Our commission is working with USIA, the Department of State, and others to resolve this dilemma in some reasonable fashion.

A third concern involves assessing the impact of public diplomacy programs. As an unabashed conservative, I am frequently urging my conservative friends on Capitol Hill to allot more funds to USIA. About every other government program I am always saying that the United States should not just throw more money at it: The same standard should hold true for public diplomacy programs. But how does one measure the effectiveness of these kinds of programs? The research operation at USIA is a step in the right direction; however, whether it is adequate and structurally sound is another area of inquiry.

Our commission is also actively interested in media training for U.S. ambassadors. In June 1985, Herb Schmertz and I were involved in launching a pilot program in London for ten American ambassadors and their public affairs officers (PAOs) from various parts of Europe. We had a major New York public relations firm send over a training team on a *pro bono publico* basis and found respective sponsors for a dinner and for lodging costs. Ten ambassadors and their PAOs experienced two days of intensive hands-on television interview training. We are still getting feedback from that program, and so far, it has all been very positive. And yet, the first question we asked ourselves was, why is this not already part of the traditional training program? Well, I hope that it will be in the future: Sometimes an outside group, like our commission, can serve as a catalyst to move policy in new directions.

Integrating and coordinating public diplomacy efforts throughout the government is another issue. For example, it came to my attention earlier in 1985 that our military attachés in Europe are not specifically assigned the responsibility of promoting the president's Strategic Defense Initiative (SDI). This seemed incomprehensible to me. Several of us talked to Pentagon officials, and it is now part of the mandate of military attachés. The reasons why this suggestion came from outside are unclear, but at least the suggestion became policy.

Another example of coordinating efforts involves the semantic infiltration issue that Herb Romerstein is currently working on at USIA and that we have mentioned in the commission's annual reports of the past several years. With such developments as the National Security Council's interagency coordinating structure for public diplomacy (NSDD-77), officials in different government sectors are now communicating with one another and considering these kinds of questions.

USIA's WORLDNET television service is also a concern, not as a concept or a theoretical ideal, but in terms of its impact: What happens when WORLDNET reaches capitals around the world? In preparing for frequent, labor-intensive WORLDNET press interviews and teleconferences, the limited staff and resources of USIA posts will be distracted from their other numerous responsibilities. What kind of new human resources do we need in the field to make WORLDNET truly effective?

These types of specific questions, and some of the underlying theoretical public diplomacy issues, are the issues on which the advisory commission focuses. Sometimes these issues are practical ones, such as representation allowances for the USIA officers who are supposed to be contacting and entertaining key opinion leaders and decisionmakers in the countries in which they serve. On this kind of issue, the commission can perhaps be of some assistance to USIA on Capitol Hill.

We work closely not only with those managing America's public diplomacy structure but also with representatives on Capitol Hill. With the possible exception of the chairman of the House Foreign Affairs Committee, Dante Fascell, until recently members of Congress have not had any sustained interest in public diplomacy. Over the last year, the commission has been attempting to rectify this situation through one-on-one contact in order to inform senators and representatives about the nature of public diplomacy.

Public diplomacy is as important in the affairs of nations as traditional diplomacy, economic capability, and military preparedness. It must be treated with the same urgency and concern. Traditional diplomats (ours included) are remiss if they fail to acquire media skills and sensitivity. The exploding communications revolution, the broadcast satellite, the shortwave radio signal, the ease of international travel, and the swift global flow of information is such that democracies and even the most rigid dictatorships cannot ignore public attitudes and concerns. Foreign perceptions of the United States and its policies may influence the policies of other countries; they will certainly affect the success of our own.

NOTES

1. United States Advisory Commission on Public Diplomacy, *1985 Report* (Washington, D.C., February 1985), inside cover.

7

FUNCTIONING OF
DIPLOMATIC ORGANS

Gifford D. Malone

The present time is unusually propitious for a discussion of public diplomacy and an examination of the institutions that are responsible for it. Today public diplomacy is in a transitional phase. The idea of public diplomacy is undergoing modification, and the institutions of government primarily concerned with it are changing in their attitudes and relationships. We are in a time of accelerating technological change, which will certainly affect the future conduct of public diplomacy. Thus, an examination of the functioning of our foreign affairs organs will help us to understand what is happening and where we may be headed.

This examination is concerned primarily with roles, relationships, and methods of operation. Obviously, the content of public diplomacy is a critically important matter, but it can be separated from the structure and functioning of institutions. This analysis focuses on governmental organs, in particular, the U.S. Department of State, the United States Information Agency (USIA), and the interagency structure of which they are a part. I have not included private sector activities, not because they are unimportant, but because they are absent from the issues under consideration. Likewise, I have not included Radio Free Europe/Radio Liberty because, although it serves an important function of public diplomacy, RFE-RL is not, technically speaking, a diplomatic organ.

Changing Characteristics
of Public Diplomacy

The Reagan administration has placed a strong imprint on public diplomacy. Without noting the general changes that have occurred since January 1981, one cannot easily understand the present functioning of our foreign affairs organs in this sphere of activity. In several important respects this administration differs from its predecessor and from others in the past.

Growing Interest and Shifting Emphasis

The first obvious difference is the extremely high level of interest, based upon a strong belief in the power of communication and ideas to effect changes in the world. Public diplomacy is seen, not as a neutral process of interaction, but as an instrument of foreign policy to achieve specified goals. Not surprisingly, there have been some exaggerated hopes associated with this outlook and occasional expectations that an all-out public affairs effort on a particular issue could turn the tide; this has done no particular harm, however, and experience seems already to have had a tempering effect.

Public diplomacy has long been regarded as incorporating two rather different elements, with varying emphasis upon one or the other: elements of persuasion, directed toward short-term policy objectives, and efforts to promote general understanding, with reliance on programs not tied to day-to-day policy concerns. Support for the second gained ground in the 1970s and reached a high point during the Carter administration, whose stated public diplomacy goals stressed mutuality of understanding and two-way communication.

The Reagan administration arrived on the scene determined to employ public diplomacy more aggressively. Although it by no means rejected educational and cultural programs—aspects of public diplomacy usually associated with promoting understanding over the long term—its first concern was the information arm. Over time its view of public diplomacy has broadened, its interest in the "softer" side has grown accordingly, and it now pays considerable attention to activities throughout the public diplomacy spectrum. Nonetheless, the Reagan administration still regards public diplomacy as a foreign policy instrument. In contrast to some of its predecessors, the current administration has been generous in its material support of this instrument: Resources allocated to public diplomacy have been substantially increased, reflecting both the executive branch's readiness to spend money on this function and Congress's willingness to provide it.

Another notable feature has been the extent to which people throughout the executive branch have become interested and involved in public diplomacy. This is evident in the cooperation USIA has received for its programs from individual administration members. The readiness of senior officials in many departments to meet foreign press representatives and to appear on international television interview programs is only one example among countless others.

Institutional Participation

The administration's distinctly activist approach to public diplomacy has also affected institutional behavior. Whereas previously the field was reserved mainly for USIA and RFE-RL, others have now become involved more directly. In addition to USIA, the current major players are the White House and National Security Council (NSC), and the U.S. Department of State. They are joined, in a more limited way, by the U.S. Department of Defense and the Agency for International Development.

The evolution in the State Department's role may be the most important. It has always had a stake in public diplomacy and, hence, an interest in the activities of USIA and the broadcasting organizations (including the Voice of America). In the past, ambassadors in the field have tended to pay attention to these activities, because USIA provided programs and events that served their purposes and because the radio organizations occasionally broadcast items that could cause them problems, or at least so they feared. Until recently, however, genuine interest in most aspects of public diplomacy within the State Department has been slight. Speeches by the secretary and other senior officers have been recognized as having importance for foreign audiences, but this is only a small segment of the total public diplomacy picture. In addition, most department officers have regarded international educational and cultural programs as, in principle, desirable; however, there was not much interest beyond that, even when such activities were managed by the department itself. The Bureau of Educational and Cultural Affairs (whose functions were transferred to USIA in 1978) was never an organization in which most U.S. foreign service officers were anxious to serve.

Attitudes within the State Department have changed considerably. From early days of the administration when State Department officers joined USIA colleagues to discuss projects related to such trouble spots as Poland and Afghanistan, public diplomacy interagency working groups have become common features of several of the State Department's bureaus. Senior officials have been appointed to direct special public diplomacy efforts, and State Department officers are now participating in a wide assortment of activities related to public diplomacy.

The Department of State was reacting, in part, to the White House, which set the tone and offered strong encouragement to public diplomacy efforts in general. The NSC established an office to deal specifically with these kinds of questions and today plays a central role in the interagency management of public diplomacy. Meanwhile, the Department of Defense established an office of its own, separate from its public affairs bureau, which, through contact with the foreign press and its role in the secretary's overseas activities, also has a public diplomacy connection. The Defense Department's efforts have included overseas conferences to discuss the Soviet military threat and the shared security concerns of the United States and its allies, foreign distribution of its annual report on Soviet military power, and internationally televised press conferences with the secretary.

The last two have been accomplished in cooperation with USIA. Early in the Reagan administration, a USIA officer was placed on the immediate staff of the undersecretary of defense for policy. The Agency for International Development (AID) has also become more interested in public diplomacy, and its representatives have been participating in interagency public diplomacy meetings. Within its own sphere of operations, AID has an interest in improving understanding abroad of its various programs. It has also entered into an exchange of senior officers with USIA.

Planning and Coordination

As different sectors of the administration increased their participation, as activities identified with public diplomacy multiplied, and as new programs were being formulated, some means of central direction and coordination other than ad hoc meetings was needed. Many kinds of activity could benefit from greater coordination, such as speech making by high officials on foreign affairs subjects, diplomatic and technical steps to improve international radio broadcasting, and efforts to counter Soviet propaganda and disinformation. Moreover, the administration was now working on a project to promote democracy abroad that would require the close cooperation of three foreign affairs agencies. Such factors all pointed to the need for some kind of well-defined interagency process. To serve this purpose, National Security Decision Directive 77

(NSDD–77), entitled "Management of Public Diplomacy Relative to National Security," was announced in January 1983.

NSDD–77 sought to bring focus and coordination to the numerous and disparate activities associated with public diplomacy.[1] The document directed the establishment of a group of interagency committees "to strengthen the organization, planning and coordination of the various aspects of public diplomacy of the United States Government relative to national security." It created a Special Planning Group (SPG) under the National Security Council, to be chaired by the assistant to the president for national security affairs and to include as members the secretaries of state and defense, the directors of USIA and AID, and the assistant to the president for communications. Senior representatives of other agencies could attend SPG sessions by invitation. The SPG was to be responsible for the "overall planning, direction, coordination and monitoring of implementation of public diplomacy activities."

The directive established four interagency committees, reporting to the SPG:

• The International Information Committee (IIC), to be chaired by a senior representative of USIA, would be responsible for the planning, coordinating, and implementation of international information activities.
• The International Political Committee (IPC), to be chaired by a senior representative of the State Department, was given broad responsibilities for "planning, coordinating and implementing" international political activities," which might include "aid, training and organizational support for foreign governments and private groups to encourage the growth of democratic political institutions and practices" or initiating programs to "counter totalitarian ideologies and aggressive political action moves undertaken by the Soviet Union or Soviet surrogates."
• The International Broadcasting Committee (IBC), to be chaired by a representative of the assistant to the president for national security affairs, was to be responsible for planning and coordinating international broadcasting activities sponsored by the United States government.
• The Public Affairs Committee (PAC), to be chaired by the assistant to the president for communications and the deputy assistant to the president for national security affairs, would be responsible for planning and coordinating U.S. Government domestic public affairs activities relating to foreign policy and national security issues.

Although there was precedent for interagency discussion of many of the types of questions now falling under the public diplomacy rubric, the structure that NSDD–77 created was innovative in form and concept. It was the most serious effort undertaken since Eisenhower's administration to establish a formal coordinating mechanism in this field.[2]

Project Democracy

The announcement of NSDD–77 coincided approximately with the unveiling of an ambitious program known as Project Democracy, or the President's Democracy and Public Diplomacy Initiative. Although as a whole this project failed to gain the approval of Congress, it deserves mention because of its connection with the evolving conception of public diplomacy and related institutional roles.

Project Democracy was intended to give programmatic substance to President Reagan's appeal, in his speech to the British Parliament on 8 June 1982, for a commitment to strengthen the "infrastructure of democracy" and to assist democratic development around the world.[3] It envisaged a broad array of programs, to be conducted by not only USIA but also the State Department and AID, and was presented as one legislative package in the USIA budget request. Although the U.S. Congress could hardly object to the principle of supporting the growth of democracy abroad, it criticized the legislative proposal and its apparent link to NSDD–77. Indeed, it is clear that a number of the functions of the International Political Committee, chaired by the State Department, were determined with Project Democracy in mind. Some members of Congress expressed concern that USIA programs might be determined by the NSC or other agencies. One major element of Project Democracy that survived the legislative process was the National Endowment for Democracy, a private, nonprofit corporation, which Congress felt to be a better vehicle than USIA for conducting some of the proposed initiatives.[4]

In retrospect, although based on an idea that most Americans would support, Project Democracy contained flaws that went beyond the various tactical misjudgments in its presentation. The implications of the proposal were never fully thought through. Mingling such a varied assortment of projects was not simply a "cosmetic" problem; it raised legitimate questions about how to preserve the integrity of long-established programs and about who would be responsible for managing them. Many projects were so vague that they created uncertainties about how they could be implemented or whether they would achieve their objectives. Although Project Democracy had laudable aims, it should not have been expected to gain congressional assent in the form in which it was conceived, and Congress was probably right in not approving it.

The Expanding Meaning of Public Diplomacy

NSDD–77 and Project Democracy gave formal endorsement to an expanded meaning of public diplomacy. Indeed, the term has never been satisfactory and has often meant different things to different people. Nevertheless, for some years it was a way—understood by the majority of those who used it—of describing collectively the various international information, educational, and cultural programs conducted by the United States. Until quite recently, few would have agreed that all of the functions assigned by NSDD–77 to the International Political Committee were a form of public diplomacy. The same is true of some of the Project Democracy proposals, such as citizens' action programs or assistance to free labor unions. Certainly one of the reasons that AID was made a member of the NSDD–77 coalition is that some of its functions fit more comfortably into a broader definition of public diplomacy than, for example, those of USIA.

Public diplomacy's meaning has expanded in other ways as well. One new and troublesome use of the term is its application to measures intended to persuade the American people of the correctness of our foreign policies. In the past, diplomacy (public or otherwise) was always assumed to be directed abroad. Public diplomacy is also now used in some quarters to mean simply techniques of public relations in the field of foreign relations. The cause of this expansion in meaning is beyond the scope of this paper, but one obvious factor is the entry of many new enthusiasts into public diplomacy, each with his own notion of its meaning and its importance. Paradoxically, the more active we have become as public diplomatists, the less clear we seem to be about what we are practicing.

USIA, THE STATE DEPARTMENT, AND NSDD–77

In the broad field of public diplomacy, the operation of three organizational entities is particularly important. The U.S. Information Agency, the State Department, and the NSDD–77 structure comprise the core of public diplomacy. Although formal members of the

NSDD–77 structure, and important in their own ways, the Agency for International Development and the Defense Department do not play a central role in the functioning of the system. On the other hand, the interrelationship of USIA, the State Department, and the NSDD–77 structure has wide implications for the management of public diplomacy.

A Brief Look at USIA

In one sense, USIA has been less affected than other government agencies by the changes that have occurred, since it would be conducting most of its present programs irrespective of NSDD–77 or the State Department's new interest in public diplomacy. These changes, however, have both immediate and long-term implications for USIA.

The current support for public diplomacy has been an important asset for USIA, which has gained both in material terms and in the cooperation it has received from the executive branch. USIA is a professional organization, with many years of experience, and it knows its business well. It is presently endowed with a strongly motivated and energetic leadership, some of whose accomplishments, such as the modernization of the Voice of America and the greatly expanded use of television as a public diplomacy tool, will be of lasting importance.

USIA is the agency chiefly responsible for conducting U.S. public diplomacy. Its mission is to explain U.S. policies abroad and, through its diverse programs, to promote foreign understanding of the United States: its people, history, culture, and system of government. The director of USIA reports to the president and receives foreign policy guidance from the secretary of state, and he is responsible for advising the president, secretary of state, and the National Security Council on foreign public opinion and the conduct of public diplomacy. USIA's programs fall primarily into the traditional categories of information, education, and culture, and they are directed toward foreign publics. Hence, the agency has been relatively unaffected in its own work by newer conceptions of public diplomacy that some others have embraced.

Obviously, to do its job well USIA needs not only the support of the president but also good working relations with other foreign affairs elements of government, above all, the Department of State. In practice, the working environment in Washington has varied from one administration to another, depending in considerable part upon the interests and attitudes of the president, secretary of state, and the USIA director. Until the Reagan administration, the historical high point was felt by many to have been reached in the Kennedy years, when Director Edward R. Murrow kept a telephone on his desk (which he called the "blowtorch") with a direct line to the president.[5]

At other times, circumstances have been different. Whereas the present USIA director regularly attends the secretary of state's morning staff meetings, this was not the custom of his predecessor in the Carter administration. Lower-level contacts—important for the daily conduct of USIA business—have depended frequently on the initiative of USIA officers who work hard to become and remain "plugged in" at the State Department and, if possible, elsewhere.

In most respects, USIA's current situation is more favorable than during any previous period. USIA officers still express frustration over problems with the State Department, but working relationships are probably closer and more extensive than ever before. NSDD–77 has benefited USIA by allowing it to participate together with senior departments in the committees and, of course, by conferring added importance on the activities in which USIA is engaged.

One other point, to which I shall return, needs to be mentioned. Despite the vigor of USIA activity, including its expanded public opinion research, and the decidedly favorable climate for public diplomacy in general, most of the interest engendered in the agencies concerned is directed toward programs. With a few exceptions, such as some interest at the NSC in a more integrated public opinion research effort, little attention has been paid to how public diplomacy concerns might be factored into policy formulation; USIA is rarely brought into the policy formulation process. Thus, USIA's responsibility to advise on the implications of foreign public opinion continues to be basically unfulfilled. The numerous converts to public diplomacy at the State Department and elsewhere have focused their attention almost exclusively upon what to do once a policy has been decided and announced.

The Role of the State Department

Probably the most important thing to be said about the State Department is that it has begun to take public diplomacy seriously. If one compares its outlook today with that of five years ago, one is struck by the difference. The State Department is involved in public diplomacy on a number of fronts in a variety of ways. Although, within the department, understanding of the uses of public diplomacy is uneven, the notion that it requires the department's attention is widely accepted. Public diplomacy is now handled through a number of mechanisms:

- As many as three senior officials, whose sole responsibility is one aspect or another of public diplomacy: a special adviser to the secretary on public diplomacy, a deputy for public diplomacy to the under secretary for political affairs, and a coordinator for public diplomacy in Central America and the Caribbean. (The first of these positions was recently abolished.) The assistant secretary for public affairs also plays a role in public diplomacy.
- Public diplomacy working groups, generally chaired by one or another bureau and including representatives of USIA and other agencies.
- Ad hoc groups to deal with special topics.
- Formal interagency committees established by NSDD–77.
- The Bureau of Public Affairs.

Through these mechanisms, as well as a multitude of individual efforts, a wide assortment of issues has been addressed.

Arms control issues have received much attention, not only because they are intrinsically important but also because public opinion is an obvious factor in the diplomatic equation. In early 1983, U.S. Ambassador Peter Dailey was brought back from his post in Ireland to coordinate public diplomacy concerning the deployment of ground-launched cruise missiles (GLCMs) and Pershing IIs in Western Europe. The significance of this move is not that it produced an outpouring of publications and oratory—indeed, at the time, it was felt to be in our interest to exercise restraint and let our allies take the lead—but that it was an early attempt to ensure coordination on a delicate and important matter. Strategic, intermediate, and other arms issues have also been subjects of regular discussion in public diplomacy working groups in the department. Although such gatherings are usually an inefficient means of creating and implementing public affairs programs, they have been useful in keeping people informed and encouraging some (who might otherwise not have done so) to consider the public aspects of arms issues. Participation of USIA officers in these meetings has meant there was a source of professional public affairs experience to draw upon when considering practical measures and has provided an additional channel (among several others) to USIA to ensure that its programs were consistent with the general thinking.

In another important policy area, Central America, the appointment of a public diplomacy coordinator invigorated the department's public affairs effort and resulted in closer coordination within the executive branch. In this case the department had tried the large working group approach and found it wanting; a full-time senior official with a staff was clearly more effective, although as will be seen, from other standpoints this model has distinct drawbacks.

The department has also concerned itself with a variety of other public diplomacy issues, in some cases playing a direct program role. For example, it initiated a program to publicize the nature and extent of Soviet "active measures," which has included the issuance of various publications and the dispatch of speaking teams abroad.[6] It played an important part, with assistance from USIA and others, in the publication of communist party documents discovered in Grenada.[7] In addition, it has worked to expose the use of toxic substances by the USSR and some of its friends and has taken a number of steps to bring the plight of the Afghan people to world attention. It has hosted various conferences, such as one on prospects for democratization of communist societies.[8]

The department has shown considerable interest in a variety of issues, programs, and activities that are difficult to categorize but, in large part, can be subsumed under "international political activities." These range from the foreign programs of independent organizations like the Asia Foundation or the AFL/CIO to events such as youth festivals or international nongovernmental conferences on specific political issues. One common characteristic, in what might seem an otherwise curious medley, is the objective of influencing publics and institutions, a theme also found in the Project Democracy proposals.

As for the actions of other government agencies, the committee structure established by NSDD–77 has been important to the State Department because it accords the department a senior position in public diplomacy councils and, together with its own bilateral contacts, a means to make its views known. Since the structure was created, the department has played an active part in the standing committees and their various subgroups.

Finally, a number of those in the Department of State with responsibility for public diplomacy have made efforts to encourage state officers overseas to take a more active interest in public aspects of foreign relations. Although this does not appear to have had much general impact, there have been a number of cases in which small department or combined teams traveling in the field have worked with embassy staffs to bring specific topics to the attention of opinion leaders and publics. Any fair assessment of the State Department's recent participation in public diplomacy leads to mixed conclusions. There have been definite accomplishments, and clearly the department's interest and involvement have greatly increased.

Yet there is much to criticize. The department's overall performance has been marked by confusion and lack of coherence. In trying to describe the process one runs the risk of making it seem more logical and orderly than it has been. Various entities have simply emerged and grown, without reference to each other. Ad hoc groups, composed largely of people unversed in public affairs or overseas information activities, have formed and reformed. Individual senior public diplomacy officials have tended to work independently of one another and of the other groupings within the department. There is no single focal point for public diplomacy and, hence, little attention to establishing priorities among the department's various public diplomacy efforts or coordinating the activities of various groups. The State Department has committed itself to a public diplomacy role; having made no effort to define that role, however, it has been striking out in various directions with uncertain intentions and results.

Although the State Department's working relations with USIA are closer than before, as the department becomes increasingly involved in various aspects of public diplomacy, the division of responsibilities between the two institutions is becoming less clear. One may question, for example, whether it makes sense for the department to be regularly convoking public diplomacy working groups, to which USIA officers are invited, when USIA itself is the institution responsible for international information programs. It is difficult for some department officers to resist the temptation to manage certain USIA programs, even though they generally know less about these matters than the USIA personnel responsible, or, as has occasionally happened, to attempt to develop programs on their own and then try to secure USIA funds to implement them.

Not only is the department directly affected by the present uncertainties about the meaning of public diplomacy, but it has also contributed to the confusion. It has blurred the distinction between domestic public affairs and foreign-oriented information programs. This is not merely a semantic problem; the knowledge, and in many cases even the techniques, required to communicate effectively with foreign audiences are different from those needed to mount an information campaign in the United States. In the former case, a sophisticated understanding of the culture and of the basic political and psychological factors in the region or country concerned is extremely important. Obviously, there is a strong relationship between the domestic and foreign sides, and in many instances the domestic and foreign information efforts may proceed in tandem. However, the frequent assertion that they cannot be separated is a vast oversimplification. Combining these functions operationally almost invariably means that the foreign side is slighted in favor of the domestic and that foreign programs become extensions of domestic programs rather than being designed for foreign audiences. Combining them, moreover, increases the risk—always present in our democracy—of pushing certain issues into the foreign arena that are actually policy disputes.

Internally, the department's mixing of domestic public affairs with public diplomacy has tended to confuse lines of responsibility, taking away from the Bureau of Public Affairs activities logically within its jurisdiction. The department has also confused matters by applying the public diplomacy label to public relations techniques, an area in which the secretary's special adviser for public diplomacy was much involved. This usage of the term has puzzled many officers attempting to understand what the department's new interest in public diplomacy actually means. In a sense, it has trivialized the idea.

Meanwhile, the deputy to the under secretary for political affairs has handled "international political activities," a more or less open-ended responsibility and one that, at times, has spilled over into the domestic front. I have noted the difficulty in defining such activities and determining how they differ from traditional forms of public diplomacy. Some of the disagreements and misunderstandings between the Department of State and USIA stem from divergent views on this subject.

One result of the department's well-meaning but unfocused approach has been that, although some important issues have been addressed, many others have not. The department has taken a scattershot approach, responding sometimes to crises and at other times vigorously attacking lesser issues or occasional targets of opportunity. It has expended considerable energy upon assorted measures to publicize the misdeeds and machinations of U.S. opponents; it has devoted somewhat less to formulating positive approaches to encourage support for U.S. policies.

There is no conceptual framework for the department's activities in this field and no rational organizational arrangement that would enable it to perform in a coordinated manner. Clearly, the department is going to remain involved in public diplomacy, and it is in the national interest that the nation's senior foreign affairs organization be involved. Consequently, there is a strong and immediate need for the department to define its role and organize itself accordingly.

It is not my purpose here to attempt a detailed prescription, but based on the experience of the last several years, certain remedial possibilities are fairly obvious. First, the State Department must consider its role in relation to that of USIA. Unless there is a possible formal reallocation of functions within the executive branch, responsibility for information, education, and cultural programs should rest with USIA. However well intentioned, efforts by the State Department to duplicate any USIA functions can only cause confusion. There is ample opportunity within the NSDD–77 committee system to make recommendations on programs, and the system could be used more for this purpose than it has been.

Second, the department could contribute to public diplomacy by assuming responsibility for identifying the main foreign policy issues and defining public diplomacy's objectives with regard to them. Working through the interagency committees, it should attempt to ensure that the members of the foreign affairs community keep their attention steadily fixed on these issues. The State Department is better equipped than any other agency to accomplish this.

Third, in terms of its organization, the department badly needs a single senior official to oversee its public diplomacy and related activities. This official should be responsible for ensuring coherence and coordination within the department and should serve as its chief representative in the interagency committees and in all public diplomacy matters in the NSC and elsewhere. In addition, the assistant secretary for public affairs should be responsible for all domestic public affairs, none of which should be called public diplomacy; that term should be restricted to activities directed abroad.

Finally, international political activities and related matters are logically the responsibility of the Department of State and should remain so. However, the department should keep its efforts in this field separate from those of USIA and resist any temptation to employ USIA programs for its own purposes. The danger of damaging the credibility of some of those programs outweighs any short-term benefit the department may hope to achieve.

The NSDD–77 Structure

NSDD–77 was a response to a practical need, and it has undoubtedly resulted in more coordination among departments and agencies. Although the four standing committees have varied in their usefulness, all have contributed in some way to the public diplomacy process. The Special Policy Group, which an administration can utilize to resolve conflict and to ensure that members address important issues, is a useful body; until recently, however, it has been underutilized. More important, NSDD–77 has provided a forum, both in the standing committees and in a small executive group, for regular discussion of matters of common concern. Exchange of opinion and information by this means has been valuable.

NSDD–77 has also drawn certain participants into the system (such as the Defense Department) that otherwise might be inclined to go their own way. During the Reagan administration, the Defense Department has cooperated closely with USIA, something that might have occurred without NSDD–77. However, given the Defense Department's broad interests, the public impact of its presence overseas, and its inevitable differences with the State Department, it is preferable to have it as a team member rather than as an outsider. Through the Public Affairs Committee (PAC), NSDD–77 also provides another potential means to help the executive branch speak with one voice in foreign affairs, although no single mechanism can accomplish this historically difficult task.

Although NSDD–77 was an important step, it has not accomplished all that its authors had hoped, and the structure that it established has not been utilized as fully as it might. Some of the original expectations were undoubtedly too great; NSDD–77 was viewed, not simply as a means to build a useful committee structure, but as a means to achieve a fully integrated approach to U.S. public diplomacy. It has proven incapable of attaining this second goal. Nor has it served as a vehicle for developing a national public diplomacy strategy (as a few had hoped it might). Whether the latter objective is possible or desirable in a country such as the United States is debatable; I believe that it is not, but in any event NSDD–77 is not able to accomplish it.

So far, however, NSDD–77 has not met its more limited, actual potential. Although the interagency mechanism has been used to address some important questions, it has never been employed comprehensively to define general public diplomacy approaches to the major foreign policy issues. In general, use of this mechanism has been episodic and more reactive than forward looking; to suggest that it could have been otherwise may be asking a great deal of a government that is normally inclined to respond to immediate crises and to attack problems on a piecemeal basis. Obviously, if the government itself has internal disagreements concerning, for example, our policy toward the Soviet Union, defining policy for public diplomacy purposes becomes even more difficult. Nevertheless, the existing structure could be utilized more effectively.

One practical step would be to provide a full-time staff for the Special Policy Group and to encourage that body to meet more often. The four committees that, theoretically, report to it would thus receive more direction and a greater impetus to their activities. Having in effect legitimized the participation of several agencies and departments in public diplomacy, NSDD–77 should also be employed to clarify their respective roles.

Conceptually, NSDD–77 fails to provide a workable definition of public diplomacy. The document states that "public diplomacy is comprised of those actions of the U.S. Government designed to generate support for our national security objectives." This formulation seems, on the one hand, to allow remarkable latitude for interpretation but, on the other hand, (unless one takes a rather broad view of "national security objectives") to exclude a whole category of USIA programs aimed at promoting better understanding of the United States over the long term, such as academic exchanges, English teaching, and American overseas libraries. It is unlikely that the authors of NSDD–77 intended to abandon such programs, but it would be helpful if this important document were clearer on the fundamentals. In keeping with recent trends, the definition quoted above makes no distinction between domestic and foreign programs.

A final deficiency is the separation of the NSDD–77 structure from the policymaking process. NSDD–77 is concerned with the mechanics of public diplomacy, that is, creating and coordinating programs. Although the notion of developing public diplomacy "strategies" for particular purposes is emphasized in the document, there is no suggestion of linking this process to that of policy formulation. This is somewhat surprising, since the idea of taking foreign public opinion into account as a part of the policymaking process has gained support in recent years. Among its advocates, the U.S. Advisory Commission on Public Diplomacy has stated the case most persuasively.[9] Although a mechanism such as the one created by NSDD–77 cannot by itself accomplish this purpose, there are ways in which it might help. The disregard of this issue in NSDD–77 points to the continued existence of mental barriers to thinking about policymaking and public diplomacy together. Although the problem is indeed old, repeated recommendations for change over the years have had almost no effect.

CONCLUDING THOUGHTS

In the 1980s we have observed an upsurge of interest in public diplomacy, sparked by the conviction that it can become a larger and more effective instrument of foreign policy. We have seen a multiplicity of efforts on the part of individuals and institutions to put this idea into practice. Not surprisingly, the government institution that has performed in the most professional manner, USIA, is the one with the requisite experience and organization. However, the expanded activities of the State Department and the NSC, and the efforts to create an interagency structure to handle public diplomacy, reflect an understanding that public diplomacy embraces a broader field of activity than that of one specialized agency. It also reflects a realization that public diplomacy needs to become a larger and more important part of the foreign policy process. How this should occur is not yet clearly understood, but there is plenty of energy and enthusiasm, and new approaches to public diplomacy are being attempted.

We are living in a time of rapid change. The communications-information revolution, whose implications none of us can fully grasp, will affect our world profoundly. Certain directions of change are already discernible. Interaction among peoples and nations will increase; public opinion will be more subject to change, more powerful in its influence upon government behavior; and probably—though this is less certain—societies will become more open. Thus public diplomacy will become increasingly important.

To make the most of public diplomacy and to employ it effectively will require substantial reorientation in thinking and behavior. In scattered ways, the process has already begun: It is evident in the convoking of this conference, in USIA's movement into the television age (obviously still experimental but acknowledging the importance of this communications medium), and in the State Department's efforts to involve itself in a new function. Much that we have described at this conference reflects a recognition that somehow the old ways will not suffice.

Yet we are far from integrating public diplomacy into the conduct and formulation of our foreign policy. Too often we seem to be floundering, ignoring central issues until they become crises, or concentrating on matters that are secondary or purely tactical. There are no easy answers to these problems, but a few general steps could be taken now to improve the situation:

- We should clarify some of the conceptual confusion about the meaning of public diplomacy. We cannot work effectively in this field if we do not have an agreed understanding of its meaning. How it is managed often depends upon how we define it.
- An interagency coordinating mechanism is certainly required, whether it be NSDD–77 or something else. As a first step we should evaluate that mechanism and seek ways to improve it.

- We must find ways to modify institutional behavior sufficiently to ensure that, as policy is developed, public opinion—the factor with which public diplomacy must ultimately deal—is considered. The participation of the USIA director in NSC deliberations could be a step in that direction, but only a small one.
- We need to start thinking about institutional reform. Although USIA, the Defense Department, the NSC, and AID could probably benefit from a review of their current operations, the State Department simply cannot avoid doing so; it cannot play its important part unless it undertakes a thorough self-examination. It must define its role, improve its organization, and clarify its relationship to USIA.

These are essentially short-term steps, which could be taken during the remaining years of the Reagan administration. There is a need, however, to think in longer terms. Can our institutions in their present form meet the challenges of public diplomacy in the future? Can we achieve real integration of public diplomacy into the foreign policy process within our present government organization?

Is the existing division of functions between USIA and the State Department suited to the future needs of public diplomacy? A strong case can be made that merging some major functions would in the end serve the national interest better than the present organizational separation of the department and the agency.[10] Although this idea was discussed at length in the 1970s, in the 1978 reorganization the Carter administration opted for continued—and, in a sense, more complete—separation. Although the subject remains controversial, it is both desirable and possible to examine it in a rational and nonpartisan manner.

In general, we need to think more fundamentally about public diplomacy—about its purposes and potentialities. Yet there is little of this basic thinking going on; presently, we are more active than thoughtful. It is difficult, of course, for those in government to think deeply about such matters, since to do so requires a degree of detachment that is hard to achieve when one is totally engaged. However, the effort should be made; those who are not operationally involved can do more. The U.S. Advisory Committee on Public Diplomacy is one organization that is thinking about these issues, and others, including academic institutions, should do so. The need is clear, and there is no more appropriate time than the present to get started.

Discussion

John R. Clingerman

In addressing the fundamental contradiction that exists between traditional and public diplomacy, I would like to share my pessimism that those most concerned about the need for public diplomacy can be brought into the policymaking process. In addition, I believe that policy guidelines that assign overall responsibility for public diplomacy will remain ill-defined. The strength and weakness of the United States as a democracy lies in the multitude of voices that intrude themselves in the formulation and implementation of foreign policy. It is a messy process, but one we will have to live with.

It is salutary from time to time to remind ourselves that the world of foreign affairs is inhabited by 157 sovereign nation states. To forget this is to risk falling victim to snares and delusions. Sovereign states are a prickly lot. They do not relish being identified as losers in *any* type of intercourse with other sovereign states; no matter how small or large, how powerful or weak, a sovereign state likes to be known as a winner. All of us know that in any game there are winners and losers. As practitioners and students of foreign affairs, we should remember a fundamental rule: Most successful negotiations between sovereign states are those in which, after the talks are completed, each party can proclaim to the world with an absolutely straight face, "I am the winner." To be able to do so means that many a deal has been cut in deepest, darkest secrecy—deals that, if given the light of publicity, would let the world know who had lost. More dangerous, publicity could reveal what made it worthwhile to a party in the negotiations to compromise on an absolutely uncompromising position.

Traditional practitioners of diplomacy avow their commitment to public diplomacy. At times, they even express a willingness to admit into their sanctums of real diplomacy communications experts from the Department of State's bureau of public affairs and from the United States Information Agency/Service (USIA/USIS). They welcome the advice of experts on the public affairs ramifications of this or that decision. However, I cannot imagine that Ambassador Philip Habib would have made USIS Lebanon or Israel privy to the innermost secrets of his Lebanese negotiations; I think he would have shuddered at the thought. When the stakes are high—as they were and are in Lebanon—any hankering after Wilsonian "open convenants openly arrived at" disappears from the traditional diplomat's computer screen. The last thing he wants is light shed prematurely on his carefully constructed edifice of compromise, which, if revealed for all to see, could prove compromising.

The traditionalist's reaction is predictable and completely understandable. He might see the desirability of a communications expert advising him on public diplomacy ramifications of actions taken during negotiations. However, he would likely weigh this desirability against the risk of possible premature exposure and opt to keep the expert on public diplomacy from the inner circle. Certainly the traditional diplomat will keep his press attaché or spokesman informed of what he, the traditionalist, thinks should be communicated to the public and no more.

The Reagan administration has shown more sensitivity to and concern for public diplomacy than many of its predecessors. There have been more concerted efforts to advance the U.S. position before the public eye both in the United States and abroad. However, in most instances the aid and counsel of public diplomacy experts have been enlisted *after* basic policy decisions had been made in Washington. The reasons for this are valid. Negotiations between the various elements that comprise the Washington political scene, on such sensitive questions as arms negotiations with the Soviet Union, are every bit as complicated as, if not more so than, those undertaken with a foreign power.

Formulating policy in our democratic way is a free-for-all that can be extremely messy; this is our strength and our weakness. Those involved in formulating policy do not routinely consult public diplomacy experts for advice on the consequence of particular decisions. Certainly they use the media to promote publicly their version of what policy should be. In this process, leaks at the top, bottom, and middle of the Washington ship abound. But, usually, only after an agreement has been reached are public diplomatists asked to explain it to audiences in the United States and abroad.

As a Department of State officer—and a believer in traditional diplomacy working at the citadel of public diplomacy, USIA—I find myself wrenched in two directions. Presently, I supervise and advise those who explain United States policy in Africa. In this capacity, I would like to believe that my agency contributes significantly in advising the Department of State and the White House on aspects of public diplomacy in negotiations and in policies that my subordinates in the field must explain. On the other hand, I understand and respect those who play the game according to traditional rules, even if this means my exclusion. If I were in the shoes of those in the Department of State and the White House, I would play my cards as close to the vest as I could. If they are prematurely exposed to the glare of publicity, meaningful negotiations between sovereign states and semisovereign elements of the United States government rarely occur.

I would like to conclude on a more upbeat note. The Reagan administration's emphasis on gaining support for foreign policy has not brought the millennium for public diplomacy. There is no tsar of public diplomacy; the advice of public diplomacy experts is not regularly sought before fateful decisions are made. And I am not sure that I would like to see a public diplomacy tsar—it goes against my democratic grain. Besides, in Washington no one can be a tsar of anything for long; forces would conspire to dethrone a tsar of public diplomacy.

However, the Reagan administration's emphasis on public diplomacy has been salutary. Public diplomacy practitioners are now given more opportunity to participate in formulating policy. At least they are notified in advance, so they can prepare themselves for an all-out effort to explain the latest foreign policy development.

Jack R. Perry

I find myself uncertain about the meaning of public diplomacy and its role in United States foreign policy. Perhaps this uncertainty is because of my checkered career, which has included tenure as a journalist, twenty-four years as a diplomat specializing in Soviet and East European affairs, and a faculty position at a liberal arts college. Journalists, diplomats, and academicians all view public diplomacy with a certain skepticism; perhaps I reflect that skepticism.

Before sharing some of my uncertainties about public diplomacy, I would like to state that I am neither uncertain about nor skeptical of Gifford Malone's excellent paper. It provides a thorough grounding in the Reagan administration's practice of public diplomacy, offers sound criticism of some American shortcomings in the fields, and points to ways of improving United States foreign policy in its public aspect. I particularly liked his statement that "paradoxically, the more active we have become as public diplomatists, the less clear we seem to be about what we are practicing."

First, I am uncertain about the proper definition of public diplomacy and about the connection between diplomacy and public diplomacy. The old-fashioned Harold Nicolson definition of diplomacy is "the management of relations among sovereign states by negotiation." This implies such things as confidentiality, willingness to reach accords with adversaries, and a certain absence of zeal that may well not jibe with some operational definitions of public diplomacy. Some modern critics would say that old-fashioned diplomacy is as dated as the idea of career diplomatic service; the idea of limits to international ambitions and a willingness to perceive the other side's interests in terms of areas of coexistence may simply be nineteenth-century leftovers.

A diplomat might reply that as long as sovereign governments seek to reconcile their clashing interests by means short of war, classic diplomacy will not go out of fashion, even if methods and personnel change radically. Winston Churchill's statement of 1 October 1939 is apropos: "Russia is a riddle wrapped in a mystery inside an enigma; but perhaps there is a key. That key is Russian national interest." If clashing national interests are to be reconciled, no amount of information activity (Voice of America and Radio Liberty broadcasts) will replace the necessity of negotiating with the Soviet government. If we expect public diplomacy to persuade governments to go against their own interests, then we are asking too much. This is not to say that public diplomacy is unimportant; its importance is great and growing. But public diplomacy is not a substitute for foreign policy.

Second, I am uncertain about the basic importance of public diplomacy (whether we call it that or use labels more popular earlier in this century, such as *psychological warfare* or simply *propaganda*—would *public foreign policy* be a more accurate term?). By basic importance, I am referring to its ability to affect historical outcomes. Did public diplomacy in this century affect the descent into the First and Second World Wars, the course of those wars, their aftermath, or the course of the Cold War? Although we stress the growing role of public diplomacy as a tool of foreign policy, do we know of instances in which it has critically affected history?

To be more blunt and undiplomatic: Did the Soviet Union win any countries, or any major victories, by means of public diplomacy? Based on my own observation of Soviet foreign propaganda in Czechoslovakia and Bulgaria (as in France and Sweden), it is singularly ineffective. In such countries, as a diplomat I felt that facts and policies—and how these affected the interests of the target states—counted far more than any amount of Soviet propaganda. What they are speaks infinitely louder than what they say.

I am talking about external rather than internal propaganda. But I do question the number of Soviet victories aided by the use of propaganda abroad. Although it is easy to cite the USSR's propaganda budget, as we imagine it to be, and state that all the broadcasts, disinformation, and rallies must be effective. But are they? And if so, where? Are people swayed by Soviet propaganda in China, the Middle East, Eastern Europe, Western Europe, or the United States? Are people perhaps less manipulated by words than we believe them to be? Perhaps this is a heretical question, but there it is.

Third, I am uncertain about some assumptions that have been made by some participants at this conference: (1) that USSR propaganda is a serious threat to American security and our national interests; (2) that this Soviet threat should be the starting point for American public diplomacy; (3) that the United States should respond in kind to the USSR; (4) that West Europeans want to be, or are being, seduced by Soviet words directed against their interests; and (5) that views of USSR representatives appearing on American television or in the press pose a danger to the U.S. public. These assumptions need to be examined.

Fourth, I am uncertain about what the basis is for a seemingly patronizing attitude toward Western Europe and Japan—an attitude that they are not as cognizant of their own interests as Americans are and that they cannot handle Soviet propaganda. Since my entire diplomatic career was spent in Europe or in European affairs, I am sensitive about this. When I was in Sweden, I was occasionally tempted to talk to my Swedish friends out of my "long experience" in Soviet affairs; but then I would remember, or be reminded, that the Swedes had been dealing rather intimately with the Russians since the time of Charles XII and even before and, therefore, did not need any lessons from Americans like myself. My own experience in Europe has led me to the conclusion that Western Europeans are generally better informed about foreign affairs than Americans are. Could it be that they understand their own interests as well as we do, or, perhaps, even better?

Fifth, I am uncertain about whether we are running the technology or it is running us. The message is more important than the medium; adding up hours of transmission time does not equate with successful foreign policy. At times, I think that people in public diplomacy are chained to a dinosaur while pretending to guide it. Although we may not like to acknowledge such paternity, Hitler and Goebbels were the pioneers of mass propaganda in the twentieth century and thus of, at least, an important component of public diplomacy. Even in the case of the Nazi regime, one wonders if the Nazis had any startling new insight into mass persuasion, or if they simply were quick to adopt the new technology available in the form of electric lighting, mass-audience microphones and sound systems, and radio. Despite this, it appeared that Nazi propaganda, though successful in Germany, had little lasting success beyond German borders.

Television and other technical wonders have added new dimensions to the panoply of instruments available to the public diplomacy practitioner; as new media have become available, practitioners have been forced to use them. The possibility of remaining silent on certain issues (for example, in a building international crisis or during a terrorist incident) becomes altogether slim. Presidents cannot *not* make news. It may also be true, or becoming true, that public diplomacy cannot *not* happen. During my years of service at the U.S. Department of State, secretaries of state had many powers, but they did not have the power to turn off the noon press briefing. To the extent that we are becoming committed to vast batteries of public diplomacy technology and obligated to utilize them, we may find it impossible to abstain from use; our diplomacy may become hostage to our public diplomacy. Undoubtedly my concern is exaggerated, but grounds for concern do exist, especially in a government that, as Gifford Malone's paper clarifies, finds it exceptionally difficult to speak with one voice.

Sixth, I am uncertain if those in government, academia, or, in general, American life always remember, when speaking of public diplomacy, that in a free society the principal function of the press (the "media" when we wish to be critical) is to report the news. Dean Rusk has wondered if the first amendment would pass by popular vote in America today; he has stated that he would like to have both a free press and a responsible press, but if forced to choose, he would take a free press. Some views have been voiced that American media are "antigovernment" or too sympathetic to Gorbachev. Could the reason for such accusations stem from preconceptions about what the news *ought* to be rather than what it actually is? Amid my uncertainties, having spent six years of my life in communist-ruled countries, I am certain that a free press, with all its faults, remains absolutely essential to the functioning of our republic.

Seventh, as Gifford Malone has alluded to, I am uncertain whether a "national public diplomacy strategy" (or even a "national strategy") is feasible, or even desirable, in the United States. I wonder whether in the realm of public diplomacy, as in some other areas, we are too pre-occupied with the Soviet threat. Perhaps we should be on our guard lest public diplomacy—enhanced by new governmental machinery, better technology, more money—seeks to usurp the place of publicly supported foreign policy. It is unfortunate when domestic promotional efforts are called "public diplomacy"—whether it is the Carter administration's efforts on behalf of SALT II or the Reagan administration's efforts on behalf of covert action in Nicaragua—but it is not surprising since the selling of policy, at home or abroad, is the point of concern.

What worries me is the possibility that the intense promotion of a particular foreign policy, such as the Reagan administration's Central American policy, will make more difficult, more painful, or more costly a shift in that policy that may occur when Congress decides to act or after the next elections. It is of no use to pretend that we have a continuity in foreign policy, when we do not. The United States may not be equipped to pursue public diplomacy strategies that last beyond a quadrennial perspective; this is not our country as we might wish it to be—this is our country as it is. Although the Soviets incorporate propaganda as a component of policy, I am uncertain whether the United States should go too far in emulating them.

Finally, I am uncertain if American divisions can be healed by means of public diplomacy, or diplomacy, to make a national strategy possible. Is the United States too large and unruly to harness itself to any effective mechanism? Does not each beast in the circus (for example, state and defense departments and the National Security Council) follow its own routine? At times, we may despair and think of the Roman empire and fear we may have flaws, even fatal flaws, that we are incapable of eradicating because our society is so massive that great internal changes are not feasible. It has been persuasively argued for a six-year presidential term or for other constitutional changes in order to make our foreign policy machinery work more smoothly; but does anyone realistically expect Americans to agree to amend the U.S. Constitution for such changes? We are what we are. Perhaps unruliness in foreign policy and thus a fortiori in public diplomacy is the price we pay for being a great democracy.

Whatever our deliberations at this workshop—and they have been most enlightening—whoever wins in 1988 (Bush, Cuomo, Kemp, Dole, or Hart) will be infinitely more important in shaping American public diplomacy over the next few years than any conclusions we reach or measures we recommend; that is how our system works. If the opposite side of the coin of our democracy is unruliness, especially in public diplomacy, then perhaps we shall have to live with that; in fact, tampering might cause harm to the things we cherish most.

My uncertainties are possibly out of phase with the confident tone of this workshop, but I hope they may be thrown as leavening into the dough. Our society and polity (that is, our way of doing things) is messy and unruly. To academics, and to those preoccupied with the Soviet way of doing things, our sloppy ways are sometimes offensive. But if this is the price we pay for being the free society that we are, perhaps we must simply try to cope and be thankful.

James D. Theberge

As specified in National Security Decision Directive 77 (NSDD–77), the Reagan administration has made the most serious effort in several decades to establish a formal coordinating mechanism for public diplomacy under the overall direction and responsibility of the National Security Council (NSC). Within the NSDD framework, the Department of State and the United States Information Agency (USIA) are obviously of central importance. As Gifford Malone has indicated, however, the Department of State's role in public diplomacy lacks focus and coherence.

In my comments, I wish to provide an operational perspective. I will briefly discuss public diplomacy as it is practiced in U.S. embassies abroad, making due allowances for the special situations of each embassy around the world. In terms of the general structure of American embassies to conduct public diplomacy, the ambassador imparts direction and leadership. A great deal depends on the ambassador's background and interests; some give higher priority than others to the instruments and ends of public diplomacy.

The key officer, usually a senior experienced USIA official, is the public affairs officer (PAO), directly responsible for preparing an annual country strategy for the employment of the available public diplomacy instruments to support U.S. foreign policy objectives in the country concerned. Normally, he reports directly to the chief of mission and is assisted by a staff that includes the press attaché and cultural affairs officer. Since the PAO is the ambassador's principal adviser concerning the form, timing, and substance of public diplomacy initiatives within the country team, the energy and skill with which public diplomacy is practiced depends critically on the quality of the PAO and his staff. Working relations between USIA and Department of State officers in U.S. embassies are closer than ever before, and the PAO has evolved into one of the chief of mission's most valuable and important counselors.

What instruments of public diplomacy are available to the ambassador in his effort to advance U.S. interests in a foreign country? There exist a wide range of resources and programs, but I shall mention only the important ones to answer this question. The range of foreign media contacts and ready access to local television, radio, and press are fundamental resources that the embassy utilizes, under the ambassador's direction, to explain, clarify, and defend U.S. policy and interests.

The Wireless File is an extremely important and valuable information service that the USIA makes available to U.S. embassies. It provides a steady stream of policy statements, news items, background articles, and other interpretive material through a radio-telephone network. The embassy uses the information for media placement and distribution to foreign opinion leaders on a selective basis. It also serves as an up-to-date background news and information service for U.S. mission personnel.

The International Visitors Program brings young foreign leaders, and potential leaders, to the United States for up to one month on an all-paid visit to meet with their American counterparts and professional colleagues. They are able to obtain a firsthand view of how the U.S. government and private institutions function and to observe U.S. elections and other public interactions. The members of the ambassador's country team select candidates for the visitor's program, and the ambassador approves the foreign visitors. Our embassies have been remarkably successful in selecting young leaders who rise to the top of their professions and to the upper echelons of their respective countries' political leadership.

Television and radio programming are increasingly important tools of public diplomacy. USIA's WORLDNET global communications system is a recent innovation; it permits policymakers in the United States, and leaders in other fields, to communicate directly with foreign audiences on vital world issues. By means of one-way video or two-way audio discussions, foreign journalists can question U.S. officials in hour-long interviews. USIA also places material on U.S. policy and related matters on local radios that reach millions of listeners, and most embassies have their own well-equipped radio stations and equipment for making live and prerecorded programs.

Educational and cultural exchange programs administered by USIA (such as the Fulbright, Hubert H. Humphrey, and Eisenhower scholarship and exchange programs) constitute a longer-term instrument of public diplomacy. They enable a select group of foreigners to live, study, and lecture in the United States and thereby gain a better understanding of the practice and functioning of America's democratic society. In recent years, these programs have been expanded considerably.

As in Washington, in the field the key to successful public diplomacy is to orchestrate effectively and make timely the range of instruments available on behalf of U.S. political, economic, and military interests overseas. In America's competition with the enemies of U.S. democratic society (above all, the USSR), public diplomacy is indispensable to our national security. It is a vitally important component of our foreign policy.

A closer integration of American public diplomacy instruments and the goals of U.S. foreign policy is needed both in Washington and in U.S. embassies. We need to train every foreign service officer about the role of ideas in the great struggle between freedom and tyranny. We need a clearer understanding of how U.S. embassies can employ, more effectively and more imaginatively, public diplomacy programs and resources. We must be less reactive and more innovative in conveying our message—freedom's message—in every country in which there are U.S. diplomatic missions. In order for public diplomacy to influence more effectively foreign leadership groups and public opinion in favor of the United States, we need to analyze more fully the attitudes, the stereotypes, and the values of differentiated target audiences.

It is awesome to observe the cumulative impact of the information and images received by foreign audiences in the increasingly complex, technologically advanced local media. Lenin and Gramsci understood the importance of repetition in propaganda; that is, they foresaw the cumulative effect of the repetition of ideas and slogans in altering attitudes, perceptions, and consciousness and in disarming politically and psychologically the opponents of international communism. The power of ideas and the persistence of ideology are undeniable.

Propaganda can modify our conceptual frames of reference. For instance, much of the world community accepts terrorist regimes—that is, states that train, arm, finance, and support armed assassins and killers who wreak havoc in other states—as legitimate governments. As a result, taking defensive action against terrorist states is widely considered illegitimate and wrong.

The United States cannot remain passive in this war of ideas and in the vast ideological struggle with the USSR and its allies; it should not, however, imitate the Soviet Union and its radical surrogates. The United States must understand Soviet and anti-Western propaganda in order to find the means to counter such propaganda in a civilized and efficacious manner.

United States public diplomacy in Latin America, at least in certain regions, is handicapped in its attempt to create foreign trust and confidence in the United States as a cooperative partner and, especially, as a security ally. Over the past two decades, successive U.S. governments (particularly the U.S. Congress) have taken actions that have undermined confidence in the United States as a reliable ally, a political-military partner, and a protector against the common adversary—international terrorism and international communism.

A profound mistrust of the United States among much of the political leadership in Latin America—even friendly, pro-Western political elites—is a result of counterproductive congressional political and economic sanctions, unreasonable restraints on military and economic aid, frequent changes of policymakers, and shifts in U.S. foreign policy. Foreign political leaders are, of course, often unreliable and irresponsible, which engenders distrust by the United States. There is, in fact, a crisis of trust in the hemisphere.

The practice of public diplomacy is, thus, only as effective as the policies that it is designed to serve and as the surrounding atmosphere (historical perceptions and expectations) permits. In Latin America, the United States operates under considerable difficulties in its effort to promote freedom and democracy, and to maintain peace and stability in that region.

Hans N. Tuch

I find Mr. Malone's paper excellent and agree with almost everything he writes, especially his recommendations. Perhaps I can best contribute to the discussion of the U.S. government's public diplomacy by emphasizing certain key issues and by raising several provocative questions. I have four principal points to make.

First, some policymakers appear not to understand what public diplomacy means, what it can do, and how to apply it to the conduct of international relations. Let me cite some examples. One is the definition of public diplomacy in National Security Decision Directive 77 (NSDD–77) as "those actions of the U.S. government designed to generate support for our national security objectives."[11] If the document had stated that this were a part or only one aspect of public diplomacy, I would accept it; however, the definition implies that such support of national security objectives is the sole purpose of public diplomacy.

Another example appeared in a 1984 *Commentary* article.[12] The author states that "some liberals would most certainly prefer to jettison official information programs altogether in favor of purely apolitical cultural exchange scholarship grants for foreign students." In yesterday's discussion, I received the distinct impression from some prominent speakers that the sole purpose of public diplomacy is to counter Soviet active measures and communist propaganda. Both examples reveal a lack of comprehension about public diplomacy.

Second, a definition of public diplomacy should be clearly stated—one that treats public diplomacy as an intellectual concept, as an academic discipline in the context of the study of international affairs, and as a profession engaging trained foreign service officers. For me, public diplomacy is the process of communication that attempts to enhance understanding among foreign publics of the ideas and ideals, of the institutions and culture, and of the national goals and policies of the United States.

Public diplomacy differs from traditional diplomacy in that the traditional approach involves the interaction among governments (in most cases, foreign ministries conducting international affairs). International relations have changed so drastically and permanently since World War Two, however, that traditional diplomacy alone can no longer regulate the peacetime affairs of nations. Public diplomacy came into its own as an indispensable component of international relations. Among the changes that have occurred are three that I consider especially significant.

One important change has been the communications revolution, which makes possible the instant transmission of all kinds of information across national boundaries, even into the tightest fortresses of thought control. Transistor radios, television, satellite transmissions, computerization of information, and data processing enable peoples everywhere to receive and pass on information that previously had taken days or weeks to transmit and often did not reach its desired destination at all. Now, governments and citizens have the same information at the same time.

Public opinion, in whatever form it might be molded, has become an important factor in international affairs, exerting a strong influence on the actions of governments—and not only on those of democracies. Totalitarian governments also recognize the power of public opinion within their own realms, since they have utilized its power in other countries. Unlike democracies, they also fear its influence; otherwise, they would not suppress it within their own dominions and try to prevent it from being affected by anyone other than their own officials.

Another principal development that has made public diplomacy a necessity in world politics is the proliferation during the past four decades of new states in the international arena—each with its own stake in the realm of ideas, politics, economics, traditions, and culture; each interested in promulgating its policies and goals before the rest of the world; each with a profile to show and a face to save—and all with the help of new communications technologies.

The third development centers on the ideological struggle between the free and the communist worlds, which has made it imperative that democracies can compete effectively in the contest of ideas and promote our views, values, and society to peoples of other cultures, traditions, and ideologies.

Public diplomacy, thus, is much broader than the mere effort to generate support for national security objectives or to counter Soviet active measures. In contrast to the view expressed in the *Commentary* article, I cannot think of a more truly "political" program to buttress public diplomacy than student exchanges. In fact, I do not believe it possible to generate much support abroad for our national security objectives (an important goal of public diplomacy) without first creating an understanding of our society and what it stands for. Such an understanding is best achieved through an in-depth familiarization with the United States, its people, and its institutions—a familiarization easily obtained through cultural and educational exchanges, particularly of the young people in an increasingly interdependent world.

In practice, public diplomacy is not a "quick fix," nor is it merely the conveyance of truthful information. It is a long-term process requiring credibility and deep understanding as solid foundations for the message (communication) that we wish to be accepted. There are three essential components for the conduct of public diplomacy:

1. Addressing the need for a sound understanding of America—its history, traditions, institutions, ideas, and culture. (This is a long-term goal, and its attainment is vital if we are to have a good chance of succeeding in our short-term goals.)

2. Addressing current objectives in the political, security, economic, and social areas.

3. Learning the attitudes and opinions of foreign audiences in order to base our approach and our programs on an understanding of the political and social dynamics of a given audience.

Having defined public diplomacy and explained its dimensions, I must ask the third of my four points: Why does the U.S. Department of State have several offices whose task is purportedly public diplomacy but that actually perform other functions? These offices include a coordinator for public diplomacy in Latin America, a deputy for public diplomacy to the under secretary for political affairs, and the recently dissolved position of special adviser for public diplomacy to the secretary of state. What are their responsibilities in the realm of public diplomacy?

We face, above all, a confusion in terminology among top policymakers that, unless corrected, will result in negative implications for the successful conduct of public diplomacy. The term *diplomacy* is commonly defined as the art and practice of conducting relations among sovereign states. Thus, the international dimension is an essential element of diplomacy, whether it is conducted privately between governments or in public.

The public diplomacy coordinator for Latin America undoubtedly considers his primary responsibility to involve promoting the administration's policy toward Latin America at home (incidentally, promoting this policy abroad is the task of the USIA). By definition, the coordinator's work is public relations, which is not public diplomacy; calling it public diplomacy merely confuses the issue. The coordinator frequently appears on domestic television, testifies before congressional committees, delivers speeches throughout the country, and disseminates materials and documentation advocating the administration's policy. The mistake, then, is in calling the office coordinator for public diplomacy, rather than for public affairs, in Latin America. Indeed, his work is similar to that of the Office of Public Affairs at the U.S. Department of State.

My final point concerns the Panel on International Information, Education, and Cultural Relations (the so-called Stanton Panel, named after its chairman, Frank Stanton), which ten years ago issued a report on the future of public diplomacy.[13] Its recommendations and those of the Commission on the Organization of the Government for the Conduct of Foreign Policy (the Murphy Commission) imbedded public diplomacy firmly into the bureaucratic structure of the U.S. Information Agency. I personally opposed this permanent organizational separation of public diplomacy from the U.S. Department of State, maintaining that policy formation and policy execution (whether in traditional or public diplomacy) belong under one agency.[14]

At any rate, today the USIA conducts public diplomacy for the U.S. government abroad, and I do not think that any other agency should be permitted to usurp the USIA's mandated responsibilities in this area. I question the need or propriety for interagency committees to conduct or coordinate public diplomacy. We have an important U.S. government agency to do this, and we have trained and experienced foreign service officers (public diplomats) to conduct public diplomacy.

I would like to close my remarks with a quotation from Edward R. Murrow, which I have repeatedly cited, because I consider it pertinent: "It has always seemed to me the real art in this business is not so much moving information or guidance or policy five or ten thousand miles. That is an electronic problem. The real art is to move it the last three feet in face-to-face communication."[15] Murrow thought of public diplomacy as an art—the art of getting the message from the loudspeaker to the mind of the foreign listeners, or from the book into the consciousness of the foreign reader. He was indeed an artist in the practice of public diplomacy, and he has served as a model for many of us.

NOTES

1. NSDD-77, originally a classified document, was declassified on 18 April 1983. The full text appears as an appendix to this volume.

2. The Operations Coordinating Board, established in 1953, was such an effort, although not an exact analogy. It was abolished by President Kennedy when he took office. (Thomas C. Sorensen, *The Word War: The Story of American Propaganda* [New York: Harper & Row, 1968], pp. 44 and 118.)

3. Project Democracy is covered in detail in various congressional documents: see, for example, U.S. Congress, Senate, Foreign Relations Committee, *Hearings on Foreign Relations Authorization Act*, 2 and 9 March and 27 April 1983, 98th Cong., 1st sess. (Washington, D.C.: GPO, 1983); House, Foreign Affairs Committee, *Report No. 98–130* (to accompany HR 2915 authorizing appropriations for fiscal years 1984 and 1985 for the Department of State, the United States Information Agency, the Board for International Broadcasting, the Inter-American Foundation, and the Asia Foundation; and to establish the National Endowment for Democracy), 16 May 1983, 98th Cong., 1st sess. (Washington, D.C.: GPO, 1983); and House, Foreign Affairs Committee, *Conference Report No. 98–563* (to accompany HR 2915), 17 November 1983, 98th Cong., 1st sess. (Washington, D.C.: GPO, 1983).

4. The National Endowment for Democracy was incorporated on 18 November 1983.

5. Sorenson, *The Word War,* p. 128.

6. "Active measures" is a literal translation of the Russian term used by the KGB and has no English equivalent. It refers, inter alia, to propaganda, disinformation, forgeries, and other covert and overt measures used to achieve a political end.

7. The enormous quantity of documents discovered by U.S. forces in Grenada constitute a unique resource for studying the development of a radical regime and Soviet and Cuban strategy in the Third World. Some have been published.

8. This conference, held during 18–19 October 1982 at the State Department, included specialists in Soviet and East European affairs, public diplomacy professionals, and others experienced in international political activities. It assessed the likelihood of change and ways in which the West might participate in this process.

9. United States Advisory Commission on Public Diplomacy, *1985 Report* (Washington, D.C., 1985), pp. 12–15.

10. I believe that we should take this course, and my recommendations are discussed in "Managing Public Diplomacy," *Washington Quarterly* 8, no. 3 (Summer 1985): 199–213.

11. "Management of Public Diplomacy Relative to National Security" (Washington, D.C.: The White House, 14 January 1983), p. 1 (mimeographed); see appendix to this volume for this document.

12. Carnes Lord, "In Defense of Public Diplomacy," *Commentary,* April 1984, pp. 42–50.

13. *International Information, Education, and Cultural Relations: Recommendations for the Future* (Washington, D.C.: Center for Strategic and International Studies, Georgetown University, 1975).

14. "Public Diplomacy in the United States Government," *Foreign Service Journal* 53, no. 9 (September 1976): 8.

15. Edward R. Murrow, interview by ABC correspondent Edward Norgan.

8

RECASTING U.S.-SOVIET EXCHANGES

Nils H. Wessell*

American public diplomacy has often been criticized for being too reactive and defensive and too oriented toward the short term rather than embodying a more aggressive approach aimed at positive results over the long run. From this standpoint, the West European parliamentary decisions to deploy ground-launched cruise missiles (GLCMs) and Pershing IIs, in the face of an unrelenting Soviet diplomatic offensive and propaganda campaign, cannot be regarded as a positive success for U.S. public diplomacy. The NATO countries merely staved off a disaster—that is, validation of the Soviet claim to the right to veto NATO's military procurement and deployment decisions.

A genuinely successful strategy of public diplomacy should be offensive; it should weaken Soviet power and influence, not simply slow down the gradual erosion of our own position. Within this context, one should regard the cultural, scholarly, and scientific exchanges with the USSR as a crucial, although modest, element in a more long-term strategy of public diplomacy. This is not to say, however, that the exchanges should be reduced to psychological warfare operations or should be regarded as a substitute for them. The exchanges have the potential to contribute to other more basic forces within Soviet society that, over

*The author is director of the Office of Research, USIA. Writing when he was director of the Foreign Policy Research Institute, he wishes to acknowledge the assistance of Tina Kaidanow in the preliminary research and drafting of this paper. The views expressed herein are the author's and not necessarily those of the Foreign Policy Research Institute or the U.S. Information Agency.

time, may weaken the overwhelming social controls of the Communist Party of the Soviet Union (CPSU). Although similar hopes for the evolution of Soviet society embodied in the doctrine of containment have been largely disappointed, a sense of realism requires acknowledging that the threat Soviet power poses to American values and interests will not disappear until the internal nature of the regime fundamentally alters.

The exchanges expose Soviet society to American scholars, scientists, students, writers, and performing artists. This exposure reinforces other, already existing trends in Soviet life, including the Soviet intelligentsia's sense of separateness from the party bosses who dominate the political system (Soviet citizens have been less impressed than the Western media with Mikhail Gorbachev's sartorial elegance). Historically, basic changes in Russian and Soviet society have been initiated from above, either by the ruler or as a result of the pent-up frustrations of the intelligentsia. Nurturing this sense of separateness should be a central objective of American participation in the exchanges.

The exchanges also reinforce the impact of the onslaught of communications technology. Scholars have traditionally thought that such technology would powerfully reinforce totalitarian control in Soviet society: Radio and television would permit the regime to socialize the populace more perfectly; telephones and computers would further centralize economic and political decisionmaking. But life itself, to borrow a Russian expression, has proven the opposite. Radio Free Europe and Radio Liberty (RFE-RL), the Voice of America (VOA), the British Broadcasting Corporation (BBC), and the reception of Finnish television broadcasts in Estonia have made it more difficult for Soviet propagandists to lie, credibly, to their own people. The next wave of technology may be direct satellite broadcasting, mass ownership of videocassette recorders, or yet another presently undeveloped means of communication. But whatever the nature of new communications technology, a larger number of knowledgeable Americans wandering the streets of Moscow, Leningrad, Kiev, and Tashkent will make it more difficult for the Kremlin to maintain its increasingly eroded communications monopoly.

After a decade in which the number of Soviet and American participants in cultural, educational, and scientific exchanges has plummeted from 2,000 in 1975 to the low hundreds, we stand on the threshold of what may be another period of expansion in American exchange programs with the Soviet Union. It is timely, therefore, to review past experience and draw what lessons we can from the achievements and frustrations of earlier interactions with the Soviet Union's closed society.

In June 1984, President Reagan announced publicly that the United States government had informed the USSR that we were prepared to initiate negotiations on a new exchange agreement covering cultural, educational, scientific-technical, and other fields of activity. The last such agreement expired in December 1979: after the Soviets had invaded Afghanistan that same month, the Carter administration suspended any further negotiations to renew the agreement. At the Geneva Summit in November 1985, Reagan and Gorbachev presided over the signing of a new exchanges agreement and agreed to a potentially significant broadening of other contacts outside the exchanges accord in such areas as sports, youth visits, and computer software.

It is easy to forget that we have accumulated nearly three decades of experience with a formal program of academic, scientific, and cultural exchanges with the Soviet Union. Since 1958, expectations about their potential impact have declined in the United States. While once lofty hopes have settled back to earth, a new and healthy attitude toward the exchanges has emerged. In my discussion, I will survey the problems and potential of the exchanges in order to suggest improvements, where possible, and restructuring, where necessary.

Although the years since the first informal exchanges in the 1920s have led to a steadily growing realism concerning cultural relations with the Soviet Union, public attitudes toward the exchanges have been cyclical. Historical perspective underscores this point. Six years after the October 1917 Revolution, Lincoln Steffens, who had found so much shame in American cities, made a goodwill tour to Soviet Russia with Senator Robert LaFollette and declared that he had seen the future and it worked. By the end of the first five-year plan, thousands of engineers from Ford, General Electric, International Harvester, and other U.S. corporations had flooded the Soviet Union with American technology, often at a financial loss to the U.S. firms.

By the 1970s, when a large number of exchange agreements were signed, few Americans found much to admire in Soviet political life. Nevertheless, the exchanges themselves were touted for contributing to improved international understanding as part of Secretary of State Henry Kissinger's strategy of building a web of vested interests in Moscow in favor of good relations with the United States. Again following a period of disillusionment, the early 1980s witnessed widespread calls for expanding nongovernmental contacts with Soviet citizens, this time to forestall what the nuclear freeze movement and others thought to be the imminent danger of nuclear war. In 1984, for instance, the National Academy of Sciences (NAS) ended a two-year moratorium on joint symposia with its Soviet counterpart. NAS members' concerns about the arms race outweighed indignation over the persecution of Andrei Sakharov. In short, both American public opinion and U.S. government policy have been moving toward expanding exchanges with the USSR.

VARIETY OF EXCHANGES

In addition to commercial relationships, U.S.-Soviet exchanges have embraced a variety of contacts:[1]

1. Academic and scholarly exchanges (private)
2. Government science and technology exchanges
3. Policy group dialogues (private)
4. Citizen action groups
5. Language training exchanges
6. Sundry cultural exchanges and other accords relevant to exchanges

Academic and Scholarly Exchanges

Although partially funded by the United States government, academic and scholarly exchanges are, for the most part, privately run. They include the exchange of individual faculty and graduate students and the joint activities of scholars in the humanities and social sciences—all administered by the International Research and Exchanges Board (IREX). The individual scholar exchanges are conducted with the Soviet Ministry of Higher and Specialized Secondary Education under the provisions of the revived cultural exchange agreement between the two governments, which the United States did not renew after the USSR invaded Afghanistan. Academic exchanges, however, were continued even in the absence of an umbrella accord, with the mutual understanding of the two governments.

The joint social science programs link the USSR Academy of Sciences with the American Council of Learned Societies and include joint conferences between U.S. research centers and the various regional institutes of the Soviet academy (principally, the USA and Canada Institute). The exchange activities of the National Academy of Sciences also fall under the rubric of private academic exchanges. Like the similarly private IREX exchanges, however, NAS exchanges are funded in part by the federal government. Although the bulk of NAS exchange activity has focused on collaborative programs, joint symposia, and individual projects in the natural sciences, in 1981 the NAS began a series of meetings with its Soviet counterparts on international security and arms control.

A third scholarly exchange, funded by the U.S. government, permits the Council for International Exchange of Scholars (CIES) to administer Fulbright lectureships for American faculty to teach at Soviet institutions of higher education. Authorized under the same cultural agreement that expired at the end of 1979, this program has also continued, sending annually as many as twenty American scholars in politically anodyne fields to such off-the-beaten-track places as Tashkent, Vilnius, and Erevan. The Fulbright lectureships are unique because they place participants in a hall full of Soviet students instead of burying them in the reading rooms of Lenin State Library.

Fourth, the State University of New York (SUNY) system operates three programs with the Institute of Foreign Languages and Moscow State University (MGU) for language study, dissertation work, and faculty research.

Fifth, the University of Missouri conducts a limited exchange with Moscow State University. Under this arrangement, two faculty members from Missouri annually teach and conduct research in Moscow, while two professors from MGU perform similar duties in Missouri.

Sixth, the Midwest Universities Consortium for International Activities (MUCIA), representing several Big-Ten schools, runs a small faculty exchange, funded by the U.S. government, with MGU.

Government Science and Technology Exchanges

A second group of interrelations with the Soviet Union, government science and technology exchanges, have been based on the eleven bilateral agreements that followed the 1972 Moscow Summit between President Richard M. Nixon and Leonid I. Brezhnev. The centerpiece accord, the Agreement on Cooperation in the Fields of Science and Technology (S&T), ultimately provided an umbrella for fourteen joint working groups in fields ranging from management application of computers to polymer sciences. The National Science Foundation financed and administered eleven of the fourteen joint working groups.[2] The United States allowed the S&T accord to expire in 1982 to retaliate for the imposition of martial law in Poland, which ended the activities of those working groups that had not already petered out. The president's science adviser had cochaired the joint commission overseeing the S&T agreement.

Not to be confused with these S&T working groups are the other ten "bilaterals," which usually have been administered by appropriate cabinet departments in the fields of environmental protection, public health, space, agriculture, world oceans, transportation, atomic energy, artificial heart research, energy, and housing. The energy and space bilaterals were allowed to expire at the same time as the S&T accord. Although several bilaterals have generally been limping along, in June 1985 the U.S. Department of Agriculture revived its accord with the USSR, agreeing to exchange 30 young farmers and information on crops. The November 1985 Summit in Geneva affirmed the importance of those bilateral accords still extant.

Policy Dialogue

Examples of policy dialogue include the conferences conducted by the Dartmouth group (once or twice a year); the United Nations' Association of the USA; and several research centers working under the umbrella of the Binational Commission on the Humanities and Social Sciences under the American Council of Learned Societies and the USSR Academy of Sciences, administered in the United States by IREX. Their focus is international security and arms control and, in some cases, regional political-military issues. The U.S. delegations often include prominent business leaders and former government officials; the Soviet side is most often represented by officials from the USA and Canada Institute, the Institute of World Economy and International Relations, or one of the regional institutes.

Citizen Action Groups

Citizen action groups include a breathtaking array of private groups seeking to "improve" U.S.-Soviet relations out of either a general interest in promoting international understanding or a fervent desire to halt the "doomsday clock." These groups usually act entirely on their own initiative, are self-financing, and at least have the virtue of demanding access to counterpart groups in the USSR—demands that occasionally rankle Soviet authorities and lead to sobering educational experiences for the American activists making it to Moscow. A small sample of the dozens of groups includes the Esalen Institute Soviet American Exchange Program, Grandmothers for Peace, Athletes for Peace, Forum for U.S.-Soviet Dialogue, U.S.-USSR Bridges for Peace, and Ground Zero Pairing Project.

Language Training Exchanges

Language training exchanges embrace a number of Russian teaching programs, the most important of which are conducted by the Council on International Educational Exchange (CIEE) and the American Council of Teachers of Russian (ACTR). Essentially apolitical, these programs have been extraordinarily valuable in training students (particularly, undergraduates) who have gone on to careers in teaching and government service.

Sundry Cultural Exchanges and Other Accords Relevant to Exchanges

These include various exhibits, artistic performances, and such matters as Aeroflot landing rights in the United States, which were revoked in 1981 but renewed in 1986; reciprocal commercial opportunities for Pan Am, which abandoned the Moscow run as uneconomic (the Soviets barred their citizens from flying Pan Am to conserve hard currency, *valiuta*); expansion of consulates (Kiev and New York in 1986); trade; technology transfer agreements; and a host of other commercial relationships. Because these accords are themselves diverse and important enough to merit fuller treatment, they will not be addressed in this paper.

GOALS OF EXCHANGE PROGRAMS

The general lack of centralization in the multiplicity of exchange programs has been a blessing and a curse, providing flexibility but creating disarray. The diversity of the exchanges helps to respond to a variety of needs and, in this respect, is beneficial. The overall lack of structure in the exchange programs, however, leads to confusion when it becomes necessary to formulate policy or to execute individual programming decisions. There is not only a general sense of haphazardness in the structure and administration of the exchanges but also a pervading lack of consensus on the exact goals of such an exchange program and on the best ways of reaching them. In light of these deficiencies, it is hardly remarkable that, faced with a comparatively well-conceived Soviet strategy toward exchanges, the United States has been less willing and able to devise a coherent approach to the welter of U.S.-Soviet exchange programs.

It is this inability to focus on what the goals of the exchange program are that prevents a clearer assessment of the program's present worth. Without a definition of success, a program cannot be evaluated or judged. If the goal of the programs is simply to exchange concrete scientific or scholarly knowledge, then one set of standards applies. If, however, the principal goal lies elsewhere, the program of exchanges can, and must, be judged by another standard.

What exactly is the primary objective of the exchange programs? This question must be considered separately for the two countries involved, since the goals of the United States and the Soviet Union in this endeavor are markedly different. Although one could endlessly dispute the rank order of Soviet goals in the exchange programs, they would certainly include the following:

1. Aboveboard acquisition of scientific and technical knowledge
2. Industrial espionage
3. Collection of political intelligence
4. Political disinformation
5. Professional development of Soviet scientists and scholars, particularly those specializing in the United States
6. Foreign travel and access to Western consumer goods by participants
7. Promotion of favorable attitudes toward the Soviet Union on the part of the American public
8. Acquisition of cultural prestige through touring Soviet performers
9. Acquisition by the state of hard currency

In the context of numerous diverse exchange agreements, the goals of the United States have been quite different from those of the Soviet Union. Although Lieutenant General James A. Abrahamson, Jr., director of the Strategic Defense Initiative Office, has noted that a particle-beam device at the Los Alamos Weapons Laboratory works because it includes three Soviet inventions,[3] access to Soviet technology has not been a central U.S. objective. American aims include the following:

1. Advancement of scholarship and language training
2. A deeper understanding of Soviet society

3. Achievement of artistic training

4. Acquisition of knowledge in those relatively few but important fields of basic science where the Soviets may be more advanced

5. The demonstration effect of American values and achievements

From the U.S. standpoint, this last benefit is the key to the exchange program. As the Twentieth Century Fund Task Force on Soviet-American Scholarly and Cultural Exchanges observed:

> The Task Force is convinced that the major benefit of the exchanges for the U.S. is that they provide an open window for viewing American accomplishments and freedoms. A good deal has been accomplished by American scholars and performers visiting the Soviet Union; even more important are the extended visits to the U.S. by Soviet scholars and repeated visits by large numbers of dancers, musicians and other performing artists. The positive view of American abundance and freedom is transmitted via the extensive Soviet "grapevine" to large numbers of Soviet citizens, especially in the political elite and in the intellectual and artistic communities.[4]

The transmission of Western standards and ideas, informational access to a previously closed Soviet society, and training of a new generation of academic specialists and government officials are the principal benefits America derives from the exchanges. These benefits would be increased by what IREX calls "more aggressive formatting," securing better access to Soviet hard scientists, policymakers, and policy analysts.

Even now, they substantially counterbalance the transfer of some scientific and technological information in the other direction, especially since Soviet access to hardware is limited by the nature of the exchanges, which are largely based in universities rather than private industry. In short, as long as the exchanges are academic rather than industrial and focus on basic science rather than applied research, the United States loses significantly less than one might, at first, fear. By the same token, however, applied research in the hard sciences (especially technology transfers resulting from industrial cooperation deals) should be excluded from the exchanges and blocked on separate but related grounds.

In 1982 a Panel on Scientific Communication and National Security (created by the National Academy of Sciences after discussions with the U.S. Defense Department and chaired by Dale Corson, president emeritus of Cornell University) reviewed these issues as part of a larger study of means to stem the flow of militarily relevant technologies to the Soviet Union. The Corson panel concluded that

> there is very little evidence that scientific exchange programs have had an identifiable adverse effect on U.S. national security. This does not imply that the flow of scientific information between the United States and the USSR through exchange is balanced. It is not. [In addition to benefits] . . . there are also some significant risks associated with exchange programs. The Soviet Union utilizes exchange programs to collect sensitive information, sometimes with highly specific aims. Heightened sensitivity among U.S. scientists to this fact is desirable.[5]

With that crucial caveat, we can say that the United States has benefited from the exchanges. They have become an indispensable aspect of the training of American sovietologists who serve in government and who, by their teaching and writing, contribute to public awareness of the realities of Soviet communism. Scientific and technological exchanges have also served to inform United States experts about the level of knowledge in given fields in the Soviet Union. On rare occasion, the United States has been able to use the results of Soviet experiments and to learn from Soviet mistakes. The program has certainly worked well enough to merit its further continuation, albeit with some significant modifications.

HUMAN RIGHTS

Even though the political value of the exchanges to the United States has been substantial, objections to continuing the program have sometimes been raised on moral grounds. In particular, many scientists and citizens have called for an official U.S. curtailment of the exchanges to protest the USSR's internal persecution of various scientists and human rights activists. Should the United States attempt to unilaterally end the program in the hope that such a curtailment would alter Soviet behavior, or at least show American opposition in principle?

In the past, this issue raised the concern of many scientists. In 1982, to protest the harassment of its foreign associate Andrei Sakharov, the National Academy of Sciences curtailed all major symposia (but not individual contacts or participation in multilateral conferences) to be convened under its agreement with the Soviet Academy. This ban lasted only two years: The moratorium ended in 1984, with Soviet troops still in Afghanistan and Sakharov forcibly exiled and isolated in Gorky. In seeking to renew contacts, the NAS implicitly acknowledged the insufficiency of its leverage over Soviet authorities—an acknowledgement all the more unfortunate in light of its earlier warning that if corrective action were not taken, additional sanctions might follow.

Although cutbacks in the exchanges may, at times, be warranted to protest especially visible abuses of human rights in the Soviet Union, the NAS experience suggests their likely futility. Moreover, if moral protest over Soviet repression is the objective, scuttling exchanges over mistreatment of one man like Sakharov, admirable as he is, scarcely addresses the worse fates suffered by Anatolii Shcharanskii, nine years in prisons and labor camps for advocating the right of Jews to emigrate; Iurii Orlov, the imprisoned founder of the Helsinki Watch Group; the 38 other Helsinki monitors still imprisoned; or, for that matter, the thousands of political prisoners consigned to obscurity in labor camps throughout the Soviet republics. Frankly, if moral consistency were the goal, the United States should maintain no contacts whatsoever with the Soviet Union.

Reducing exchanges may also be counterproductive in several ways. Curtailing the exchanges affects primarily those Soviet scientists and members of the intelligentsia who crave Western contact. Through them, Western ideas are most effectively spread, and through the exchanges more information is available on the persecution of Soviet dissidents. Curtailing exchange programs to protest Soviet repression would mean an end to one of the few means at our disposal to influence Soviet society—thus accomplishing the opposite of the effect intended. Instead of altering Soviet behavior by discontinuing the exchanges, the United States would lose one of its few opportunities to strengthen commitment to its own ideals in the heart of Soviet society. The cause of human rights is best served by continuing to maintain as many contacts with the Soviet intelligentsia, including dissidents, as possible.

FOREIGN POLICY CONSIDERATIONS

One of the most hotly debated questions about the exchanges is the degree to which they should be subject to political considerations. In the past, the argument has often seemed to polarize government officials and the academic community. Government officials, who have supported a large number of the exchange programs through public funds, often tend to believe that exchanges are valuable primarily as a political carrot to be extended to the Soviets as an incentive for better bilateral relations. When those relations have turned sour in the past (as in the months after the Soviet invasion of Afghanistan) the carrot was withdrawn as the governmental exchanges were terminated or diminished to signify American disapproval of Soviet actions.

Scientists and other scholars frequently argue that the subordination of science and learning to political considerations is inconsistent with the traditions of American government and the needs of scientific progress. They note that governmental interference is reminiscent of the Soviet modus operandi. In the aftermath of the declaration of martial law in Poland, for example, the U.S. government terminated the S&T agreement and the bilateral agreements on cooperation in space and energy. Washington also decreased funding for other exchanges. The announced restrictions, however, failed to further any specific policy objectives, beyond giving vent to a general irritation with Soviet policy.[6] They satisfied neither scholars nor proponents of the sanctions. Echoing their counterparts in the arms control community who insist on the importance of controlling arms to the exclusion of other values, such as defense, and who believe in the independent value of dialogue for its own sake, some scholars wedded to the exchanges have argued that they are both too important to abandon and too harmless to curtail.

While the scientists' fears of governmental interference in scholarly exchanges are not to be dismissed out of hand, a different reason for allowing the exchanges to continue despite political fluctuations is far more persuasive. Curtailing the exchanges would mean an end to the benefits that accrue to the United States. These benefits, discussed earlier, lie in the demonstration of American ideas and achievements in Soviet society and the channel of information made possible through the exchanges. If the exchanges are to be used as a political tool, the loss of such benefits is a substantial cost to bear.

The Panel on Scientific Communication and National Security stressed that across-the-board cutbacks are particularly undesirable when they have an impact on exchanges in select fields in which Soviet science can contribute to American research; for example, plasma physics, condensed matter physics, and fundamental properties of matter. Accordingly, the panel urged greater selectivity in the future with respect to which programs should be the object of sanctions and suggested that White House science officials take part in decisions affecting the bilaterals.

Finally, there is something slightly pathetic about responding to the invasion of another country by discontinuing ballet performances, athletic contests, and learned symposia. If the objective of United States policy is to frustrate the Soviet regime's efforts to extend its dominion abroad, a policy of arming the Afghan insurgents is more likely to achieve the goal.

IMPROVING THE EXCHANGES

Despite the political utility of the exchanges, certain improvements in the current program are desirable. Although such exchanges are more valuable to the United States as modes of cultural and social interaction than as tools to gain scientific and technical knowledge, heed should be paid to the common complaint of American exchange participants that their access to scholarly and scientific resources in the Soviet Union is far more limited than the access of their Soviet counterparts in the United States. This asymmetry requires an increase in the reciprocity of the exchanges, to ensure that the Soviets are sending fully qualified participants and are permitting American scholars free access to needed resources.

More important from a national standpoint, American agencies administering the exchanges need to coordinate more effectively policy and action. Given the degree of centralization under which the Soviets operate, they can effectively delineate what they want to achieve through the program (including intelligence missions), whereas no such coherence is evident on the American side. The confusing array of administrative bodies, both private and governmental, prohibits the formulation of a set of principles that should govern such a program of exchanges and, concomitantly, of a well-defined strategy of action. The resulting lack of synthesis permits a certain flexibility in the creation of exchange opportunities and allows the private exchanges to retain their identity free from governmental interference. However, as a whole the exchange programs would benefit from a greater amount of discussion and consultation among government agencies, between them and private sector groups, and among private sector groups themselves.

Reciprocity

The often urged proposals to insist on U.S. access to human and material resources in the USSR equal to the access that Soviet scholars enjoy in the United States bear reiteration. Similar demands have been voiced that the Soviet side broaden the areas of research permitted in political science, public administration, and sociology—not to mention the hard sciences. From a scholarly standpoint, we do not need many additional studies on the role of local soviets, but we do need more research on the process of technological innovation in the Soviet Union, the mechanisms of government liaison with religious organizations, relations between ethnic groups within republics, and the party's relationship to society. Although no one should hold his breath waiting for Soviet authorities to provide access to these areas for Western field investigations, there is every reason to continually demand that such research be permitted. Without such pressure, no progress can be made.

Likewise, the extension in recent years of visits by American scholars to cities outside Moscow and Leningrad should go still further. Efforts should be made to broaden the narrow circle of Soviet *institutchiki* who are beginning to form their own mini-*nomenklatura*, receive foreign visitors, and are allowed to attend foreign conferences (and shop) in the West. Exchange critics are undoubtedly correct in suggesting that more exchanges should be held in areas where Soviet knowledge is equal or superior to Western expertise. Mathematics is a prime example.

As this list of recommendations suggests, there has been no shortage of proposals to improve the exchanges at the micro level, but such suggestions are not a panacea. First, they are microsolutions. As such, they can be adopted only piecemeal, and their impact will be exceedingly gradual. American institutions administering exchanges should probably be more ready to terminate their relationships with Soviet counterparts when reciprocity breaks down. This observation applies not only to IREX, and the American groups operating under the IREX umbrella, but also to other groups.

The problem, however, is that participating American institutions lack the necessary leverage over their Soviet counterparts to realize even these piecemeal improvements. This is partly because many American sellers confront one Soviet buyer. If the hypothetical American Center for Soviet Research in Gotham demands a higher level of reciprocity from the not-so-hypothetical USA and Canada Institute in Moscow, the Soviet institute can redirect its energies to another eager American group at Stanford or Berkeley or in Cambridge or Washington, D.C.

It is also a case of private American groups having an institutional need to continue the particular exchange in question or a philosophical commitment to dialogue either for its own sake or for the cause of peace, disarmament, or conflict resolution. Probably, Soviet authorities do not find themselves subject to similar pressure (here is an area in which useful research might be performed). The problem of organizational asymmetries suggests the importance of addressing organizational questions in the U.S.-Soviet exchange relationship.

Measures to Improve Coordination of Action

The variety of American exchange programs and administrative agencies places the United States at an organizational disadvantage vis-à-vis the Soviets, who can pursue a strategy of dealing with those American groups it wishes to. These American groups have distinctly fewer Soviet institutions from which to choose, all of them regulated by central party organs, primarily the International Department of the Central Committee. Faced with a relatively coherent Soviet exchange strategy, the diversity of American groups could use a greater measure of coordination in their actions, at a minimum in terms of discussing long-range goals and the best methods of achieving such goals in light of Soviet objectives and organizational processes.

Recently, IREX has taken a useful step in this direction by convening periodic informal meetings of U.S. nongovernmental organizations involved in continuing policy-related discussions with Soviet counterpart specialists in international affairs. To compare experiences in order to correct many of the above-mentioned deficiencies, American participants in discussions sponsored by the Bilateral Commission on the Humanities and Social Sciences of the American Council of Learned Societies, the Kettering Foundation (Dartmouth conferences), the United Nations Association of the USA, and others have met with representatives of the U.S. Embassy in Moscow, the National Security Council, and the U.S. Information Agency.

Although Soviet exchangees are often well informed about the nature of the research establishment in the United States and the work of their American counterparts, this kind of knowledge is often lacking in participants from the United States. The most common lacuna in American understanding of the Soviet institutions and individuals with which we deal relates to the domestic political context in which their institutions operate. It would, therefore, be particularly enlightening to make available to American scholars an authoritative guide to the role of the institutes of the USSR Academy of Sciences in the Soviet political system. Such a study, presently being compiled under the auspices of the informal group mentioned above, would enumerate the political and intelligence functions of the institutes, trace the political and family connections of institute directors and researchers, and assess the influence of these institutes in the Soviet policymaking process. At least one

Soviet defector has already provided illuminating insights into several of these questions.[7] A comprehensive study available to all exchange groups would contribute to a more sophisticated understanding of the semiofficial tasks of the quasi-academics participating on the Soviet side.

A biographical register might also be kept on scholars and scientists in the Soviet hierarchy and on the nature of the work they have done, including their publications.[8] This biographical knowledge would be especially useful since the Soviets tend repeatedly to exchange many of the same individuals as a function of their privileged positions.

These measures would eliminate several of the Soviet advantages in negotiating with American groups. On a programwide basis, however, greater measures may be needed to improve coordination of action and lessen the impact of Soviet centralization. To address this need, some have suggested the advisability of re-examining the proposal of the Twentieth Century Fund Task Force to create a Cultural Exchange Advisory Council, which could easily extend its purview to scientific and academic exchanges as well.[9] As originally proposed, such a council was to be modeled after the National Council on the Humanities, which is the advisory body of the National Endowment for the Humanities. Such a council might have two dozen members, appointed for overlapping terms by the president or the Congress. Its function would be to monitor and review programs, make recommendations, and advise on policies and basic goals. Its members should be committed both to the basic value of the exchanges and to the principle that the exchanges should be conducted in a spirit of reciprocity. Such a council, whose recommendations might be nonbinding, could serve as the coordinating force behind the American side of the exchanges. While allowing individual programs to maintain their integrity, and avoiding the creation of a new bureaucracy, this council would be able to provide the necessary overview that the smaller programs need. Basic goals and policies would become clearer and, accordingly, the required negotiating tactics vis-à-vis the Soviets.

With the notable exception of a few causes célèbres (such as the persecution of Soviet physicist and Nobel Peace Prize winner Andrei Sakharov), American faculty members, scientists, and cultural figures strongly prefer that U.S.-Soviet exchanges be treated as nonpolitical. The general conviction that the heavy hand of government should be kept off cultural matters lies at the heart of traditional American conceptions of the limited role that government should play: That government governs best which governs least.

The Soviet approach to cultural and scientific exchange is the polar opposite. It has been so since 1925, when Lev Trotsky's sister (and Moscow party boss L. B. Kamenev's wife) was put in charge of the Society for Cultural Relations with Foreign Countries, the early Bolshevik monopoly for cultural imports and exports.[10] As is true in so many areas, the Soviet approach—which includes rationing foreign travel to reinforce domestic social controls—makes this common aspiration of Americans a regrettably utopian hope. Athletes deplore the politicization of the Olympics; arms control experts urge the insulation of the Geneva talks from the broader political relationship; farmers insist that grain is too important to be embargoed for political purposes; and bankers and businessmen contend that trade should determine political relationships rather than vice-versa.

The academic community similarly seeks special exemption for matters of special concern to it. Like athletes, academics are unlikely to exert sufficient political leverage to insulate their chosen activity from political crosscurrents. It is, therefore, all the more in their interest to protect the exchanges by developing the informal techniques and mechanisms to enhance coordination among themselves and maximize their leverage vis-à-vis their Soviet counterparts, toward the end of securing greater reciprocity in the exchange programs.

CONCLUDING OBSERVATIONS

With respect to Russian-language exchanges, few would dispute their value and most would urge their expansion on general educational grounds, but there are also important political implications of which we should be mindful. Obviously, to acquire and assess all kinds of data on the Soviet Union, Russian-language expertise is indispensable; and in light of the vastly superior Soviet system of teaching English, language exchanges directly serve important American interests. For example, the recently reported and long overdue plan to replace many Soviet citizens with American citizens in "clerical" jobs at the U.S. embassy in Moscow can be smoothly accomplished only if American competence in the Russian language is greatly improved. Alarmed critics have warned that unless such training is expanded, we may eventually have to rely on Soviet interpreters for all government-to-government discussions.

There is another important, and much broader, objective that the United States exchange program promotes. As suggested above, it involves efforts to encourage the evolution of Soviet society in a direction less inimical to American interests and values. While there may be no

Thomas Jefferson in the United States today, and the Alexander Radish-chevs of the USSR reside chiefly in the Gulag Archipelago, the possibility to reinforce existing preferences of key elements of the Soviet intelligentsia in favor of greater professional autonomy and openness should not be casually dismissed. Although it is hardly conscious of American concepts of civil liberties, the successor generation of the present Soviet intelligentsia is keenly interested in expanding its knowledge of the outside world, its own range of material choices within Soviet society, and for those individuals not eagerly seeking to be co-opted, its autonomy vis-à-vis party authorities. These aspirations represent an opportunity for politically significant fallout from deeper and broader contact with American counterparts.

As the People's Republic of China's newly declared receptivity to foreign investment, technology, and expertise suggests, even communist regimes—if graphically confronted with the undeniable relationship between economic freedom and national prosperity—are potentially capable of experimenting with economic decentralization reforms. One of the consequences of such fundamental reform may be greater openness to foreign concepts of the central requirement of technological innovation: the liberation of the individual's entrepreneurial instincts. If and when this relationship between economic freedom and technological advance is assimilated by a communist elite, an important door has been opened for the penetration of a political idea, namely, that greater economic freedom is impossible without greater political freedom. The cultural, scholarly, and scientific exchanges offer the United States the opportunity to promote the seepage of these two ideas, economic and political freedom, into Soviet political culture. There is no country in the world as well equipped as the United States to wring this advantage from exchanges with the Kremlin.

Finally, one often-ignored benefit of the exchanges—greatest, ironically, when the exchanges are most lacking in reciprocity—is their cumulative impact in acquainting American scholars and activists, firsthand, with the USSR Committee for State Security (KGB) and its dense network of border guards, agents, informers, and assorted freelancers. The educational value of such exposure cannot readily be quantified, nor does it figure in most net assessments of the mutual benefits of the scientific and other exchanges. The critically important value of the entire exchange program is to provide influential segments of American society with direct experience of the Soviet apparatus of repression. Its persuasiveness rarely fails to impress Western exchange participants, particularly those who reside in the Soviet Union for several months at a time.

This benefit—generally not regarded as such by those most fervently devoted to "improving" U.S.-Soviet relations—is sufficiently compelling that in any recasting of the exchanges an effort should be made to increase the relative weight of protracted visits and to decrease the proportion of short-term visits of a month or less, particularly brief scientific symposia. Although longer visits permit Soviet vacuum cleaners to gather information and impart disinformation, they also force party and police officials to face the painful dilemma of either significantly exposing Soviet society or showing the veiled hand of repression.

But realistically, the United States cannot hope to succeed in creating genuine reciprocity in its exchange relationship with the Soviet Union. The generally closed nature of Soviet society, the paranoia of an insecure ruling elite, and the centralized political institutions characteristic of Marxist-Leninist systems in historically authoritarian societies are, fortunately, not likely to be duplicated in the United States. These hallmarks of the Soviet system will make it impossible in our lifetimes to establish equal degrees of freedom and opportunity for American scholars in the Soviet Union.

Discussion

Catherine P. Ailes*

I would like to compliment Dr. Wessell on his interesting paper, which raises many of the key issues surrounding U.S.-Soviet exchanges and provides several valuable suggestions for enhancing their effectiveness. My remarks will focus specifically on scientific and technical exchanges between the two countries; particularly, those that took place between May 1972 and July 1982 under the U.S.-USSR Agreement on Cooperation in the Fields of Science and Technology (S&T Agreement).

This was one of eleven bilateral agreements signed following the Moscow summit of May 1972. Although official exchanges of scientists and engineers between the United States and the USSR date back to the late 1950s, the S&T Agreement broadened significantly the scope of cooperation and expanded markedly the number of scientists participating in such exchanges. Prior to 1972, only very modest and restricted exchange programs existed, and these were often hampered by lack of effective focus and coordination in negotiating with Soviet counterpart organizations. In contrast, the S&T Agreement represented a basic change in the approach to develop scientific interaction with the USSR.

Activities were programmatically organized, with teams of scien-

*This paper is based on research supported by the international programs division of the National Science Foundation, the full results of which are described in Catherine P. Ailes and Arthur E. Pardee, Jr., *Cooperation in Science and Technology: An Evaluation of the U.S.-Soviet Agreement* (Boulder, Colo: Westview Press, 1986). Any views or opinions expressed herein are the author's and do not necessarily reflect those of SRI International, the National Science Foundation, or the U.S. government.

tists collaborating over extended periods of time on specified project areas. The subjects selected for joint exploration under the S&T Agreement were diverse and covered a broad spectrum of basic and applied sciences. The topically focused working group programs provided an opportunity for intensive joint project activity, exchange of test data and samples, and sharing of facilities and equipment by teams of scientists in the two countries. Given the highly centralized Soviet system, these opportunities could not have been effectively initiated by the academic or industrial sectors and would not have been feasible under individualized exchanges.

A large number of scientists, representing a broad and diverse set of institutions, participated from each country. On the United States side, participants included academic scientists from most of the major research universities and a broad representation of scientists from industry, government, and research institutes. Although the organizational representation was less broad than in the case of the United States, large numbers of top Soviet scientists were directly involved from key technical institutes and ministries, the State Committee for Science and Technology, and the USSR Academy of Sciences and its research institutes. During the ten-year period in which the agreement was in effect, more than 1,000 scientists from the United States participated in over 400 organized activities, which included joint meetings, long-term visits, and conferences and symposia. More than $22 million was provided by the United States government to support these activities, and some 300 publications resulted from these exchanges.

For each country, the principal motivation underlying the initiation of the S&T Agreement in 1972 differed significantly: Economic motives were particularly strong for the USSR, whereas political factors were predominant for the United States. In the years after the agreement was signed, however, it became increasingly evident that neither of these expectations was being met, and both sides began to shift in their objectives for the cooperative science exchange.

As the exchanges progressed, it became clear that cooperative programs provided only for the exchange of information and the development of joint research projects and that the United States intended to keep it that way. The Soviet leadership, thus, began to shift the level of its expectations for acquiring United States technology through Soviet participation in the exchanges and to develop a general appreciation of the advantages of cooperation in scientific research with the United States.

In the United States, high expectations of the early period of détente were succeeded also by a disillusionment that altered the original objectives of the exchange. With this shift, the notion of the United States as superior to the Soviet Union in many areas of science and technology increased concern that the United States must be relinquishing more than it was receiving in return. This concern resulted in a closer scrutiny of individual projects under the agreement to ensure that the principle of mutual benefit and reciprocity was being applied in the exchange of scientific and technical information and capabilities.

Nevertheless, the S&T Agreement never totally escaped its original linkage with political objectives; scientific and technical exchanges always remained a hostage to U.S. foreign policy interests. Although closer attention was given to selecting and implementing individual projects to maximize the scientific outcomes, the worsening political relationship between the two countries (exemplified by the periodic interruption in cooperative programs for political purposes) led to a "yo-yo" fluctuation in program continuity, the willingness of U.S. scientists to continue to participate, U.S. funding support, and, ultimately, the scientific quality of the exchanges.

During the period in which the S&T Agreement was in effect, the National Science Foundation (NSF) served as the source of support for eleven of the fourteen working groups that had been established under the agreement. These eleven working groups were the principal focus of an extensive review and evaluation of the S&T Agreement that was conducted by Stanford Research Institute (SRI) International for NSF. To evaluate the agreement, this review used surveys of U.S. participants in the program; evaluations by panels of experts with substantive knowledge in the various fields addressed, but not formally associated with, the programs; and information contained in joint protocols, annual and semiannual reports, publications, and other records of working group activities found in files maintained by NSF and the U.S. Department of State.

It was agreed that all of the working group programs significantly broadened the knowledge of U.S. scientists about Soviet scientific capabilities. In many cases, U.S. participants learned not only about the directions in research and the specific procedures followed by Soviet scientists but also about the organization and direction of Soviet activities. Such knowledge is significant to the United States as a nation, because it is useful in assessing the plans, trends, and prospective accomplishments of the USSR, which in turn can be used to formulate the general policy of the United States toward the Soviet Union.

In terms of the impact of the exchanges in increasing U.S. scientific capabilities, varying results were produced in different fields. In general, the United States benefits substantially in terms of increased scientific knowledge in those areas in which Soviet expertise was equivalent to that of the United States, or in which Soviet resources were concentrated in specific areas or methods of research neglected by U.S. scientists because of emphasis on other topics or techniques. On the other hand, in those areas in which Soviet expertise lagged well behind that of the United States, there was a negligible (or nil) benefit in terms of increasing U.S. scientific capabilities. In some cases, however, the impact on U.S. scientific knowledge was limited, not because of wide discrepancies in the state of the art in the respective countries, but because of political sensitivities that inhibited the full cooperation of the Soviet side of the working group. The predominant forms of cooperation utilized by the working groups were more important than relative levels of scientific expertise in the two countries. Benefits of this type concentrated on those areas that emphasized intensive joint project work and extensive contact between scientists of the two countries.

In general, the following six factors are important in maximizing the effectiveness of programmatically organized scientific exchanges with the Soviet Union:

1. *Careful selection of areas for cooperative research.* In terms of the impact on U.S. scientific capabilities, the degree of success of the various working group programs depended largely on the degree to which Soviet research in the field was behind, equivalent to, or ahead of the current U.S. state of the art. Because of this, the enhancement of U.S. scientific capabilities from cooperation with the USSR was not evenly balanced across fields. In those areas in which U.S. scientific capabilities and expertise far surpassed those of the Soviet Union, there was little or no benefit to the United States in a strictly scientific sense. However, the Soviet Union has focused on specific areas of science and technology in past years, whereas the United States has concentrated on other techniques and research approaches. In exchanges focused on areas in which Soviet scientific capabilities and techniques were as advanced as or more advanced than those of the U.S., the latter benefited significantly. Recently, in order to maintain more of a mutual balance, the United States has selected projects from those areas of the S&T Agreement in which scientific achievements are most evident and has focused increasingly on joint, as opposed to parallel, research.

2. *Access to USSR institutions and scientists.* Access to Soviet individuals and institutions working in the most important and productive fields was a problem that plagued almost all of the working group programs to some extent and was a key factor accounting for

their relative degree of success. Many of the programs suffered because of insufficiently broad organizational representation on the part of the Soviet project teams. In the later years of the agreement, the problem became less severe; negotiators and participants from the United States began to demand increased access to certain individuals or institutions considered to be doing some of the most outstanding work in the Soviet Union, and some programs were reorganized to require such access.

3. *Appropriate institutional linkages.* From the U.S. perspective, a major problem involved determining and establishing the best institutional linkages for cooperative research. Often there were problems in matching the interests of U.S. specialists with the areas of competence of Soviet participants who had been assigned to the program. The United States encountered difficulty in obtaining information in many cases because it was unclear with whom the U.S. participants were working or should be working. When the United States could determine and specify appropriate institutional linkages at the outset of a joint project, which it often could as experience under the agreement progressed, it was able to avoid major delays that were caused by a change in the principal Soviet counterpart organization once cooperation was initiated.

4. *Agreement on concise and concrete project objectives.* On the U.S. side, more preliminary work was often needed to define clearly the specific purpose and objectives of the proposed research prior to negotiation with Soviet counterparts. It was often difficult to reach mutual agreement about what research was important; in some cases, projects were incorporated into the joint program because one side had little or no interest. Consequently, many projects were only loosely defined in advance and lacked a specific focus and concise objectives. The U.S. participants thus found it difficult to obtain from their Soviet counterparts information that had been originally anticipated; the results of many projects, particularly those that involved parallel research, were not really comparable. The United States also found it difficult to determine the point at which specific projects had reached a natural conclusion so that new ones could be introduced. However, problems have been kept to a minimum recently by carefully examining prior project objectives and approaches and assuring that a consensus existed about them before projects were initiated.

5. *Advanced preparation for meetings and exchanges.* A frequent complaint of U.S. participants concerned insufficient preparation for joint meetings and workshops. The Soviet participants generally

knew in advance exactly what information they sought and often came to joint meetings with protocols drafted in advance. Participants from the United States did not allocate enough time prior to joint meetings to define their objectives, establish the information they sought to obtain, and present a unified front. Frequently, this gave the Soviet participants an advantage in terms of decisions about directions for project activities and about desired information.

6. *Early and regular evaluation of project results.* In the later years of the S&T Agreement, the National Science Foundation regularly reviewed cooperation on individual projects under the working groups and determined progress toward achieving specific finite objectives. The reviews were intended to determine existing problems that might suggest terminating or gradually circumscribing certain activities. Although this review process ultimately led to eliminating certain projects or combining less successful projects with those in which the Soviet participants had been more cooperative (usually because of political pressure to continue certain programs), an inordinate amount of time was devoted to remedying problems before deciding to terminate particular programs. As resources devoted to the S&T Agreement dwindled and pressure increased for reciprocity, projects were readily terminated after a reasonable amount of effort had been expended to correct problems hindering the progress of cooperation.

NOTES

1. The following catalog loosely follows the scheme in *U.S.-Soviet Exchanges: A Conference Report* (Washington, D.C.: The Kennan Institute, 1985). In his remarks on 27 June 1984 to the meeting of heads of major American exchange programs, President Reagan indicated United States readiness to initiate negotiations on a new cultural exchange agreement with the Soviet Union, replacing the accord that expired in 1979, and called for private initiatives to expand contacts.

2. For a comprehensive assessment of the operation of the working groups sponsored by the National Science Foundation, see Catherine P. Ailes and Arthur E. Pardee, Jr., *Cooperation in Science and Technology: An Evaluation of the U.S.-Soviet Agreement* (Boulder, Colo.: Westview Press, 1986).

3. "Space Arms Projects Ignite Debate on U.S.-Soviet Science Exchanges," *New York Times*, 1 July 1985, p. D-10.

4. Twentieth Century Fund Task Force on Soviet-American Scholarly and Cultural Exchanges, *The Raised Curtain* (New York, 1977), p. 8. Members of the

task force, chaired by Harry C. McPherson, Jr., included Richard Pipes and Hans J. Morgenthau, among others.

5. Panel on Scientific Communication and National Security, National Academy of Sciences, *Scientific Communication and National Security* (Washington, D.C.: National Academy Press, 1982), p. 62. This is also called "the Corson Report."

6. For a discussion of similar questions, see Felice D. Gaer, "Soviet-American Scholarly Exchanges: Should Learning and Politics Mix?," *Vital Issues* 29, no. 10 (June 1980).

7. Galina Orionova, interviewed by Nora Beloff, "Escape from Boredom: A Defector's Story," *The Atlantic*, November 1980, pp. 42–50.

8. William F. Scott, "A Proposal to Enhance the Value of Exchange Visits Between American and Soviet Scholars," an unpublished paper.

9. Twentieth Century Fund Task Force, *The Raised Curtain*, p. 15.

10. J. D. Parks, *Culture, Conflict and Coexistence: American-Soviet Cultural Relations, 1917–1958* (Jefferson, N.C.: McFarland, 1983), p. 21.

9

New Broadcasting Technologies

Allen M. Peterson

For the past half century international radio broadcasting has depended upon high-frequency (HF) radio transmissions that reach distant points on the earth by means of successive reflections at the ionosphere and at the surface of the earth. Since it depends on the ionosphere, which varies during the day, the season, and the eleven-year sunspot cycle, the performance of HF radio systems is highly variable. Under ideal conditions, modest power levels permit satisfactory communication to distant points.

In international broadcasting, on the other hand, ionospheric conditions are often far from ideal; noise levels at the receiver are often high, and at many locations deliberate jamming must be contended with. Under these circumstances, very high-powered transmitters and large high-gain antennas are required to achieve satisfactory broadcast reception. It is also important to choose the correct radio frequency for a given path and ionospheric conditions. Together with real time ionospheric sounding techniques, modern computer-generated ionospheric predictions can significantly improve the performance of HF broadcasting systems. When permitted by technology, broadcasting from satellites in a variety of frequency bands will offer an opportunity to overcome some of the problems associated with present-day HF broadcasting.

HIGH-FREQUENCY
IONOSPHERIC BROADCASTING

At frequencies between 3 and 30 megahertz (MHz, HF Band) and distances greater than about 200 kilometers (km), radio transmission depends primarily on sky waves reflected from the ionosphere. The ionosphere is a region in which the rarefied air is sufficiently ionized to reflect and/or absorb radio waves. The ionosphere consists of the following layers or regions:

- At heights from about 50 to 90 km, the D layer exists only in the daylight hours and the ionization follows the elevation. This layer partially absorbs HF signals.
- The E layer (at about 110 km) is important for daytime propagation at distances less than about 2,000 km. The ionization of the normal E layer follows the elevation of the sun. Irregular areas of unusually high ionization density (called sporadic E) occur frequently in this region of the ionosphere. Sporadic E occasionally prevents frequencies that normally penetrate the E layer from reaching higher layers and causes occasional long-distance transmission at very high frequencies.
- The F1 layer occurs at heights between about 175 and 250 km and exists only during daylight hours. This layer is the reflecting region for HF waves that penetrate the E layer, but usually oblique incidence waves that penetrate the E layer also penetrate the F1 layer and are reflected by the F2 layer.
- At heights between about 250 and 400 km, the F2 layer is the principal reflecting region for long-distance HF communication. The height and ionization density of the F2 layer vary diurnally, seasonally, and over the sunspot cycle. Ionization of the F2 layers does not follow the elevation of the sun, and at night the F1 layer merges with the F2 layer at a height of about 300 km. The layers are said to exist where the ionization gradient is capable of refracting radio waves back to the earth. Obliquely incident waves follow a curved path in the ionosphere because of gradual refraction or bending of the wave front.

Depending on the ionization density at each layer, there is a critical or highest frequency (f_c) at which the layer reflects a vertically incident wave. Frequencies higher than f_c pass through the layer at vertical incidence. At oblique incidence, the maximum usable frequency (for reflection) is given by

$$muf = f_c sec\phi$$

where ϕ is the angle of incidence at the reflecting layer. Both f_c and height (for a given distance) vary for each layer with local time of day, season, latitude, and with the eleven-year sunspot cycle. Ionospheric losses during propagation are a minimum near the muf and increase rapidly for lower frequencies during daylight. High-frequency waves travel to distant points by reflection from the ionosphere and earth in one or more hops.

In designing an HF system, it is necessary to determine optimum frequencies, system loss, signal to noise ratio, angle of arrival, and circuit reliability. Manual methods for calculating such parameters have existed, but modern computer programs such as "Ioncap" (the U.S. Commerce Department's "Ionospheric Communications Analysis and Prediction Program") permit more detailed analysis.

Listeners to HF broadcasts must contend with both natural and man-made noise. At high frequencies, natural noise is of both cosmic and atmospheric origin. Under most circumstances, atmospheric noise that originates from electrical discharges in thunderstorms is the predominant source of noise. Man-made noise results from both incidental sources and from deliberate jamming. In urban areas, man-made noise usually exceeds natural noise and field strengths of a few microvolts per meter are normal. In some parts of the world, deliberate jamming is the most serious problem confronting the listener (jamming mitigation techniques are discussed in a later section).

A number of options exist for improving the transmission systems of HF broadcast stations. Individual transmitters can achieve power levels in excess of 500 kilowatts (kW), and still higher powers can be obtained by feeding a single antenna array from two or more transmitters. Control of antenna radiation patterns and elevation and azimuth directions can be accomplished through the use of phased arrays or physically moving antenna structures. Separate antennas with their transmitters can be phased to maximize power density on particular listener regions. Speech processing can be used to increase the apparent transmitted power of the broadcast signal. Eliminating or reducing the peaks in the speech spectrum, so that the peak-to-average power ratio is reduced, increases loudness. In effect, this places more power in the intelligence bearing sidebands. In addition, by shaping the voice frequency spectrum, emphasis can be placed in that portion that aids in word recognition.

Real-time management of the transmission facilities, based on knowledge of HF propagation conditions, can enhance broadcast system performance. Capabilities that make this possible include real-time monitoring or signals received in the listener region and the use of data provided by networks of vertical incidence and oblique incidence ionospheric sounders. Networks of oblique incidence sounders that already exist in various parts of the world could be used, the performance of which could be enhanced by adding more receivers. Backscatter sounding of the transmission path—using signals scattered back to the transmitter site from distance illuminated regions of the earth—can also be used to determine proper frequencies for transmission.

Broadcasting from Satellites

Satellites in earth-synchronous or other desirable orbits have a number of attributes that appear favorable for international broadcasting. In particular, they do not suffer from the time-varying vagaries of the ionosphere. On the other hand, not all of the technology needed for broadcasting is available, and international agreements concerning broadcasting from satellites are still unresolved.

For international broadcasting, it is important that receiving equipment be widely available to listeners at the frequencies proposed for use. As a result, the following appear particularly attractive: the upper end of the HF band (26 MHz), the frequency modulation (FM) broadcast bands (66–72 MHz, 87–100 MHz, and 88–109 MHz), and the television (TV) bands (49–99 MHz and 175–229 MHz). The sound portion of a TV channel without video could provide an option that might be used for broadcasting.

In order to estimate the characteristics of suitable satellite systems the signal strengths required in the receiving regions must be known. For the HF band we will use the values suggested by the Voice of America, that is, 1 millivolt per meter (mv/m) in regions without jamming and 2.5 mv/m in regions subject to jamming. For FM broadcasting in the United States, 3.16 mv/m is suggested for the minimum field strength over the principal community to be served. For TV series (grade A) in the United States, 2.5 mv/m is required for channels 2–6 and 3.5 mv/m for channels 7–13. These values of field strength provide reasonable guidelines for estimating the required broadcast satellite system parameters.

HF Satellite Broadcast System

An estimate of the required transmitter power and antenna size for a synchronous-orbit satellite (with a range from earth center $R = 40,000$ km) can be based upon the desired area coverage at the earth and the 2.5 mv/m field strength required for a jammed environment. We will assume a large satellite antenna of linear dimension L with an area $A = L^2$. The beamwidth of such an antenna can be written approximately as

$$\tau = \lambda/L.$$

At the earth the width of the beam is approximately

$$w = \tau R = \lambda R/L.$$

If a region on the earth of area $w^2 = 2,000 \text{ km} \times 2,000$ km is desired, then

$$w = \lambda R/L = 2,000 \text{ km} = 2(10^6)m$$

and

$$L = \lambda R/(2 \times 10^6).$$

For $\lambda = 11.5$ meters, $L = 230$ meters. The area of this HF satellite antenna is

$$A = L^2 = (230)^2 \text{ square meters.}$$

The directional gain of this antenna is

$$G = 4\pi A^2/\lambda^2 = 4\pi(400).$$

The power density generated at the earth by radiation from this antenna is

$$S = PG/(4\pi R^2) = P/(4 \times 10^{12}) \text{ watts/square meter.}$$

If $E = 2.5$ mv/m is the required electric field strength at the earth, as is assumed for a jammed environment, then

$$S = E^2/(377) = P/(4 \times 10^{12})$$

and

$$P = 66 \times 10^3 \text{ watts.}$$

System parameters for other satellite broadcast frequencies can be estimated in the same manner used for the HF band. Table 9.1 shows required antenna sizes and transmitter power levels for synchronous-orbit systems in the HF band (26.1 MHz); in the FM band (72 MHz); and in the TV band (200 MHz). It should be noted that, for broadcasting to quiet locations without jamming, much lower transmitter power levels and/or smaller antennas could be used for satellite systems. For example, if a field strength of E = 0.250 mv/m were satisfactory instead of 2.5 mv/m, which is suggested for a jamming situation, the power levels shown in Table 9.1 could be reduced by a factor of 100. Alternatively, the antenna dimensions could be scaled down by a factor of 10 (areas reduced by a factor of 100). Reducing the antenna sizes would, of course, increase the area covered on the earth, which may not be desirable.

Satellite orbits other than the synchronous (24-hour period) orbit may be useful for some purposes. The Molniya orbit (12-hour period, perigee 500 km, inclination 65 degrees, apogee 40,000 km) can provide better coverage of polar regions than can a synchronous equatorial orbit.

TABLE 9.1   SYSTEM PARAMETERS FOR VARIOUS
SATELLITE BROADCAST FREQUENCIES

Frequency (MHz)	Antenna Size (m)	Transmitter Power (kW)	Coverage Area (km × km)
HF band	230	66	2,000 × 2,000
(26.1)	153	149	3,000 × 3,000
	115	264	4,000 × 4,000
FM band	84	66	2,000 × 2,000
(72)	56	149	3,000 × 3,000
	42	264	4,000 × 4,000
TV band	30	66	2,000 × 2,000
(200)	20	149	3,000 × 3,000
	15	264	4,000 × 4,000

A spacecraft in a Molniya orbit spends most of its time moving slowly at high altitudes near apogee. Another possible orbit is an inclined 8-hour circular one at an altitude of roughly 8,000 km above the earth. Both of these alternative orbit systems would result in more complicated, less flexible broadcast scheduling.

The power levels necessary for even a single high-power HF broadcast (such as those in Table 9.1) are greater than presently available in spacecraft, and for solar systems the cell array size might well exceed that of the large antennas. The U.S. departments of defense and energy, and the National Aeronautics and Space Administration (NASA), are investigating nuclear power supplies that might provide the necessary power. In particular, the SP-100 reactor project could provide a solution to the primary power requirements. For multiple simultaneous program broadcasting, however, even the SP-100 might not be adequate. High-power reactors are, of course, possible.

Presently, the large antenna structures needed for HF broadcasting exceed demonstrated capabilities in space. In the future, the NASA space station program and various requirements of the Defense Department's Space Defense Initiative ("Star Wars") may provide the technology to launch and/or assemble the necessary structures in space.

JAMMING MITIGATION

In parts of the world, jamming of broadcast signals is so widespread that it cannot be completely avoided. Through technological and operational means, however, significant improvements over present capabilities should be possible. The goal of the Voice of America (VOA) is to produce a signal-to-jam power ratio at the listener's receiver so that at least 90 percent sentence intelligibility is achievable for 90 percent of the potential listeners. This will be a difficult goal to achieve.

Methods for improving the signal-to-jam ratio (S/J) include (1) transmission system enhancements, (2) frequency management and propagation tactics, and (3) receiver system enhancements. The VOA engineering staff has estimated that a total S/J improvement of 74 decibels (dB) might be attainable through these methods. Table 9.2 gives a breakdown of possible improvements. Transmission system enhancements and propagation tactics are under control of the broadcaster and should be achievable with state-of-the-art system improvements.

Receive-system enhancements must be carried out by the listener. The broadcaster, however, can provide the listeners with methods for achieving improvements. Dr. Oswald G. Villard of SRI International is

TABLE 9.2   SUMMARY OF S/J IMPROVEMENTS
WITHIN THE STATE OF THE ART

Method	Description	Improvement (dB)
Transmission system	Combining transmitters to feed separate elements of a phased array (maximum of two transmitters into one antenna)	3
	Combining up to six separate antennas to form a phased array (9 dB increased directivity and 8 dB increase in transmitter power)	17
	Audio processing	up to 9
Propagation tactics	Using real-time ionospheric measurements to select optimum set of relay stations, frequencies, and radiation patterns	up to 25
Receiver	Rejecting jammer signal because of polarization	up to 10*
	Effects of local environment on S/J	up to 10*
	Total	74

NOTES: *These values are estimated reductions in the effective jammer power at the output of the listener's receiver.

conducting a study of methods for reducing the jammer signal. He is developing simple receiving antennas for nulling out the signals of both skywave and groundwave jammers. The SRI antenna designs are simple enough so that directions for their construction and use could be transmitted to interested listeners via regular broadcasts, pamphlet, or word of mouth. Jam-resistant antennas of any sort will probably not be of much use to listeners living within a few kilometers of a jammer with overwhelmingly strong signals. Outside these areas, however, the new antennas may well enable listeners to receive broadcasts that are presently being jammed.

DISCUSSION

Oswald G. Villard, Jr.

I am particularly happy to comment on Professor Peterson's paper at this meeting because my first paid job as a graduate student in electrical engineering at Stanford during the period 1939–40 was to record shortwave broadcasts from Asia for the Hoover Library, as it was called in that time. Since war had already broken out in Europe, there was a need to assess the mood of Chungking, Saigon, and Tokyo, respectively, by means of monitoring their broadcasts (the work was funded, I believe, by the Rockefeller Foundation). This activity was one of two that led to the formation of the Foreign Broadcast Information Service. I presume that the transcripts of those early broadcasts exist somewhere at the Hoover Institution, which is hosting this workshop.

The possibility of direct broadcasting from satellites has aroused considerable current interest, and Professor Peterson's paper makes a valuable contribution to clarifying the numerous complex tradeoffs that must be considered. However, as a result of the Voice of America's modernization program, the United States is substantially increasing its investment in conventional shortwave broadcasting. Anything that can be done to help the United States get more mileage out of "good old HF" (high frequency) seems worthwhile.

In that connection, I would like to describe a new development in broadcasting—or, more accurately, broadcast listening—that assists those behind the Iron Curtain to find ways of reducing the effectiveness of jamming, with which they must otherwise contend. This can be achieved by means of directional receiving antennas that take advantage of certain differences between broadcast and jamming signals in order to discriminate against one and favor the other. Such discrimination is routinely performed using physically large antennas at professional receiving installations, such as the one at Voice of America's relay base in Munich. However, the new development consists of compact forms of these antennas—easy to build, easy to use, easy to conceal, yet nevertheless effective ("compact" indicates something about the size of an accompanying radio). Another important step forward involves the discovery that, by appropriate design, the antennas can be made to function reasonably well indoors, rabbit-ear style; it is not necessary to take them outside or to mount them on top of a mast.

The hope, therefore, exists that instructions on how to build and use these devices can be conveyed to listeners by articles, pamphlets, and, of course, broadcasts. There are two kinds of jammers—groundwave and skywave. Groundwave is effective but expensive and is used only in larger urban areas; skywave is less effective but can cover the entire rural area of a given country.

An antenna that counters the first kind of jamming has been developed by Radio Free Europe/Radio Liberty, under the auspices of Mr. Hugh Fallis, vice president for engineering. It has been tested in Austria, near the Slovak capital of Bratislava, where both kinds of jamming can be heard in full measure. The design has been published, and descriptive pamphlets can be obtained from RFE/RL.[1]

I have been concerned with reducing skywave jamming, which turned out—to my chagrin—to be more challenging than I had initially thought. However, there now appear to be at least three designs that will do this work. I will play you a recording of one whose performance was taped in Vienna, Austria, during July 1984. The antenna—which consists of two plates, a coil, and a capacitor—is not much larger than the receiver. If desired, the plates could be made of metal foil mounted on cardboard. The coil and tuning capacitor are the same as those found in most radios; a set, therefore, that has been scrapped should make an excellent source.

The modus operandi of the device (which has been dubbed a "twin plate") can be described in several ways. Perhaps the easiest involves thinking of the plates as producing a radio shadow; when interposed between a receiver and a radio transmitter, the twin plates produce a shadow, or dead spot, surrounding the radio and its normal whip antenna. However, if the plates are on the "downstream" side (that is, radio waves flowing away from the transmitter), the radio receives normally. Consequently, the device works as long as the jammer and the transmitter are not in exactly the same direction. This is generally true in the European part of the Soviet Union and in its satellite countries. Free world broadcasts come from the West; skywave jamming comes, for the most part, from the East.

The recording you are about to hear was made in a Vienna hotel of normal reinforced concrete construction. The time of day was 7 A.M.; the frequency, 11,855 MHz; and the transmission, a Czech language broadcast over Radio Free Europe from either Spain or Portugal. The antenna was mounted on a plastic turntable, so that its direction of fire could be aimed like a search light. With the "beam" pointed to the West, the broadcast is clearly audible; pointed to the East, only jamming can be heard. If a nondirectional antenna, such as a whip, had been used in place of the directional setup, a mixture of the two signals would have been heard. (Comparable results have been obtained in other locations and on other occasions.) One of the curiosities of this antenna is that it is not an antenna in the usual sense—that is, it does not connect to the set by means of wires. Installation is, therefore, particularly simple; however, wire connections can be used in situations where they may be preferable.

What lies ahead is to optimize these designs, quantify their performance, and choose the best for conveyance to interested listeners. There seems to be little the jamming network can do to counter the use of jam-resistant antennas, except to increase the power and/or the number of the jamming stations. Another option would be for the regimes to make illegal the use of such antennas to receive foreign broadcasts. However, the antennas are likely to find some application since they are also quite useful in rejecting unintentional cochannel interference and noise from leaky power line insulators and fluorescent lights. Consequently, ownership of one of these antennas would not automatically mean that it had been used to uncover "forbidden" foreign broadcasts.

Richard C. Levy

While superpower representatives debate and capture headlines on SDI and the uses of space for military purposes, the battle of ideas proceeds quietly, almost unnoticed by American politicians and the press alike. State-of-the-art satellite technology, which allows the instantaneous transmission of words and images around the globe, has proved to be an extraordinarily powerful and persuasive new medium.

Recognizing the enormous potential of this new technology in the struggle to influence people, governments are positioning themselves behind the scenes for a major information offensive via satellite. In Europe, for example, several national broadcasters have joined forces to combat what many are calling the "MacDonaldization" of the air over the continent.

TV-5 is a satellite partnership among the French, Belgians, and Swiss that carries French language programming throughout Europe via cable television systems. A similar device, 3-SAT, is offered in the German language by the governments of Austria, Germany, and Switzerland.

The German worldwide shortwave radio service, *Deutsche Welle*, is reported to be preparing for entry into the satellite television era. And the USSR is already offering news and cultural programming in Russian via its *Ghorizont* satellite. However, rumors have it that in the near future the Soviets will begin other language services, including English.

The British Broadcasting Corporation (BBC) is considering a world television service similar to its external radio service. The TV service would likely start with satellite broadcasts in English, but other languages (including Arabic, French, and Spanish) are under consideration.

But the most impressive and innovative demonstration of the effectiveness of this means of international communication has been the U.S. Information Agency's WORLDNET, the first global television network and America's most important new foreign policy communication tool since the Voice of America went on the air 40 years ago. WORLDNET has demonstrated conclusively the power of satellite communication as a device for public diplomacy and, in doing so, has single-handedly changed the way in which government information services do business.

The United States of America is presently at least one year (if not more) ahead of other countries in the development and implementation of this new medium, thanks to the leadership and imagination of USIA Director Charles Z. Wick. The creator of WORLDNET and its driving force, he has transformed USIA's underutilized television production studios into a full broadcast operation that today puts on the most frequent and complex global teleconferencing of any organization in the world.

WORLDNET's engineers and producers are writing the book on how to produce "interactive" satellite teleconferencing. In addition to the president and vice president, WORLDNET's guests have included almost every cabinet member, members of Congress, and distinguished Americans from all walks of life.

An acknowledged landmark in the history of international communications, USIA's entry into the age of "video diplomacy" began on 3 November 1983. On this date an innovative international press conference took place linking journalists in five European countries interactively with U.S. Representative to the United Nations Jeane Kirkpatrick, deputy assistant secretaries of state Craig Johnstone and James Michael, and prime ministers M. G. Adams of Barbados and John Compton of St. Lucia. The topic was the United States action in Grenada.

Since this first satellite telecast, WORLDNET interactive programs have generated over 100 hours of foreign television coverage. More than 2 billion television viewers worldwide have seen local rebroadcasts of all or parts of WORLDNET programs. The 100 hours of air time is a commodity that would not be available to USIA at any price. These programs also have reached some 120 million radio listeners and an estimated 63 million newspaper readers.

As culled from post reports, the following are some outstanding examples of media usage of WORLDNET interactives by television, radio, and newspapers around the world.

Europe and EURONET. President Reagan's 16 January 1984 WORLDNET speech on disarmament was broadcast to an estimated 100 million television viewers. In West Germany, over 40 million people saw excerpts from the program via local rebroadcast.

In Great Britain, BBC-TV's nightly news and current affairs program, "Newsnight" ran a six-minute excerpt of Treasury Secretary James Baker's 24 April 1985 WORLDNET program for an estimated audience of 1.2 million. The same program used five minutes of the 21 March WORLDNET broadcast with Senator Richard Lugar and Congressman Dante Fascell.

Latin America and ARNET. Colombian television pre-empted regular programming to telecast the entire U.S. presidential candidates' debate on foreign policy on 21 October 1984. The estimated television audience was 8 to 10 million with 6 to 8 million radio listeners. In Brazil, TV Globo broadcast the same video feed to an estimated 30 million viewers.

Excerpts from Treasury Undersecretary Beryl Sprinkel's 25 September 1984 EURONET/ARNET transmission reached audiences of 12 million in Mexico, 30 million in Brazil, and 8 million in Venezuela through local rebroadcast.

East Asia and EANET. Secretary of State George Shultz's interview of 8 April 1984 was broadcast in its entirety to some 12 million viewers in the Philippines and approximately 8 million in Korea. A discussion of the artificial heart with Drs. Robert Jarvik and William

DeVries on 25 February 1985 was aired in full by Philippine station MBS-Channel 4.

Middle East and NEANET. The pioneering NEANET program on hypertension with leading American cardiologists and their Middle East counterparts on 10 March 1985 was shown in its entirety on local television in Jordan and Bahrain, receiving front-page newspaper treatment in these countries and in the United Arab Emirates.

Africa and AFNET. An AFNET program on U.S. aid policy with AID Administrator Peter McPherson and Office of Foreign Disaster Assistance Director Julius Becton on 18 December 1984 was broadcast in a 33-minute edited version on Senegalese television and in full on Radio Television Gabon.

These figures tell only part of the story. Equally impressive has been the reaction of USIA field posts, the media, and WORLDNET guests who see for themselves the dramatic impact of immediate global communication.

The United States Information Service (USIS) in Belgrade, Yugoslavia, reported that, thanks to WORLDNET programming arranged in connection with the 1984 presidential election, they "were able to reach and inform, in some cases even influence significantly, a far greater segment of our participant audience than ever before."[2] From Dakar, Senegal, our USIS representative commented that WORLDNET's broadcast of the presidential candidates' debates on foreign policy enabled the Senegalese "to experience full force the vitality of our political system unexpurgated, undiluted, and unfiltered through other editorial eyes."[3]

Reporting on "Astronet #1" (featuring President Reagan, Chancellor Helmut Kohl, and the Spacelab astronauts), USIS Rome cabled that "100 people packed the American Library's conference room" for the reception hosted by U.S. Ambassador Maxwell Raab in conjunction with the program. Numerous dignitaries were on hand, including a Supreme Court justice, two foreign ministry under secretaries, a member of Parliament who is one of Italy's most prominent social critics, and the dean of the Space Engineering School.

As U.S. Ambassador Paul Nitze stated, following one of his WORLDNET appearances, "I know of no more effective way for our policy spokesmen to reach foreign media and opinion leaders . . . than by timely WORLDNET programs."[4]

Commenting on the introduction of WORLDNET on its editorial page, the *Wall Street Journal* wrote that "the USIA has gone high-tech to allow European journalists to reach out and touch U.S. officials . . . It looks as if USIA is up to some good, and putting American officials directly before European questioners and audiences is bound to increase the understanding of all concerned."[5]

Belgium's *Western World* carried an editorial stating that "in the long run, this communications linkup between Western Europe and the U.S. may prove more important to the Alliance than the 'coupling' of the defense of two continents by the stationing of American Pershing II and cruise missiles in Europe."[6]

In the Philippines, influential columnist Teodor Valencia of the *Daily Express* praised the WORLDNET technique in his comments following the first East Asia EANET with Secretary of State George Shultz: "WORLDNET permits world leaders to meet the international press on instant notice to explain earthshaking world developments. The USIS calls it WORLDNET. By whatever name, it's a spectacular show."[7]

USIA's long-range goals and objectives for WORLDNET fall into two categories: the programmatic and the technical. Under "programmatic objectives" our goals are similar to those of the U.S. Information Agency as a whole:

- To strengthen foreign understanding and support of United States policies and actions
- To promote foreign awareness and knowledge of American society
- To counter hostile attempts to distort or frustrate the objectives and policies of the United States
- To provide state-of-the-art interactive or passive television satellite communication with overseas posts and staffs and share these facilities with other government agencies
- To give American policymakers a chance to speak directly to foreign audiences, amplified through replay in local television, radio, and newspapers

Under technical objectives our goals are the following:

- To systematically equip all overseas missions with TVRO dish antennae on a prioritized basis, in consultation with the Department of State and other government agencies
- To lease satellite time at the most reasonable available rates to enable USIA and other government agencies to maintain 24-hour video and audio communication with overseas posts for program and administrative purposes

•   With the cooperation of the Department of State and other government agencies, to develop a worldwide satellite television network as a means for instantaneous communication between government headquarters in Washington and our overseas missions during times of emergency

EUROPEAN SERVICE

The introduction of daily WORLDNET service (ten hours a week) to Europe occurred on 22 April 1985. This is in addition to the ongoing series of interactive programs transmitted to other areas of the world. Daily delivery of this same programming behind the Iron Curtain commenced on 4 October 1985.

WORLDNET's daily service is telecast from Washington, D.C., from 8:00 A.M. to 10:00 A.M. Eastern Standard Time (EST, 1300–1500 GMT). The first hour of European service is designed for cable television systems (CATV), satellite master antenna television (SMATV), and hotel closed-circuit systems. Giving the fullest possible representation of American society, a typical day's program schedule includes a half-hour news and feature broadcast, *America Today*, and an exciting mixture of short segments and documentaries on science, the arts, business, and sports. The second hour offers interactives (one-country and multiple-country) plus an array of public affairs programs.

Commenting on the inauguration of daily WORLDNET service to Europe, President Reagan stated that "science and technology have given humanity many gifts. The American people want to share this latest technological marvel with others, not only to tell America's story, but to listen to and heed what is said, in the interests of peace . . . I congratulate the United States Information Agency and its Television Service on this memorable occasion."[8]

Plans are underway to expand WORLDNET's daily service into Latin America (Spanish), the Middle East (Arabic), Francophone Africa, and Asia (English). Since its inception, USIA's Television and Film Service has been a secondary delivery system, that is, one requiring rebroadcast by primary delivery systems (for example, national television networks) to reach target audiences. But when WORLDNET is ultimately combined with Direct Broadcast Satellite (DBS) technology, USIA will, for the first time in its history, be capable of transmitting directly into households worldwide. This should be possible within the next couple years in Europe.

To effectively fulfill its mandate, it is essential that the United States

Information Agency utilize the most powerful communication tools available. As House Foreign Affairs Committee Chairman Dante Fascell stated, "as the United States approaches the 21st century, USIA will play a vital role in determining the success or failure of our foreign policy efforts. The advent of satellite broadcasting—now a reality for some twenty years—has put the need for dynamic television and film service beyond dispute."[9] USIA has taken a giant leap forward in its continuing efforts to bring American society, in all its complexity, to foreign publics worldwide. The days of the town crier are over at USIA-TV.

Robert B. Fenwick

Audio broadcasting plays an important role in the lives of many people, and international programming plays an integral role in public diplomacy. Relatively few people, however, listen extensively to international broadcasting—indeed, it is likely that most Americans never listen. This is partly because, in a strictly technical sense, it is not of consistently high quality and cannot be tuned in reliably.

Knowledge is currently available, however, to improve the technical—as opposed to program—quality of international broadcasting. There are two targets of special interest: (1) improving the quality of the present broadcast technique and (2) introducing a totally new one. For present international audio broadcasting, terrestrial radio stations use medium frequency (MF) and high frequency (HF) radio bands. Both of these methods suffer from serious defects that drastically limit their usefulness.

MF broadcasting is the traditional amplitude modulation (AM) band that most Americans have in their homes and cars. Although reliability is unsurpassed, its range is very short—typically a few hundred kilometers, at most, during the daytime. Another serious problem with MF is inadequate bandwidth, that is, only about 100 to 150 stations can be heard at a given place. In addition, the type of modulation is restricted, which renders, for example, quality stereo difficult but not impossible. Although the distance covered by MF could be increased somewhat through technology, given the latter two problems (inadequate bandwidth and restricted types of modulation) and interference among multiple users of a given channel, this approach is impractical in international broadcasting.

HF or shortwave broadcasting overcomes the distance problem of

MF broadcasting, but other problems make it less pleasant to listen to. Highly variable and frequently unsatisfactory signal propagation and noise conditions cause a dynamic listening environment; consequently, few American radios have shortwave listening capability and, of those that do, relatively few are actually used by listeners. HF broadcasting can be improved substantially through such modern technology as higher effective transmitter power and real-time adaptation of transmission equipment to the propagation environment. Shortwave broadcasting, however, will never achieve the status of amplitude modulation (AM) or frequency modulation (FM) because of such fundamental problems as unreliability, intermittently poor technical quality, and the limited number of broadcast stations operating into a given area.

In addition to those current problems of MF and HF audio broadcasting, certain broadcasts in particular regions of the world experience intentional interference or jamming. Today's technology provides the broadcaster with a number of tools to compete effectively with the jammer, but such technology is limited primarily by expenditures. For the U.S. government to spend substantial sums of money to combat jamming directly, however, is of dubious wisdom because of the following five factors:

1. Jamming promotes education in English, since English-language programs are not normally jammed.
2. Jamming calls attention to our broadcasts, so there must be something interesting being said.
3. Jamming costs the jammer a great deal of money that otherwise might be used for more harmful purposes.
4. Jamming is an annoyance to most regions of the world in which support of the United States and the jamming country are sought.
5. Most important, no amount of money spent on overcoming jamming will lead to an audio broadcast of a desired higher quality.

Combating jamming does not innovatively use funds for improving international broadcasting. So, what can affordably be done to dramatically improve the quality of, and listener interest in, international radio broadcasting? The answer lies in direct satellite audio broadcasting.

Almost everybody has one or more radios that receive AM or FM. Although these two bands are technically similar in many respects, AM has greater range and FM has better quality. Today, it is technically possible to add a unique third band to all radios, which I shall call the International Broadcasting Band (IBB). On such a widely available, quality band (quality comparable to present-day FM bands), the nations of the world could compete in a more enjoyable manner—certainly in a more acceptable way than warfare, and probably of wider and more consistent interest than athletic and other games. The IBB proposed here could eventually have hundreds of easily (that is, digitally) selectable channels, received in any given area—far more channels than AM or FM and a greater variety. Channel 331 might be Nepal!

The quality and reliability of IBB would be superb. Although jamming or destruction would be relatively easy if done simultaneously for all channels, it would only be done at a high political penalty to the jammer. Jamming of selected channels would not be trivially difficult. The cost to produce broadcasts for listener radios would not differ significantly from that presently experienced and, in fact, might be less. (Table 9.3 summarizes the suggested technical details of the *ultimate* and *initial* IBB systems.) The technical problems of this IBB system are minimal, except, perhaps, for the power generation in the eventual system (presently, nuclear power plants or multiple solar-cell plants could do this).

The number and placement of uplink ground stations, and the access to the broadcasting channels, would be primarily political issues. Since the cost would not be significantly different from the present costs of international transmission and reception, and might actually be less, the problems hindering the IBB system are essentially political in nature. "Listenability" would be far superior to current broadcasting.

A Third World–intensive consortium, similar to Intelsat, might have to initiate such a program and its system control. Although totally private sponsorship might be considered and even private programming might be permitted, international approval of these options is unlikely. Undoubtedly it will take several decades to bring the IBB to reality, but each year delays this reality and adds that much time until its inauguration.

Hugh Fallis

Since I am an engineer with the responsibility for ensuring that Radio Free Europe/Radio Liberty, Inc. (RFE-RL) transmissions to

TABLE 9.3   SUGGESTED TECHNICAL DETAILS OF THE
ULTIMATE AND INITIAL IBB SYSTEMS

Category	Ultimate	Initial
Frequency band	2.5–2.69 GHz	2.5–2.69 GHz
Present band allocation	International satellite broadcasting	International satellite broadcasting
Portion of frequency band used	All	Any contiguous 20 MHz
Number of satellites	3 geosynchronous	1–3
Number of channels per satellite	Ca. 900 (maximum)	100
Power per channel	5, 50, 500 W selectable	5W
Modulation	Compatible with FM stereo	Compatible with FM stereo
Received areas major dimension	200, 600, and 2,000 km selectable	200 km
Receiver size	Comparable to FM receiver today	Converted to 88–108 MHz FM band followed by standard FM receiver
Receiver cost	Comparable to FM receiver	A few tens of $U.S. above that of FM receiver
Receiver antenna size	2-inch-long dipole	2-inch-long dipole

Eastern Europe and the Soviet Union are heard over jamming, I have found the presentations and discussions on new broadcasting technologies particularly interesting. Professor Villard's report about his anti-jamming antenna is right on target. If a few of the concepts discussed at this workshop can be developed into new high-tech equipment, then the ability of the Voice of America (VOA) and RFE-RL to combat jamming will be significantly improved.

I would like to summarize RFE-RL plans to modernize its existing transmitting stations and to build new ones. The present RFE-RL short-wave transmission system consists of 45 transmitters with a total capacity of 7,500 kilowatts (kW). Although it fulfills the 1977 National Security Staff Memorandum 245 (NSSM-245) technical standards for coverage of Eastern Europe and the USSR's European area, the present system does not reach the entire landmass of Soviet Asia. In addition, RFE-RL is

TABLE 9.4 AVERAGE TECHNICAL EFFECTIVENESS OF RFE SERVICES, 1980–1984

	1980				1981				1982
	Winter	Spring	Summer	Fall	Winter	Spring	Summer	Fall	Winter[a]
Polish Program									
Effectiveness	52.4%	58.4%	54.1%	53.9%	46.8%	46.2%	37.6%	37.6%	35.1%
kW/program hour	692	682	680	698	695	670	697	1078	1405
Average no. frequencies	5.3	5.4	5.6	5.6	5.3	5.6	5.6	6.5	5.5
Czechoslovak Program									
Effectiveness	18.6%	23.6%	11.6%	16.9%	21.0%	13.8%	10.6%	20.0%	41.7%
kW/program hour	535	576	551	546	512	723	732	914	617
Average no. frequencies	5.5	6.0	6.3	6.0	5.8	5.8	6.3	6.0	5.1
Hungarian Program									
Effectiveness	88.0%	87.4%	79.3%	85.7%	73.1%	70.0%	75.4%	82.0%	71.0%
kW/program hour	426	437	484	448	440	488	463	515	584
Average no. frequencies	4.5	4.7	5.0	4.5	4.5	4.7	4.6	4.3	4.5
Romanian Program									
Effectiveness	77.3%	77.9%	69.4%	80.2%	74.7%	79.2%	74.4%	79.0%	77.7%
kW/program hour	450	512	533	440	417	608	550	479	642
Average no. frequencies	4.4	4.5	4.4	4.4	4.4	4.8	5.3	4.4	4.4
Bulgarian Program									
Effectiveness	46.5%	35.3%	20.4%	38.3%	45.5%	34.9%	19.8%	31.6%	47.2%
kW/program hour	365	381	388	389	438	428	444	430	500
Average no. frequencies	3.4	3.6	3.5	3.6	3.6	3.6	3.5	3.6	3.6

	1982			1983				1984	
	Spring	Summer	Fall	Winter	Spring	Summer	Fall	Winter	Spring (4–17 March only)
Polish Program									
Effectiveness	21.4%	13.0%	21.2%	25.6%	31.0%	26.4%	27.1%	31.6%	34%
kW/program hour	1462	1348	1358	883	940	1254	1034	1098	1177
Average no. frequencies	5.6			6.1	6.7	8.0	7.0	6.8	7.6
Czechoslovak Program									
Effectiveness	55.9%	34.9%	44.6%	56.0%	35.8%	31.8%	44.1%	45.9%	50%
kW/program hour	830	858	1030	820	850	946	990	943	914
Average no. frequencies	5.2			5.2	5.2	5.6	5.3	5.3	4.6
Hungarian Program									
Effectiveness	76.4%	76.6%	71.4%	76.6%	60.9%	82.2%	73.5%	73.8%	69%
kW/program hour	487	524	526	603	576	557	665	553	506
Average no. frequencies	4.7			4.5	4.9	4.9	4.4	4.4	4.9
Romanian Program									
Effectiveness	61.7%	80.0%	70.0%	64.5%	70.3%	71.9%	63.3%	61.4%	64%
kW/program hour	696	800	592	546	546	573	606	616	626
Average no. frequencies	4.8			4.3	4.6	4.4	4.2	4.3	4.4
Bulgarian Program									
Effectiveness	56.1%	14.6%	47.2%	52.4%	44.7%	44.1%	48.2%	41.4%	61%
kW/program hour	494	550	513	525	629	699	677	626	685
Average no. frequencies	3.6			3.4	4.0	4.0	3.8	3.5	3.9

SOURCE: RFE, *Technical Monitoring Reports*, 1979–1984.
[a]Martial law went into effect in Poland in late December 1981.

losing signal effectiveness in its European broadcast area because of increased jamming and spectrum congestion and because of the influx of shortwave transmitters with power outputs greater than 250 kW.

Under the present system, during priority listening hours, every transmitter is in use; there is no reserve capability for maintenance or contingency needs. The system is thus "gridlocked" and cannot accommodate requirements for additional programming; for period enhancement of transmitter schedules during unforeseen political events, such as the recent occurrences in Poland; or for the resumption of jamming of Hungarian or Romanian programs. Hence, under the existing transmission system, effective contingency planning is impossible: All these factors, including significant changes in the electromagnetic environment since 1977, underscore the need for a new plan. There is strong scientific evidence, however, that the technical standards of NSSM-245 are not valid for the electromagnetic environment in which RFE-RL currently must operate.

Table 9.4 depicts the technical effectiveness of the five RFE broadcast services as evaluated at respective monitoring sites in Berlin, Vienna, and Salonika. For each of the five RFE broadcast schedules from winter 1979–80 through spring 1984, this table shows the technical effectiveness, the average power, and the average number of frequencies scheduled. This time span corresponds to the period just before the new transmitters specified by NSSM-245 began to come into service.

Prior to examining this table, it would be helpful to summarize portions of the technical standards established by NSSM-245. For language broadcasts not subject to jamming, NSSM-245 established that an effective coverage region would require a monthly median signal of not less than 1.0 millivolt per meter (assuming broadcast operation at the highest frequency that propagates on 90 percent of the days of a given month). For language broadcasts subject to jamming, a monthly median signal level of not less than 2.5 millivolts per meter would be required to define an effective coverage region (using the same assumption).

The Presidential Report NSSM-245 defined additional technical standards on which to base a transmitter network:

- When propagation conditions permit, a minimum of three shortwave transmitters where the size of the intended reception area is less than a single time zone, with one transmitter assigned to each of three different bands.
- Five transmitters where the area spans two time zones.
- Six transmitters where the area spans three time zones.

- Seven transmitters where the area spans four or more time zones.
- An additional transmitter per time zone spanned can be added for language broadcasts that are subject to jamming.

A close examination of the average technical effectiveness indicates that RFE-RL programmers have found it necessary to schedule more frequencies than NSSM-245 specifies (see Table 9.4).

Since martial law was declared in Poland in December 1981 and jamming subsequently intensified, it has been necessary to schedule almost twice the number of transmitters specified by NSSM-245 for the Polish service; this unplanned scheduling of transmitter resources, however, did not check the loss in effectiveness. Although average transmitter powers have increased because of NSSM-245 modernization, there is a general disturbing downward trend in effectiveness.

These data emphasize the need to develop a new set of standards for dimensioning the number and power levels of the transmitters that RFE-RL needs in the future. Since these new standards have not been formulated and tested, however, RFE-RL engineers have used NSSM-245 standards to redimension the RFE-RL transmitting system in order to ring the USSR. This approach is justified because of the urgent need to boost RFE-RL signals in Europe and to establish a new presence in Asia.

RFE-RL must maintain a strong and effective radio presence in its audience areas in the future for geopolitical reasons. The Soviet Union has never before confronted such a formidable web of internal economic, societal, and demographic problems as those presently confronting Kremlin policymakers; Soviet leaders themselves have begun to speak of their regime as being at a turning point. A strong Radio Liberty could play a particularly positive role at this crucial juncture.

In Eastern Europe, the traditional Western policy of differentiation has been clearly fruitful. In varying degrees, not only are individual countries seeking greater independence from the Soviet Union, but their publics are also seeking a greater measure of freedom internally. This irreversible process makes it all the more important that East Europeans have full access to the unique information and analysis that Radio Free Europe provides.

By signing the Helsinki Final Act, the United States has committed itself to the free flow of information and ideas across borders—another cogent factor supporting the RFE-RL modernization plan. Having secured the formal assent of the Soviet and East European regimes to this principle, the United States must now convince them that they have no real alternative but to practice it. The Eastern man in the street views

TABLE 9.5   RADIO FREE EUROPE/RADIO LIBERTY
TRANSMITTER MODERNIZATION AND
POWER ENHANCEMENT PROJECTS, 1985–1995

Project	Location	Transmitters	kW
1*	Gloria, Portugal	8	250
2*	Maxoqueira, Portugal	6	500
3*	Biblis, West Germany	1	100
4*	Lampertheim, West Germany	2	100
5**	Pals, Spain	1	250
6**	Pals, Spain	7	500
7***	Far East	8	500
8***	Near East	10	500
9***	Middle East	8	500
10***	Europe (Ireland and/or Sardinia)	12	500
Total		63	

SOURCE: *RFE-RL Ten-Year Modernization Plan* (March 1984).
NOTES: *Funding for projects 1 through 4 were made in FY 1986 budget requests; funding for the remaining projects will be requested as soon as negotiations are completed successfully with potential host countries.
**May be a single new installation containing 8–500 kW transmitters.
***Proposed as joint project with VOA (these are BIB requirements).

America as a land inhabited by technological wizards whose present achievements offer a glimpse of his distant future. He believes that, if the United States so desires, it can place a radio signal into his technologically backward country that eludes even the most determined jamming. It is, therefore, in the interest of the United States, and the free world, to confirm the East's stereotypical image of American prowess.

To overcome the deficiencies mentioned, RFE-RL has recommended the installation of 63 new shortwave transmitters (fifty-one 500 kW, nine 250 kW, and three 100 kW) during the period 1985–1995, at an estimated cost of $900 million (in 1984 dollars). These transmitters will permit RFE-RL to reach almost the entire Soviet Eurasian landmass and to enhance considerably signals subject to jamming. In addition, they will be able to accommodate five additional program networks and will provide a 10 percent reserve transmitter capacity. During the period 1985–1995, RFE-RL will thus be able to withdraw 23 obsolete transmitters.

Upon completion of the proposed modernization and enhanced transmission system, RFE-RL will have available a total of 85 shortwave transmitters (compared with the present 45) with a total capacity of

33,400 kW (compared with the present 7,500 kW). This improved capacity will allow RFE-RL not only to maintain a strong and effective radio presence in Europe but also to inaugurate a new presence in Asia. (Table 9.5 summarizes the ten different transmitter modernization and power enhancement projects recommended for the period 1985–1995.)

The success of this transmission modernization program primarily depends on the willingness of strategically located host countries to provide adequate sites for the proposed transmission facilities, on sufficient frequencies for their operation, and on U.S. government funds. Considering the complex political problems involved and the critical shortage of frequencies, Washington, D.C. must negotiate vigorously, at the highest level possible, with host countries.

NOTES

1. It is featured in the *1985 Annual Report* of the Board for International Broadcasting (Suite 400), 1201 Connecticut Avenue, N.W., Washington, D.C. 20036) and has been discussed in RFE/RL broadcasts.

2. USIS Belgrade official cable to USIA headquarters in Washington, D.C.

3. USIS Dakar official cable to USIA headquarters.

4. Letter from Paul H. Nitze to Charles Z. Wick, dated 14 March 1985.

5. *The Wall Street Journal*, op/ed, 27 December 1983.

6. *Western World* (Belgium), 19 November 1983, as reported by USIS Brussels in official cable to Washington, D.C.

7. Teodor Valencia, *Daily Express* (the Philippines), 18 April 1984, as reported by USIS Manila in official cable to Washington, D.C.

8. Quote taken from special videotaped message delivered by President Ronald Reagan at inauguration of daily European service on 22 April 1985.

9. Dante B. Fascell, "Dynamo or Dinosaur," *Foreign Service Journal* 61, no. 1 (January 1984): 31–35.

10

RESEARCH ON PUBLIC DIPLOMACY

Richard E. Bissell

The subject of public diplomacy research in the United States has received inordinate attention in recent years, largely as a result of the efforts of the Advisory Commission on Public Diplomacy. In each of its recent annual reports, the commission chaired by Edwin J. Feulner, Jr., has identified an essential role for research and recommended a major enhancement of the research budget of the United States Information Agency (USIA). In its 1985 annual report, the commission said that "USIA's resources are insufficient to provide the research capability that national security requires and that the Agency needs to make its resource management and programming more efficient." Indeed, the administration (including the Office of Management and Budget), the Congress, and the USIA have cooperated to enable a rapid expansion of research resources on public diplomacy. In some cases, this has meant doing more of what the USIA has been doing for years; in other cases, it has allowed research in new areas to be undertaken.

An underlying theme is that this expansion in research was guided not by a renovated and coherent vision of "public diplomacy" but by the need to allocate marginal increases in fiscal resources in substantive areas. On the basis of that experience, we have an opportunity to define what has been accomplished and, hopefully, to contribute to a better sense of where we go from here. The institutional focus of this paper is on the United States Information Agency, since it is mandated by law to survey foreign public opinion in order to inform U.S. foreign policy of public diplomacy needs. As the notion of public diplomacy has expanded, other agencies have become involved in research, and their roles are noted as appropriate. But the USIA is the core agency for research in this field.

This background is not meant to suggest that the recent augmentation of USIA research resources has been wasted for want of a grand strategy. On the contrary, recent experience shows that the increased funding might have been better spent in an even more unstructured manner to allow greater attention to new areas of research as well as the existing research programs to which it was allocated. The fact that the USIA leadership used the criterion of supporting ongoing programs would not surprise anyone who has worked in or with that agency; its "action orientation" is legendary, and USIA leadership would naturally be impatient with the uncertain payoff period associated with more basic research. Such basic research is of interest not simply out of pursuit of some misguided intellectual hedonism; rather, the fact that so many people disagree about the meaning of and appropriate guidelines for "public diplomacy" indicates that some basic research in the field, in both broad and particular sectors of the field, might contribute greatly to a more strategic approach to public diplomacy.[1]

The purposes of this paper are both descriptive and prescriptive: to put in perspective the progressive development of research in public diplomacy, especially in recent years, and to identify several avenues of possible future development, especially as public diplomacy is seen as an increasingly integrated aspect of U.S. foreign policy.

BACKGROUND

Research has been a constant and frequently unnoticed component of foreign information efforts of the United States government, dating back to the founding of USIA and, even beyond, to the experience of the Office of War Information (OWI). Spanning the World War Two years, the OWI experience established certain methodological precedents that have been influential in successor organizations but largely ignored by those attempting to understand the promise and perils of American public diplomacy. For instance, OWI research focused heavily on the "enemy" and on the need to understand a state of mind hostile to the United States and to devise propaganda that would weaken the resolve of enemy publics to resist United States power.

As that mission was gradually transformed into that of successful occupation of enemy territory, the challenges to research became great. Extremely difficult questions were raised by policymakers: What kind of reception would occupation soldiers receive? What political expectations will be held by former enemy populations? How can their political views be rehabilitated from authoritarian to democratic? How can we measure the success of the occupation effort? The shift from relatively clear-cut criteria of success in wartime to the uncertain political sands of the postwar world created major challenges for the information effort. Models for dealing with the "enemy" could be applied to the communist bloc (with radios being the principal tools), but new and complex approaches had to be devised to convert former enemies in Western Europe and Japan into allies.

The challenge of converting former enemies into allies forced public diplomacy research to draw on new and experimental social science ideas in the United States. Major intellectual resources were attached to the U.S. occupation forces in Germany and Japan, in an effort to use social scientific models for social engineering. Given the paucity of literature on those experiences, we do not have a reliable way of assessing its success.

The earlier experiences, however, did have a major impact on the eventual organization of research in the USIA. One research component focused on the Soviet Union and its satellites; another powerful component drew on the quantitative methods of social science for the design of information efforts among United States allies. In the meantime, the Department of State was forming the long-term component of public diplomacy (that is, educational exchange), but research was not an important aspect of the program. The effort was to move people rather than to measure their impact. Finally, the research effort was intermittently given the task of internally evaluating programs on the basis of scientifically measured impact in the field, but it was under constant attack from program elements of USIA given the implicit threat from evaluating programs.

Some important aspects of those research efforts need to be emphasized. First, it should be noted that the existence of USIA separate from the Department of State (aside from the Bureau of Education and Cultural Affairs until the late 1970s) meant that USIA research had a difficult time attracting attention in other foreign policy agencies. The institutional bias against the product of other agencies, combined with a tendency in the Department of State to view public diplomacy as a public relations exercise, meant that research was rarely heeded. Only when particularly powerful directors of USIA, such as Edward R. Murrow, were able to use their connections was research given an appropriate role in policymaking.

On other occasions, research obtained more attention than it wanted. During the Vietnam War, for instance, the White House became quite agitated over the findings emanating from public opinion in Western Europe and attempted to suppress the adverse results from circulation both within and outside the government. Bad news could command a great deal of attention for research, and to a significant extent, the USIA research office was unprepared for that kind of attention.

The change in international social science also took its toll on the role of USIA research, especially in measuring attitudes among allied populations. In large part, the United States and social scientists from this country were responsible for the development of scientific polling in postwar Europe and Japan. It was the enthusiasm of the American occupation authorities in Germany that gave rise to a domestic polling industry in West Germany, which today has the most developed marketing groups outside the United States. Commercial polling firms cannot earn a living examining attitudes on foreign policy. There is far too little work in that area to support a standing social scientific effort, with trained interviewers and data analysts. But the development of mass marketing techniques in most West European countries and Japan, combined in recent years with more active use of polling firms for domestic elections, has meant that there now exists in major West European countries a substantial autonomous capacity for examining and reporting public attitudes on international issues.

In a sense, USIA research has spawned competitors all over the world, some of whom (especially the Japanese) may be more aggressive and productive in undertaking attitudes measurement on foreign policy issues than is the USIA itself.[2] For instance, in the course of the German debate over INF deployment in 1982–83, the various German polling firms inadvertently prompted a national debate over the fairness of the polls, over the appropriate release of results, and the possible manipulation of public opinion that might result. Clearly, that debate had been converted from a foreign policy into a domestic policy issue for the West Germans, and thus, significant polling resources were devoted to attitudinal measurement, both by supporters and opponents of deployment.

Likewise, for several years a massive multinational effort has been underway in Europe to conduct surveys that measure attitudes that assess social, political, religious, and cultural values; the implications of the findings of such surveys for USIA work could be enormous. As a result, USIA now has a growing challenge to monitor research not commissioned by USIA and to analyze it, not only for its intrinsic intelligence value but also for aiding USIA's entrance into foreign public debates over the significance of the data. This is a difficult role for USIA to play, having always operated bureaucratically in an unclassified, but shaded, environment in order to maximize its effectiveness.

Finally, there is enormous pressure for research in USIA to change in response to methodological improvements in the profession. In terms of analytical techniques, political and media polling in the mid 1980s has moved light years from the 1950s, when many of USIA's fundamental research approaches were established. In the last decade, the changes in data gathering and analysis have been products of technologies whose capabilities are just beginning to be tapped. If there is a state of the art to be defined in the polling world, one has to look at the major corporate marketers (especially on the media side of the business) or the pollsters serving the presidential campaigns in the United States.

For instance, the ability of Richard Wirthlin, president of Decision Making Information, to undertake a national, detailed (by voting ward) analysis of preferences in terms of personalities, issue themes, and public relations approaches in a timely way has created an enormous challenge for USIA research to catch up. One of the great frustrations for recent White House occupants has been the inability of research at USIA to make that methodological leap from the 1950s to the 1980s. From experience in presidential campaigns and from changes in White House data management, the staff of the National Security Council has a clear notion of what would make a logically integrated data system for public diplomacy. Over time, that frustration is likely to effect major changes in the research processes at USIA.

Research in public diplomacy has also assumed an unavoidable technological character. The telecommunications revolution has intruded on public diplomacy in ways that are not yet fully understood. How can we properly track public diplomacy channels in the Middle East, for example, in the wake of videocassette recorder (VCR) proliferation? We know that Khomeini had an unprecedented channel of political communication in the form of cheap, easily duplicated tape recordings of his speeches among his followers in Iran before the revolution. We have some rough surveys of material used on VCRs in the Persian Gulf countries but virtually no ways of influencing trends.

Technology of various types is disseminating television images to an unprecedented extent; satellite dishes in backyards are just one manifestation. The uneven process by which such technologies proliferate in different countries and regions of the world have a direct, profound impact on the success of United States public diplomacy. It is uncontroversial to point out that we are in the midst of an even greater telecommunications revolution than when the transistor, battery-powered radio appeared on the global scene. How USIA should respond to that revolution, however, generates great heat, little light, and, hopefully, sufficient research in the near future to guide changes in USIA's programs and formats.

From Analysis to Action

Each of the mandates for public diplomacy research noted above (media and media-use analysis, attitudinal polling, internal USIA program evaluation, and monitoring the telecommunications revolution) has a descriptive aspect and a possible prescriptive role. Before delineating a strategy for public diplomacy research, it is essential to clarify the extent of these two characteristics in each type of research.

The Media

Foreign media, especially the printed press, have been a long-term staple focus for U.S. public diplomacy efforts. Basic programmatic efforts of the USIA include placing stories abroad, providing news to major foreign media outlets, arranging interviews between foreign journalists and U.S. foreign-policy makers both abroad and at home, and feeding video material to foreign television systems. An essential element of any public affairs officer's annual analysis of his working environment is the structure of his country's or region's media. In many embassies, the public affairs officer (PAO) is basically viewed, and sometimes described, as the "press officer." In large American embassies, care has been taken to identify the second-ranking United States Information Service (USIS) officer (officially the information officer) as the principal press contact, so that the PAO can pursue the broader public diplomacy goals.

As a result, USIA research on media is both long-standing and carefully harmonized into the current structure of programming. For instance, it is no longer necessary for the USIA to undertake studies of print/video media use in most foreign countries, since commercial firms have long ago taken over such work; demographic figures on media use are thus available commercially to USIS officers. On the other hand, exotic media that have not yet approached commercial proportions may indeed have to be the focus of USIA efforts. An example would be the extent of VCR ownership and program use in areas (such as the Middle East) where commercial marketing firms are relatively rare. The findings of a 1982 survey—that 61 percent of Saudi households and 53 percent of Kuwaiti households had VCRs—is important for public diplomacy priorities.[3]

The other area where media use has to be USIA-monitored is in shortwave, noncommercial radio. Audience surveys for the Voice of America have to be commissioned by USIA. They are expensive (especially in relatively remote Third World areas) and the results not always reliable given the small market shares listening to the Voice of America (VOA). Some outside help for improving the reliability of such figures can be obtained from the BBC or Deutsche Welle, which also conduct regular surveys and check on listenership (as does USIA) of competing government broadcast services.

Reasonably close working relationships have been developed in recent years with those services to share research results and to share costs by collaborating on surveys. It must be said, however, that the reliability of USIA figures on VOA listenership has fallen considerably in the last decade, and the restoration of valid listener numbers is likely to take at least five years.

Within the last two years, VOA and USIA research agreed on a major program of updating listener figures that will require the allocation of more than $1 million to accomplish. It may sound like a great deal of money, but relative to the capital costs of new VOA transmitters meant to reach an unknown audience, it is likely to prove to be research well worth the investment. On some occasions, USIA is also required to research the nonreception of VOA and other United States media. Its research reports on East Bloc jamming of U.S. broadcasts have been definitive studies used within the government for assessment of the problem.[4]

The other type of media research given great prominence in recent years is the analysis of actual media content overseas. A special unit was created some years ago in the USIA Office of Research to conduct "media reaction analysis," whose major product evolved into the "Morning Digest." That digest of news coverage and editorial comment from major newspapers abroad has been a major interagency tool during the Reagan administration. Its early-morning character means that the director of USIA has used it as his briefing source for daily meetings at the White House and the Department of State.

The growing attention of United States administrations to foreign press coverage of U.S. policies and events has increased the visibility of such analysis—almost to the point of expecting more than it can deliver. Such research depends, after all, on a daily overnight flow of excerpts reported by USIS officers to Washington. Those officers have variable standards as to what they report, basically sending more of what they see appear in morning reports. That creates its own dangerous centripetal momentum, such that reports cover fewer topics and are sent by fewer USIS posts. Third World countries, for instance, are discouraged from sending media reaction reports unless the United States president is visiting. European and Japanese posts tend to focus only on the "crisis of the week" rather than using the opportunity to sensitize USIA/Washington and other foreign policy agencies to issues they may have overlooked. Coverage of specific issues is also not consistent over time.

Those faults of the media reaction system would not matter greatly if its only purpose were to produce daily summaries. In fact, a broader purpose has been identified in the last few years—namely, to analyze foreign media trends through uncomplicated surveys of coverage or eventually through content analysis. This area holds great promise in providing "one-step-back" analysis of where specific media are moving in their coverage of issues and United States policies. It would be particularly useful to individual PAOs in the field and, for purposes of special-issue publications emerging from Washington, in the identification of emerging issues that need broader multicountry treatment. The availability of such analysis would have been particularly useful in the context of the INF deployment agony, which was such a protracted challenge to United States public diplomacy.

Attitudinal Research

Over the years, research on the attitudes of foreign publics and elites toward the United States and its policies has grown from being one aspect of USIA's research to being the dominant element. It consumes the lion's share of its budget, a majority of the professional analysts spend full time on it, and it is seen by the departments of state and defense and the White House as USIA's unique contribution to the policymaking process. Despite that prominent position, it can be argued that it is underfunded and behind the times methodologically, and inadequately affects foreign policy.

The public opinion surveys focus only on foreign countries; through a division of labor based on custom more than law, the Bureau of Public Affairs at the Department of State researches and reports to the various agencies on domestic United States attitudes on foreign policy issues.[5] The USIA surveys are conducted by host-country contractors through unclassified arrangements, which necessitates a form of political clearance by regional bureaus in USIA and the Department of State, and by relevant American embassies, to ensure that foreign public knowledge of such surveys will not have an adverse effect on the United States presence in that country. That aspect of attitudinal surveys has always limited the nature of the polling to a relatively dry social scientific approach. Any hint of Soviet-style "active measures" through the use of doctored questions would result in an immediate scandal involving the foreign polling firm, the American embassy, USIA, and United States bilateral relations with that country.

Polling can only be done in relatively democratic countries that tolerate people walking up to strangers and asking questions. The core of USIA's polling has always been in Western Europe and Japan. It has been intermittent in Latin America, depending on the type of government in power. One of the unnoticed side benefits of recent democratization in Latin America has been dramatically increased access to countries in that region for polling by the United States. Aside from Japan, access in Asia fluctuates depending on relations with the United States. A case can be made that the willingness of host governments to approve USIA-commissioned research in their countries is a reliable barometer of the working relationship with the United States.

The Soviet bloc poses a special problem. In the last decade, the growth of social science institutes interested in public opinion polling has been significant in Eastern Europe. Although such institutes are not yet collaborating directly with USIA—for obvious reasons of policy sensitivity—the indirect communications have been encouraging. In the Soviet Union itself, the USIA has devised various indirect methods of assessing and reporting on elite and public opinion. Since 1981, the Office of Research has posted an assistant cultural affairs officer in the American embassy in Moscow to find innovative ways of distilling changes in public opinion. At the elite level, major surveys of surrogates have been done to provide a profile of attitudes—once around 1980 and, more recently, in 1984.[6] Research on the East bloc, however, inevitably suffers from comparison with the wide-ranging efforts of the intelligence agencies. As a result, it has attempted as much as possible to focus on issues of immediate relevance to USIA: media, cultural and educational programs, and propaganda and disinformation.

The *Research Reports* issued by USIA research analysts vary greatly in their scope and audience. Some will focus on a single country and even a single issue within that country.[7] Others will be quite sweeping on both scores, sometimes reflecting a single comprehensive survey and at other times a summary of a year's worth of surveys and analysis.[8] Generally, the broader reports reflect research undertaken at the initiative of the research analyst and office in order to keep data up-to-date on a country or region, whereas more specific research results reflect priorities set by the director of USIA or another agency.

A pleasant coincidence of both interests in research occurred in West European research during this administration. The crisis in alliance confidence over INF deployment created a policy-level need for frequent updating of European public opinion, and a cadre of first-rate specialists in European defense issues had been assembled in the USIA Office of Research. The result was an outpouring of research findings and analysis that set new standards for public diplomacy research.[9]

The common element of all such reports from USIA research is that they simply report findings. They do not include recommendations: When implications of actions recommended for USIA creep into reports, they are generally weeded out in the vetting mechanism. Disputes between research and other offices of USIA over the right to make recommendations in past decades left a very clear demarcation of mission for the Office of Research. Description is the object of attitudinal research, and any effort to include prescription is strongly resisted by the geographic bureaus and the Office of Policy Guidance.

The new methodologies in attitudinal research, in fact, make possible an exceedingly sophisticated form of program prescription based on polling data. This has been demonstrated in recent American presidential elections (not to mention recent experiences in French, German, and British national politics). Outside consultants and several recent research directors have urged the use of new methodologies by USIA researchers. The resistance throughout the USIA organization to such a renovation of research and its role, however, was widespread: ranging from the desire of USIS officers in the field to retain operational autonomy and the right to make judgments intuitively; the desire of other offices in USIA to retain their bureaucratic authority over program design; and a sense among research professionals that an ambitious agenda might jeopardize the recent gains in budget and personnel if rebuffed by higher authority. Yet it was argued that the adoption of new research methodologies would be essential to bridging the gap between research and the policymaker, with implications for foreign policy spelled out in detail. The consideration of options on domestic issues is much more sophisticated in process than those on foreign issues, so that public diplomacy has to adopt some of the domestic policy methodologies to get a fair hearing from the White House.

Ironically, the sidetracked effort to prescribe public diplomacy programming through attitudinal research found more effective channels. In order to disseminate the findings through interagency channels, the Foreign Opinion Research Advisory Committee (FORA) was established under the direction of the National Security Council (NSC). Monthly meetings provide a prominent opportunity to present findings and their implications to NSC staff members and representatives from the departments of state and defense.

In addition, during recent years on-site briefings have increased enormously for other foreign policy agencies on the range of priority topics engaged by foreign public opinion: NATO, INF deployment, U.S. policy in Central America, and the Geneva arms control talks. The opportunities to engage in discussions of programmatic and policy implications of findings have made ample use of increasingly sophisticated polling done by the USIA Office of Research.

Some of the controversy within USIA about allowing the Office of Research to engage in prescription goes back to old divisions over the role of propaganda and truth in USIA's mission. Many of the proponents of the 1978 reorganization into the United States International Communications Agency (USICA) believed that the agency could thereby finally eliminate its association with "propaganda" by focusing on the old platitude that truth is the greatest public diplomacy weapon in the hands of the United States. In that context, to use attitudinal research to find out what the target audience likes and dislikes is seen as inviting USIA to bend its message into propaganda—telling foreign publics what they want to hear rather than the truth about the United States and its policies. Others think it quite foolish for the United States to miss an opportunity to present, in the best light, the truth about U.S. foreign policy and about American society—in some cases, to balance free American media that consistently point out the problems of United States society.

With modern polling techniques, we have not only a portrait of foreign public opinion but also its reasons for maintaining certain values—with what intensity, and if given tradeoffs between various policies, which it would favor. We can also determine subliminal themes that affect its attitudes toward rational policy choices, right down to what color tie the president ought to wear in France to convey the right message (that is, conciliation, strength, friendship, or informality). To deny the use of such tools in this media age is not to remove the United States from the public diplomacy arena—it simply means that the United States readily makes mistakes in its ignorance. If foreign publics are exposed to American leaders and policies, their views will be affected.

The massive amount of information bombarding publics from all media means that somebody is packaging the truth (in the best case) to suit his or her needs. It would be a strange rejection of the late twentieth century for USIA to not engage in tailored packaging of the truth. Just as the United States learned that it could not walk away from major military conflicts in the 1930s, so it is likely to decide that it cannot avoid becoming engaged assertively in the public diplomatic arena in the 1980s.

Internal Program Evaluation

The traditional involvement of USIA research in the evaluation of program efforts by various offices within the agency was largely abolished in the late 1970s by then-Director John Reinhardt. Budget pressures on USIA forced a setting of priorities, and from the foreign service perspective, the judgments reached by the Office of Research were of less value relative to the ability of a skilled USIS officer to evaluate the success of his or her program. The agency was also on the brink of a major effort to provide program monitoring and evaluation on a real-time basis. The leadership of the Program Bureau created a distribution and record system (DRS) designed to computerize the transactions of program elements in Washington and the USIS offices in the field. This attempt to quantify program results on a rolling basis was widely resisted and yielded even less success than the more traditional set-piece evaluation efforts by the Office of Research.

By whatever method, for its success program evaluation depends on the willingness of the senior officials of the agency giving effect to the results and recommendations of reports. Few directors of USIA have ever given much attention to the results of program evaluation, either as a basis for internal reform or for setting priorities. In recent years, the Office of Research has maintained its skills through a trickle of studies on specific publications or exhibits and intermittent monitoring of exchange programs. Separately, the Bureau of Educational and Cultural Affairs has tasked a few officers to oversee the census counting of educational exchanges and to explore new ways of assessing the effectiveness of specific programs within that bureau. However, enthusiasm for the effort is clearly not present, and one could not expect that bureau or the agency generally to foster serious program evaluation unless results are genuinely applied in a manner that demands attention of officers at all levels.

In its 1985 annual report, the Advisory Commission on Public Diplomacy recommended that "USIA increase its utilization of the Office of Research to assess the impact and effectiveness of Agency products and programs." As pointed out in that report, the Office of Research has, in fact, recently requested expanded funding and personnel slots to engage in such an evaluation—especially in new and innovative areas of USIA programming, such as television, new broadcast services, the expanded educational exchanges under the Pell Amendment, and proposed magazines. Although an expansion of that evaluation work has been approved in principle, the follow-up resources have not yet been approved. If public diplomacy is to expand its efforts as envisioned by the Advisory Commission, this administration, and others in the field, then it will also require monitoring by serious evaluation efforts.

Telecommunications Developments

The rapid technological changes in the last decade have left both USIA and the rest of the U.S. government struggling just to monitor the large contextual changes for public diplomacy. Attempting to play a central role in shaping those technological changes has been far beyond the capability of the U.S. government, and in an era of deregulation, there has been active opposition in parts of the U.S. government to doing so. And yet, the telecommunications revolution is changing the world in which U.S. public diplomacy is attempting to make an impact.

In every part of the world, the processes of communication being put in place have the potential for undermining USIA programs established since World War Two. Examples are almost too numerous to begin to cite: the shift of radio listeners in many parts of the world from shortwave to medium wave bands; the explosive growth in access to video materials (whether through new national television systems, direct broadcast satellites, or videocassette recorders); changing access to information and data, making old processes obsolete; and the potential computer revolution in the Soviet Union and Eastern Europe.

The private sector is doing a great deal to monitor these developments. Specialized magazines and newsletters have been springing up to provide a synthesis of information about technological changes.[10] But following changes abroad is particularly difficult, given the number of national environments that independently change their rules and regulations with impunity.

And on the American side, the rule has been decentralization; two years ago, a Congressional Research Service report stated that, "in the United States, more than in any other nation, Government authority for international telecommunications and information policymaking is dispersed among different departments and agencies."[11] When a United States delegation recently visited Japan to discuss telecommunications issues, it had to include representatives from the Department of State, the Federal Communications Commission, the National Telecommunications and Information Administration of the Department of Commerce, and the Office of the U.S. Trade Representative. And that was a small, working-level delegation![12]

All of this activity has left the major agency with responsibility for public diplomacy (USIA) attempting to track not only developments abroad but also the initiatives of the other United States agencies that may impinge on USIA activities. The Reagan administration created a small, two-person office at USIA to increase the agency's involvement, but even that atrophied for lack of clout relative to the Department of State, where an entirely new bureau was being created under Diana Lady Dougan's leadership to deal with this area (accomplished in the summer of 1985).

To supplant and make more effective that USIA effort, the Office of Research organized a meeting of the various agencies in the summer of 1983, devoted to examining the telecommunications research effort throughout the United States government. Its success, in making the various agencies aware of the limited and highly fragmented effort of such research, resulted in 1984 in the USIA Office of Research setting aside limited funding for award to outside contractors for assessments of foreign telecommunications efforts. The first awards from that funding were made in late 1984, and staff attention to telecommunications research began to increase in the Office of Research. The high-level attention to such research, if properly focused, was bound to follow, given the importance attached to increased dissemination of television material, a sector consistently subject to the greatest and most arbitrary regulation overseas.

To turn the assessment research on telecommunications changes into a basis for action will inevitably require remedial education for USIS officers and the strong injection of USIA's perspective into the deliberations of the Department of State. The former has already begun, with the creation of special seminars for USIS officers on home leave and in the field. To get the attention of Department of State policymakers, however, will require a greater effort, especially by senior USIA officials able and willing to make the necessary, periodic demarches on their colleagues in Foggy Bottom.

WHERE DO WE GO FROM HERE?

On the positive side, public diplomacy research is recovering rapidly in terms of resources: Funding for research in USIA and in related efforts in other departments and agencies is on the increase, and even in an administration dedicated to reducing the federal work force, there have been allocated additional people to carry out the work. At the applied level, there is scope for additional work in attitudinal research and a growing appreciation of media research, and the government now realizes the extent of the challenge in tracking the changes in telecommunications. As a result, we now witness more of the same kind of research traditionally done by public diplomacy agencies, as well as some limited forays into new types of research.

The negative side is equally impressive, however, and should be properly grouped into an agenda for those interested in public diplomacy research:

• The nongovernmental constituency for public diplomacy research remains abysmally weak. A major exception is the work done by the U.S. Advisory Commission on Public Diplomacy. Otherwise, the academic sector is engaged in little research relevant to public diplomacy; to hire someone for the Office of Research at USIA is to look for a person with basic methodological skills and to hope to be able to train them in the applied requirements of the positions. A small effort was made to draw universities into the effort on telecommunications policy research. The response was not large, and only time will tell whether a constituency for such work exists. More work is being done by the private sector in monitoring the technological changes of the field, but only insofar as public policy influences the potential for profitable exports and imports.

• The constituency in government outside USIA for public diplomacy research remains more limited than it should be. The obeisance to the role of such research in foreign policy formation remains largely ritualistic. Attention is paid in time of crisis, when the Department of State reluctantly realizes that public opinion overseas will have a measurable impact on the outcome of a problem. But it becomes too late to construct information flows, the understanding of statistical output, and the kind of bureaucratic responsiveness that everybody wants suddenly. FORA may help overcome that problem, but only with additional leadership from the National Security Council.

• USIA methodologies are under attack by public opinion itself. The widespread skepticism about the role of public opinion polls in the United States is spreading abroad. And with the proliferation of unsophisticated skepticism ("it's all how you phrase the question!"), increasing hazards complicate USIA relations with foreign contractors and the surveyed publics. American attitudes, however, set the fashion in this regard, and the field has many fences to mend in the United States if it is to restore the respectability that it earned in the first few decades of its existence.

- If the USIA Office of Research is to take on, once again, expanded responsibilities for program evaluation, it probably needs to be moved within the agency. It is currently located in the Bureau of Programs and isolated from the other bureaus. It is appropriately located for conducting and reporting on foreign polling, but for any other responsibilities, the director of the office should be made an assistant director of the agency, reporting directly to the director and deputy director of the agency. It would thus be recognized that the director appreciated the output of program evaluation and that the broad trend analysis (telecommunications and media) was meant for agencywide consumption and application. Presently, that message is not conveyed.

- The application of new polling methodologies and related political campaign designs needs to go forward rapidly. If existing personnel are not able to adapt, it may require the creation of new bureaucratic units to accomplish that. The need for rapid analysis, reaction, and application into highly maneuverable public diplomacy strategies is clear, especially as the speed of global communications accelerates. The private section has shown the way forward (for example, multisite television programming, theme-analysis political campaigns, and large-scale data bank accessibility) in a manner that cannot be simply imitated by the United States government. It must look ahead to the next generation of methodologies and invent them on its own (through basic research) if it is to have an independent impact in shaping images of the United States held by the rest of the world.

DISCUSSION

Kathleen C. Bailey

Had analysts in the United States examined the pamphlets produced by Iranian mosques as early as February 1978, they would have noted the antishah and pro-Khomeini themes and the demands for an Islamic government.[13] Moreover, if they had surveyed the opinions of the man in the street or the clergy (community leaders at the neighborhood level) in Iran, they would have better gauged the depth of discontent with the shah and the receptivity of Khomeini's messages. Because there was no such public diplomacy research—that is, methodical research about what information was circulating, what media were being effectively used, and how the public was responding to the information—United States foreign policy decisionmaking suffered.

Without the insight provided by such research, American officials depended heavily on subjective evaluations by Western scholars and diplomats on the scene. One academician who had met Khomeini described him as a virtuous and beneficent philosopher-statesman, free of corrupting power drives or personal ambitions.[14] The United States ambassador to Iran predicted that the Shah could maintain power. Using such impressionistic data, American officials did not perceive Khomeini's fundamentalism and his extreme distaste for the United States, nor did they correctly assess the strength of popular opposition to the Shah. They were thus ill-prepared to respond to the 1979 revolution and, later that year, the hostage crisis.

Today there is another crisis in the Third World that may yield a revolution—this time in South Africa. As in Iran, the policies and actions of the United States government will be crucial. American policymakers already have acknowledged their need for public diplomacy research on South Africa. During debate in the U.S. Congress about whether economic sanctions should be imposed on South Africa, amendments were introduced first to provide for an opinion poll among nonwhite South Africans to determine their views on United States divestment.[15] In addition to surveys of black and colored public opinion on a variety of issues, public diplomacy research in South Africa should examine white opinions to help assess policy options and, possibly, predict behavior of that community. Government and opposition media should be analyzed to pinpoint major issues and possible solutions to problems.

Also as in the case of Iran, there has been virtually no public diplomacy research conducted on South Africa that would enable United States officials to make more informed decisions regarding the growing crisis in that country. There are no up-to-date analyses of the media; not in any of the South African communities, white or nonwhite, do we track continually the information and disinformation that drive the actions and reactions. Existing assessments of public opinion either do not focus on relevant issues or are unreliable.

Last year, a university professor surveyed opinions of black South Africans on several economic issues of direct concern in the current crisis.[16] One of his findings—that 74 percent of the respondents opposed disinvestment—would have been useful in the congressional debate cited above. However, the opinion survey was dated and had been somewhat discredited, because of both its methodology and the close association of the author to blacks who are known to oppose disinvestment. Other surveys on related questions have been conducted, but they are even less useful. Thus, American decision makers have only the statements of the very few outspoken nonwhite leaders as indicators of public opinion on any issue.

There are, of course, other examples of Third World countries where the results of public diplomacy research could be of great use to United States policymakers. Yet, the resources of USIA, the agency responsible for conducting such research, have been focused primarily on industrialized, democratic countries. My remarks today probe some of the reasons for that focus, and I argue that the need to understand the public diplomacy environment and public opinion in Third World countries is increasing.

THE INCREASING NEED FOR
RESEARCH IN THE THIRD WORLD

The public opinion environment in Third World countries is undergoing a transformation that will increase the need for USIA-sponsored public diplomacy research in those countries. These changes can be roughly categorized as (1) an increase in availability and use of electronic media, (2) the new generation of leadership in many of the countries, (3) stronger public diplomacy efforts by the USSR, and (4) the "internationalization" of United States foreign policy. Each of these will be discussed below.

Spread of
High-Technology Communications

As Dr. Bissell stated, the flow of information and disinformation in Western industrialized countries has increased exponentially with the development and spread of high-technology communications and media. Although this has increased concurrently the tools available to the public diplomacy process, it has greatly complicated the challenge of portraying United States policies and creating a favorable image abroad. This high-tech revolution necessitated better United States policy planning and more careful integration of marketing strategy into the foreign policy process.

Only in the past few years has the communications revolution spread widely in the Third World, creating vast new audiences for the flow of information, as well as disinformation. India now has an indigenous space program enabling it to design, build, and launch satellites.[17] Several other Third World states, including Indonesia and a consortium of Arab countries, have had communications satellites put up for them by the United States and Western Europe. Television sets are everywhere. Surveys in Bangkok, for example, reveal that up to 90 percent of that city's residences have sets.

In many of the Third World countries, the impact of spreading communications technology will be mitigated by strong governmental control over the content of broadcast and print media. However, because of limitations on their abilities to create their own programming and to gather international news, most of these countries will have to rely on imports for the short term. In Arab countries, for example, 42 percent of the television programs are imported; approximately one-third of this number comes from other Arabic countries, and the rest predominantly from the United States and Western Europe.[18] The international wire services based in the West are still heavily relied upon for news.

Resentment of their dependence on Western information and programming has grown in the Third World, resulting in attempts to place legal restraints on transborder communications and to develop "Third World news reporting." Several Third World states, with strong Soviet backing, have attempted to create domestic and international laws that would help reduce the impact of Western media in their countries. To the extent that such barriers are erected, United States public diplomacy will be a more difficult process. Not only will the flow of Western programming and information be stymied but it is also likely to be replaced by less objective, possibly anti-Western, news and entertainment.

In addition to providing analyses of the publicly available media, United States public diplomacy research should also focus, to the extent feasible, on the "private media" of audio and video cassettes. As evidenced by the pivotal role of audiocassettes in conveying ideas and instructions from Khomeini during the Iranian revolution, such media can have tremendous impact on what the public perceives as truth and how it reacts to events. In countries where the public media are limited in what they can provide (such as African countries) or are willing to provide (viz. Saudi Arabia), cassettes can be a greater source of information than the public media. Research can provide estimates on the use of cassette players in a given country and can help answer questions about the kinds of information the public is receiving via these media.

Thus, as Third World countries acquire electronic and high-technology communications, the public diplomacy environment becomes more complex. There will be more information available, and the way in which it is delivered or slanted will increasingly be influenced by the Third World governments themselves, and perhaps by the Soviet Union. There is thus the need for research to monitor the Third World communications revolution, to analyze media content, and to assess the impact on public perceptions.

NEW GENERATION OF LEADERSHIP

When Gorbachev came to power in the Soviet Union, commentators quickly pointed out that he is too young to have participated in World War Two. Because that conflict had been the event that shaped a generation of leaders in the USSR and other countries, people wondered whether Gorbachev and his generation would be substantially different from their predecessors. The question about Gorbachev is a good one and should be a topic of research on any new generation of leadership, including those in Third World countries. Many of the new leaders have less understanding of the West than their predecessors, and some are openly hostile to Western philosophies and policies. The attitudes and policies of these new leaders can make it more difficult for the United States to cultivate a positive image abroad and to ease the way for acceptance of its foreign policies.

India, a country that has always seemed a difficult challenge for United States public diplomacy, may be an example. Following independence from Britain, the top positions in the new government of India were filled by party leaders and civil servants who were heavily influenced by British values and philosophy. Despite strenuous USSR efforts to sway the Indian leadership, India has remained outside the Soviet camp on many issues and has pursued nonalignment. To some extent, the cultural, linguistic, and philosophical heritage of the colonial period probably has tempered India's left-leaning policies.

India's young prime minister, Rajiv Gandhi, is forcing older politicians aside and is bringing in the new generation, many of whom were not even born until after independence. Not having shared the colonial experience, they do not have the political and emotional ties to the West that the retiring politicians have. Public diplomacy research could help determine the philosophical orientation of the new leadership and help pinpoint areas in which the United States needs to improve dissemination of information about itself and its policies.

Similar research should be done in other countries. The young South Koreans are not yet being brought into government in large numbers, but when they do come in, their policies may be less closely tied to American interests. The new generation does not have firsthand memory of alliance with the United States in the Korean War, and many will view the U.S. as synonymous with their current autocratic government.

In Argentina, young politicians' view of the United States has been affected by two important events: The Falklands-Malvinas War (in which the United States sided with Britain) and the crushing foreign debt crisis (much of which is owed to American banks). It is, therefore, quite possible that the task of public diplomacy in Argentina will be much more difficult in coming years. Research can help reveal the extent to which the new generation has been affected by these events and can assist in developing strategies to overcome the problem.

The above examples demonstrate three basic facts that make the new generation in many Third World countries different from the old. In those that were previously Western colonies, power is now passing to younger politicians and bureaucrats who do not have the same political-emotional ties to the former metropole. In most Third World countries, there has been no wartime alliance, in the memories of the new generation, that would bind their sentiments to the United States or other Western countries. In fact, in the minds of many new politicians in the Third World, there have been negative events that cause them to disdain the United States.

STRONGER PUBLIC
DIPLOMACY BY THE USSR

One of the strongest messages of this workshop is that the Soviet Union has recognized the value of public diplomacy. As Paul Smith has said, the USSR propaganda effort is "a modernized weapons system of equal rank to other instruments of strategy."[19]

The Soviets expend considerable effort to disseminate in the Third World their own version of international news events and to provide favorable information about their own activities. In addition to regularly placing stories in media throughout the Third World, the USSR has enlisted the support of many countries in trying to define a "new world information order"—which is essentially defined as a world free from the influence of Western media.

Along with its "legitimate" public diplomacy efforts, the USSR actively promotes disinformation—a complex process of deception involving transmission of false and misleading information, and active measures designed to shape popular perceptions and to impact directly or indirectly on Western policies.[20] Although used in developing and developed countries alike, Soviet disinformation is usually far more effective in the Third World. There, the populations are relatively less educated and the news media are less rigorous in delineating fact from fiction. Dramatic events of 1979 in Pakistan illustrate this.

During that year, religious fanatics from a dissident tribe attacked and occupied a Moslem holy shrine in Saudi Arabia. Shortly thereafter, in Pakistan, also an Islamic country, word spread rapidly that the assault on the shrine in Saudi Arabia had been sponsored by the United States. In response, angry mobs of Moslem peasants and students attacked the U.S. embassy in Islamabad, the capital of Pakistan. One United States marine and several Pakistani embassy personnel died in the fires that swept the embassy compound. Later analysis of the incident showed that the rumor of American responsibility for the events in Saudi Arabia was disinformation spread in Pakistan by the Soviet Union.

As the USSR generates more information and disinformation in the Third World, the image of the United States and its policies is likely to worsen. To counter this, research must be conducted on what Soviet public diplomacy efforts are underway and how the public is responding. In addition, research on general public images of the United States enables American diplomats to counter misperceptions about the United States and, hopefully, creates an environment in which disinformation campaigns by the USSR will be less likely to succeed.

INTERNATIONALIZATION OF
UNITED STATES FOREIGN POLICY

United States foreign policy in one country or region of the world is increasingly of concern to other countries or regions. Thus, U.S. policy in Central America is an issue to West Europeans; U.S. nuclear weapons in Europe are of concern to Japan and Australia. Often U.S. policy is a contentious one, and opponents portray it negatively in the foreign media to create pressures on the United States to alter or abandon the policy. Although this internationalization of American foreign policy is not, by any means, a product exclusively of Soviet efforts, the USSR has exploited the process. Recent events involving India provide a good example.

In late 1984 and early 1985, United States officials noticed that some low-ranking Soviet officials were delivering speeches in India, in local dialects, on the subject of the United States budget for research on the Strategic Defense Initiative (SDI)—an American program to develop a defensive shield against attacking nuclear missiles. Research on SDI is strongly opposed by the USSR. Ordinarily, one would not think that such speeches would be of interest to Indian audiences and would not warrant the effort that is required for the Soviets to prepare and present the speeches in local dialects. Yet, upon closer look, it is obvious that the campaign did make sense, and it was successful.

The theme of the Soviet speeches was that the millions of dollars being spent on SDI research should be spent instead on Third World development—an argument that would appeal to Indian peasants and government officials alike. The success of the Soviet public diplomacy effort soon became apparent. At several international conferences, including the recent United Nations' conference on women held in Kenya, Indian representatives made an issue of the "misspending" of money on SDI research and asserted that, instead, the funds should be spent on Third World development.

As a result of internationalization, United States public diplomacy efforts in Western Europe and other industrialized countries must now be integrated with its public diplomacy strategy in the Third World. Research can be useful in a number of ways. It can help identify the following: (1) which United States policies toward a Third World country or region are being actively opposed in another country or region, (2) which non–Third World policies, such as SDI, are being opposed in the Third World (usually by the Soviets or at their instigation), (3) how the target public is responding to the opposition campaign, and (4) what efforts the United States should undertake to present its position clearly and fairly.

Bernard Roshco*

Public diplomacy is like the elephant that the blind men tried to describe; how they described the creature depended on the part of it they touched. Alan Rubin, for example, points out that private citizens can be effective practitioners of public diplomacy. Although I do not question their effectiveness, I do deny they are engaged in "diplomacy," if what we term "diplomacy" is to survive as more than a metaphor. And although private citizens can promote good will and better understanding among nations—perhaps better than professional diplomats—diplomacy is nonetheless a governmental activity.

Mark Blitz cogently defines key aspects of public diplomacy but restricts his overview to persuasive efforts aimed at foreign publics. Although this usage once was accurate, current practice has overtaken it. As Gifford Malone points out in his paper, the Reagan administration directs what it defines as "public diplomacy" to the domestic public and to foreign publics.

A term that becomes an umbrella for such diverse efforts is already a catch phrase whose definability is evanescent. Because so many products can be bottled under the label of public diplomacy, the label can be inherently misleading. It intimates that public diplomacy complements what we presumably should call "private diplomacy." Such definitional dualism suggests—erroneously, I believe—that contemporary diplomacy can proceed successfully on two discrete tracks.

Discussing public diplomacy as an enterprise that successfully can function apart from mainstream, private diplomacy obscures a key historical development. Fundamental changes in the current practice of conventional mainstream diplomacy have led, as one result, to the de-

---

*Bernard Roshco's views are his own and do not imply the concurrence of the U.S. Department of State or the United States government.

velopment of a set of ancillary activities. Such labeling generates the prevailing, yet mistaken, assumption that the techniques, methods, instruments, and practices that comprise what is currently dubbed public diplomacy can be employed autonomously and successfully outside the purview of mainstream diplomacy. The act itself of discussing public diplomacy as a discrete enterprise obscures a vital point: twentieth-century communication technology has forced mainstream diplomacy to go public.

Our discussion and definition of public diplomacy comprises a set of forces that increasingly impinge on the practices of traditional, unpublicized diplomacy. Instead of defining public diplomacy as an enterprise apart from conventional diplomacy, perhaps we ought to examine how practices in the domain of public diplomacy actually describe the extent to which traditional diplomacy is now conducted using the type of publicity traditionally shunned by diplomats. Traditional diplomacy is private in that it is a closeted enterprise; its formalities and mannerism are therefore subverted by just about everything implied in the definitions and practices of public diplomacy. Hence, it is not surprising that conventional, mainstream diplomatic practitioners often want to be a part of it.

If mainstream diplomacy is, indeed, in transition and increasingly becoming a publicized enterprise, then the advocates of a broader role for public diplomacy are misguided in suggesting that it function parallel with conventional diplomatic practice. The techniques and tools comprising public diplomacy are increasingly necessary for the successful practice of contemporary diplomacy. As Richard Bissell indicates in his paper, denying the use of such tools in the media age does not remove the United States from the public diplomacy arena but simply demonstrates that, in its ignorance, the U.S. government readily makes mistakes. It is as if a contemporary candidate for national office tried to eschew polls and television appearances; and, if induced to appear on television, insisted that he did not care how he looked or sounded. That would hardly be an effective way to campaign, and it is hardly an effective way to practice contemporary diplomacy.

As John Clingerman states so pithily, even though the values and behavior of many diplomatic practitioners are not changing, the publicity that increasingly accompanies diplomacy indicates that the norms of diplomatic practice are changing. In general, all professions resist changing their long-practiced procedures; given the centuries it has taken to develop the norms and procedures of traditional diplomatic practice, such resistance should be expected. When diplomats go public in the contemporary manner, they violate a central norm of traditional diplomatic practice. Whereas at one time only the product was publicized, now the process is publicized; consequently, negotiations must be conducted differently because publicized diplomacy impinges in direct and disturbing ways on the negotiating process. This was illustrated by Soviet attempts to shape popular impressions and expectations prior to the Reagan-Gorbachev summit in November 1985.

When the adequacy of traditional diplomats' skills are questioned, this leads to further resistance to the new norms that follow in the wake of publicized diplomacy. Going public requires enlarging and revising the professional skills brought to bear on the process of negotiation. Publicized bilateral negotiations, for example, are conducted before a third party—an audience of ratifiers, legislative and electoral, and foreign and domestic. One wonders how a Talleyrand would fare in the present negotiating environment.

Richard Bissell answers a key question underlying our discussion: Why is research so important for the effective practice of public (that is, publicized) diplomacy? As Bissell notes, research is important because the massive amount of information with which the media assails publics demonstrates that someone is packaging the truth to satisfy his or her needs. Trained researchers usually do not participate in this packaging process. This exclusion is not only because of policymakers' unawareness of the insight well-done research can provide but also because of, more significantly, the competition intrinsic to the policymaking process. Those privy to the action are rarely concerned about inviting those not included. In terms of the present structure of policymaking, researchers are outsiders.

Until research is "in," because its findings are deemed a necessary contribution to the early stages of policymaking, researchers will remain outside the policy formulation and implementation processes. The packaging role, in which Bissell wants researchers to participate professionally, will therefore be conducted by those likely to be incognizant of the potential contribution of research. Consequently, efforts to develop persuasive presentations of the rationales underlying specific policies—the intent of much of what is designated as public diplomacy—will, for the most part, continue to be based on an unarticulated trio of propositions:

1. In devising and implementing specific aspects of policy, one can usually postpone considering the likely reaction of most of the public, both foreign and domestic.
2. If the need arises, one can attract the respectful attention of this previously unconsidered public.

3. On fairly short notice, one can then persuade a sufficient proportion of this previously inattentive or unpersuaded public to accept your viewpoint and thereby carry the day for a beleaguered
policy.

Enunciated baldly, the fallacies inherent in these propositions become apparent. They prevail presently, partly because they are unex-
amined and undiscussed. Appropriate research of the type Richard
Bissell describes will have a full-scale, full-time opportunity to demonstrate its utility only after they have been recognized, examined, and
discarded. At that point, we will not have to define public diplomacy;
it will have melded into the mainstream of policymaking and diplomatic
practices.

Ronald H. Hinckley

In his paper, Richard Bissell charts the course that public
diplomacy research has followed within the USIA over the last half decade. In discussing the progress and identifying the key obstacles to further advancement, he indirectly comments on public diplomacy itself;
that is, the success of a public communications program is intertwined
with the quality of the research behind that program. He notes that the
recent expansion of public diplomacy research at USIA was unrelated
to any strategic vision of public diplomacy. American public diplomacy
lacks a grand strategy; it is tactical and narrow in focus and, consequently, so is the research associated with it.

Bissell's revelation about the lack of visionary public diplomacy is
more critically related than he acknowledges to the obstacles to sound
public diplomacy research, which he does identify. Although he implies
that the cart (sound public diplomacy research) should follow the horse
(strategically designed public diplomacy), the opposite is also true; that
is, sound public diplomacy research is critical to strategic public diplomacy. American public diplomacy lacks a grand strategy precisely because its creators ignore basic research on the public.

By its very nature, research is foremost a tool of strategy; it collects
and records information about factors in the environment that are likely
to affect policymaking. Research information enhances the choice of objectives and subsequent actions consistent with an organization's external and internal environments; policymakers can, then, not only pursue

their objectives within their organization's capabilities but also respond effectively to changes in the external environment.

Politicians or executives generally never instigate communication campaigns without initially researching the competition and the target public. Likewise, diplomats entering negotiations use research information to verse themselves thoroughly on the nature of a given topic and on the attitudes and beliefs of the opposition. Many contend, nevertheless, that public diplomacy can be designed and executed without primary, high-level consideration of research information on the targeted publics.

Hence, Bissell understates his suggestion that broader basic research might contribute greatly to a more strategic approach to public diplomacy (I would draw attention to much of the existing research about public opinion). The U.S. vision of public diplomacy will only expand insofar as we acquire, interpret, store, retrieve, and present basic public diplomacy research to responsive policymakers.

Bissell identifies several changes relating to the USIA Office of Research that must occur for public diplomacy to become strategic in nature. One involves improving the office's bureaucratic location. He notes that only when powerful USIA directors, such as Edward R. Murrow, were able to use their connections was research given an appropriate role in policymaking. My own investigations into strategic research and information units in various public and private institutions reveals that those organizational units tied directly to the top are the most effective. Those located lower in the hierarchy, whose work is filtered by several layers of bureaucrats, have little strategic impact.

We should seriously consider Bissell's suggestion to relocate the USIA Office of Research out of the Bureau of Programs and to have its coordinator report directly to the agency's director and deputy director. Only such an organization is consistent with the nature of research and the strategic information it produces. A bureaucratic repositioning would alleviate some of the other obstacles identified by Bissell. With greater independence, the Office of Research would be better situated to take "bad news" positions, which would produce better public diplomacy. Such positing includes identifying the incompatibility of certain public diplomacy efforts with the public environment they seek to affect. Weighing environmental factors would, then, help to determine what should be communicated to which people and in what manner.

With a more strategic role, public diplomacy research would have to focus on findings other than self-generated data. The office could monitor research from sources that it did not commission. Integral to these enhanced responsibilities is the need to upgrade the office in terms of technology and methodology of the 1980s; constant contacts with other research activities would assist this process. The need to deal with strategic public diplomacy issues would also induce the modernization of information handling; required speed and flexibility would put enormous pressure on the office.

Although modernization would help solve other problems, it also further demonstrates the chain-linked nature of the problems Bissell identifies with USIA research. As he notes, media research, particularly foreign press coverage of U.S. policies, creates its own dangerous centripetal momentum, which reduces topics covered and discourages Third World reporting of items that would help sensitize Washington to matters it may be overlooking.

Modern methodologies and technologies could be used to establish rules for media research that could be followed by USIS officers, adding reliability and validity to their currently ad hoc efforts. In addition, it would not be necessary for someone to read everything that came in overnight from a post; instead, it could be stored in data bases that can be machine-scanned and manipulated to identify anomalies or emerging patterns in the media coverage. This would put research activities on the Third World and the developed world on equal bases, because machines would store the information until someone had the time, need or interest to review it.

The current-events nature of the media reports would not be lost, but the longitudinal research value (not currently existing) would be added. In the long run, the longitudinal data would be more important than the current-events analysis, because it would permit patterns, trends, or anomalies to be identified. Such identification would facilitate quick and accurate public diplomacy responses.

Bissell singles out USIA research reports as a problem: They tend to be purely descriptive in nature, and any effort to prescribe is strongly resisted. Bureaucratic turf battles determine the scope of research and levels of analysis, since geographic bureaus and policy guidance staff resist interpretive research analysis because it infringes on their respective territories. This limitation on research analysis is contrary to the basic nature and value of research.

It is possible and desirable to have interpretive analysis that goes beyond description (the simplest and least valuable type of analysis) but avoids policy prescription (the hardest and most controversial). The USIA Office of Research needs to be able to free its officers to perform data synthesis, integration, and evaluation. These analytic levels assemble a complete picture out of component parts and give meaning to the data without prescribing what should be done.

Granted, evaluative and integrative analysis will establish parameters within which policy will have to operate to be effective. This should not be seen as binding the policymakers but, rather, freeing them from some potentially ineffectual policy choices. In the private sector, research emphasizes this goal, that is, to identify the parameters for effective decision making. Within government, the opposite often occurs: Bureaucrats oppose the restrictions that analyzed research information can place on their policy options. It is assumed that not spelling out the implications will produce greater leeway in policy choice; it only produces poor policy.

Limited (that is, descriptive) public diplomacy research analysis also results in public diplomacy that occurs without considering the public. As Bissell indicates, this restriction on analysis stems from fears that the USIA is engaging in propaganda rather than the truth. Ironically, in a country with the oldest tradition of public opinion molded for political, marketing, and educative purposes, a group arises within the government that denies that country this right in the world arena. To cede this is to engage in a different public diplomacy game than that played on both the American and the world political stages.

Research on public diplomacy is misunderstood within the USIA and ineffectively positioned. This explains the recent inordinate attention to research by the U.S. Advisory Commission on Public Diplomacy. The commission's constant focus on the role of research demonstrates that these people, from outside the government, understand both the strategic role research must play in effective public diplomacy and the shortcomings of public diplomacy and research as designed and practiced by the USIA.

In the most recent USIA annual report, space devoted to research activities is greater than that concerning any other activity. Together with the advisory commission's report, Bissell's paper points to more than the need to rectify some problems with public diplomacy research. They stress the need to reformulate public strategy, with major contributions from old and new public and media research.

To achieve this, the bureaucratic independence of the USIA Office of Research must be established so that modern technology, methodology, and analysis can be used effectively to determine public diplomacy strategy and tactics. The problems of public diplomacy and public diplomacy research are so integral to an understanding of the role of research that they must be treated as one large problem and not many smaller ones addressed individually. This requires visionary leadership from those engaged in directing public diplomacy and public diplomacy research.

Carnes Lord

Initially, I would like to focus on three issues that Dr. Bissell did not see fit to surface or, at any rate, emphasize in his paper: (1) methodologies for public opinion research, (2) opinion research versus attitudinal research, and (3) public diplomacy with respect to the communist world.

METHODOLOGIES FOR
PUBLIC OPINION RESEARCH

Dr. Bissell's discussion is oriented toward quantitative survey research concerning the opinions of broad publics in modern advanced and democratic societies. Leaving aside the problem of the feasibility of such research in nondemocratic societies (communist or Third World), the utility of survey research is questionable for countries in which levels of public education and political participation are extremely low. In those countries (that is, most of the world, excluding Europe and a few advanced nations elsewhere) in which public opinion, for the most part, is the opinion of a small and readily identifiable elite, different approaches to gauging opinion would seem more appropriate and promising—approaches involving more qualitative and in-depth interviewing of selectively targeted audiences.

In the extreme case, this would entail a revival of old-fashioned political reporting by embassy officials from various agencies, especially those from the Department of State. Even in cases where the targeted audience is fairly broad, approaches could be devised based on relatively random sampling of individuals from different occupational and social groups. Dr. Bissell mentioned the USIA studies of Soviet elite opinion using a surrogate interview method. Apart from obvious risks in such techniques, in principle, there is no reason why valid approaches could not be designed.

OPINION RESEARCH
VERSUS ATTITUDINAL RESEARCH

Dr. Bissell's plea for more attention to basic research and long-term strategies points to the problem but does not address it explicitly. If we define opinion as an essentially short-term phenomenon that is reactive to events in the world, often the U.S. government simply cannot react in time to developing opinions in order to influence them effectively. But opinions are directly (or indirectly) shaped by attitudes that are more persistent—if often more vague and more difficult to isolate. These underlying attitudes are often bound to fundamental and unspoken characteristics of a country's political culture or national style.

The more radical the differences between our own political culture and that of another country, the more important it is to try to understand these differences and to exploit this understanding effectively for the purposes of United States policy and public diplomacy. Of course, this involves an effort at self-awareness that will always be difficult. No one claims we do this well, or even to any significant degree, at the present time. However, over the long run the effectiveness of our public diplomacy has to derive its sensitivity to the deep currents of attitudes and ideas throughout the world and a constant awareness of the danger of mirror-imaging (that is, projecting distinctively American attitudes to audiences that do not share them). This is probably the most profound limitation and challenge facing United States public diplomacy today.

PUBLIC DIPLOMACY WITH RESPECT
TO THE COMMUNIST WORLD

Survey research techniques are of limited use here. The study of the communist opinion industry is as important as the study of opinion in communist-ruled countries. Soviet propaganda and disinformation is a rich and neglected area of investigation, with a potentially high payoff for policy. There remains an urgent need to create and sustain sophisticated data bases that will permit timely analysis and exploitation of communist propaganda efforts. Historical studies in key areas, such as arms control, could be extremely useful. The USIA's *Soviet Propaganda Alert* is a step in this direction, but only a step.

Let me make a few final remarks on the agenda sketched by Dr. Bissell at the end of his paper. He is absolutely right in identifying the lack of a nongovernment constituency for public diplomacy research as a critical weakness of such research. There is virtually a complete vacuum of interest in the academic world in almost every area of research pertaining to public diplomacy—from intercontinental media trends to propaganda and disinformation. This vacuum places a heavy burden on the United States government and, in particular, on USIA and makes it all the more necessary to undertake the basic research in this field that

Dr. Bissell mentions. Given the inevitable limitations of the government in such endeavors, however, it is highly desirable to encourage the establishment of independent academic or policy-oriented organizations that can undertake such research.

Dr. Bissell is also correct in calling attention to the problems USIA continues to encounter in marketing its research to other agencies of the U.S. government and, more generally, in affecting how other agencies (most notably, the Department of State) conduct the nation's business abroad. It is encouraging that a high-level interagency coordinating group has been formed under the auspices of the National Security Council (NSC) to oversee public opinion research. It is unlikely, however, that public opinion data will play a significantly greater role in policy formation without sustained and high-level attention to this problem at both the Department of State and the NSC, and structural changes to support such policymaking.

Finally, Dr. Bissell is on the mark with his plea for new research methodologies incorporating the latest advances in communications and data-processing technologies and designed to support what he calls "highly maneuverable public diplomacy strategies." In addition to the need for data bases dealing with communist propaganda (previously mentioned), there is a desperate need for data bases that will support flexible and rapid response to developing events by United States public diplomacy and policy organizations. And, to return to Dr. Bissell's fundamental point, there is a need for genuine strategic planning in the public diplomacy area that builds on and benefits from a revitalized research base.

NOTES

1. Some literature on the subject does exist, although its quality is uneven. Among the most recent efforts to give public diplomacy a meaningful context are Allen C. Hansen, *USIA: Public Diplomacy in the Computer Age* (New York: Praeger, 1984); Gifford D. Malone, "Managing Public Diplomacy," *The Washington Quarterly* 8, no. 3 (Summer 1985): 199–216; and John M. Oseth, "Repairing the Balance of Images: U.S. Public Diplomacy for the Future," *Naval War College Review* 38, no. 4 (July/August 1985): 52–65.

2. See, for instance, "Poll Finds French Support Reagan; Germans and Britons Split," *The New York Times*, 31 October 1984; Gregory Flynn and Hans Rattinger, *The Public and Atlantic Defence* (London: Croom Helm, 1984); Peter Schmidt, "Public Opinion and Security Policy in the Federal Republic of Germany," *Orbis* 28, no. 4 (Winter 1985): 719–42.

3. U.S. Information Agency, "Videocassette Use in Saudi Arabia and Kuwait," *Research Memorandum* (Washington, D.C., 17 January 1984).

4. See, for instance, U.S. Information Agency, "Jamming of Western Radio Broadcasts to the Soviet Union and Eastern Europe," *Research Report*, R-4-83 (Washington, D.C., April 1983).

5. These are done through a memorandum format; for instance, see U.S. Department of State, "Overview of the American Public's Attitudes Toward U.S.-Soviet Relations," Information Memorandum S/S to the Secretary from John Hughes, assistant secretary for public affairs (Washington, D.C., 9 March 1984).

6. The latter results are reported in U.S. Information Agency, "Soviet Elite Attitudes and Perceptions: Domestic Affairs," *Research Report*, R-25-84 (Washington, D.C., November 1984); and USIA, "Soviet Elite Attitudes and Perceptions: Foreign Affairs," *Research Report*, R-4-85 (Washington, D.C., February 1985).

7. See, for instance, U.S. International Communications Agency, "Most Britons Uninformed About El Salvador Conflict," *Foreign Opinion Note* (Washington, D.C., 6 March 1981).

8. See, for instance, USIA, "Public Opinion in Four Countries in Central America, 1983," *Research Report*, R-1-84 (Washington, D.C., January 1984).

9. See, for instance, USIA, "Public Image of U.S. Policies Worsens in Britain; German Opinion Remains Largely Negative," *Research Memorandum* (Washington, D.C., 6 February 1984).

10. See, for instance, *Telematics and Informatics: An International Journal* (New York, Pergamon Press); *Connections: World Communications Report* (New York, *The Economist* and Television Digest, Inc.); *Chronicle of International Communication* (Washington, D.C., International Communications Projects, Inc.); and *Communications Daily* (Washington, D.C., Television Digest, Inc.).

11. Congressional Research Service, Library of Congress, *Report on International Telecommunications and Information Policy: Selected Issues for the 1980s*, prepared for the U.S. Senate, Committee on Foreign Relations (Washington, D.C., September 1983), p. 16.

12. See U.S. Department of State, *Press Release*, no. 249 (Washington, D.C., 8 November 1984).

13. Shaul Bakhash, *The Reign of the Ayatollahs: Iran and the Islamic Revolution* (New York: Basic Books, 1984), p. 15.

14. Richard Falk, "Trusting Khomeini," *The New York Times*, 16 February 1979, p. A-17.

15. Danny L. Burton, U.S. representative from Indiana. U.S. House of Representatives, amendments nos. 65 and 68, offered and failed in the Committee of the Whole on 4 June 1985.

16. Lawrence Schlemmer, *Black Attitudes, Capitalism, and Investment in South Africa* (Durban, South Africa: Center for Applied Social Sciences, University of Natal, August 1984).

17. Jerrold F. Elkin and Brian Fredericks, "India's Space Program: Accomplishments, Goals, and Politico-Military Implications," *Journal of South Asian and Middle Eastern Studies* 7, no. 3 (Spring 1984): 46–57.

18. Tapio Varis, "The International Flow of Television Programs," *Journal of Communication* 34, no. 1 (Winter 1984): 143–52.

19. Paul Smith, "Propaganda: A Modernized Soviet Weapons System," *Strategic Review* 11, no. 3 (Summer 1983): 65–70.

20. Hans Graf Huyn, "Webs of Soviet Disinformation," *Strategic Review* 12, no. 4 (Fall 1984): 51–58.

PART THREE

THE VIEW FROM WESTERN EUROPE

11

USA/USSR: A DIPLOMACY OF DIFFERENCES OR A DIFFERENCE IN DIPLOMACIES?

Monique Garnier-Lançon
Translated from the French by Margit N. Grigory

What is diplomacy? Some define it as the science of agreements that govern international relations; this definition, however, is somewhat didactic and restrictive. An alternative definition is the means of representing one's country vis-à-vis a foreign country in, for instance, international negotiations; without being exhaustive, this notion captures more of diplomacy's evolutionary nature from the beginning of recorded history to the present.

Even though diplomacy has existed as long as certain states, only with the establishment of permanent missions during the sixteenth century did diplomacy assume its traditional role. From ancient times to the twentieth century, the practice of diplomacy has evolved from the personal initiatives of sovereigns to the establishment of international organizations, such as the League of Nations and the United Nations, charged with arbitration of international disputes. Without radically changing the objectives and the role of diplomacy, this gradual evolution has profoundly modified the conditions of its practice. In recent decades, mass communication has helped to mold the present-day notion of public diplomacy through the transformation of the traditional means of communication, the increased and ceaseless growth of technical data, and the instant dissemination of this information.

How the United States and the Soviet Union have implemented their respective interpretations of public diplomacy is the most important issue facing the free world today. Not only world peace but also the survival of liberty itself depend on the interaction of these two interpretations, which have confronted one another since the First World War on a battlefield whose boundaries are losing ground each day. The three essential differences between American and Soviet diplomacy concern nature, appraisal, and means.

A Difference in Nature

There is a fundamental difference in the nature of the American and Soviet political regimes. The United States is a democracy—in fact, the model of democracy. Hence, the problems that concern the nation and its people—even those who are least able to understand and to judge foreign policy and defense matters—should be accessible to everyone, despite varying levels of education and responsibility. Most serious decisions require policymakers to spend months or even years closely examining and rigorously studying them, and to feel a weighty and torturous responsibility—a process that, to be valid, must often be conducted in secret. When surrendered to the public scrutiny of citizens generally unprepared to undertake such a task, the decisionmaking process becomes difficult, and the subsequent decisions do not necessarily command the citizenry's respect.

This is, however, the greatness of democracy: Citizens have not only a right but also a duty to participate in the life of their country. This American tradition of democracy, however, only reinforces the impact of the media, who tend to extend themselves beyond their role and explain information in order to become a major influence or, for certain ones, the principal power. Too many recent examples demonstrate the abuse of this power.

With its regular turnover of elected officials and their respective retinues of power, the democratic regime unfortunately gives American diplomacy discontinuous character. Each renewal of mandate is a genuine renewal, and those who make decisions in areas that normally require permanence and continuity succeed one another too rapidly to establish a line of efficient and coherent doctrine.

The Soviet Union, on the other hand, is a totalitarian regime in which everything to the smallest detail, the smallest place, and the smallest remark is regulated by the party's omnipresence. Consequently, only Politburo members have the means and the power to make decisions. Even among this cloistered elite, only a few are true decision makers; other members are asked to assent, and decisions are subsequently transmitted to those who will execute them. In a feeble public gesture, the decisions are forwarded to the party *apparatchiki* and from them, all across the country.

There are, of course, no media problems within the USSR. The media only publish what they are ordered to publish for domestic consumption and for the proper functioning of the party's authority; for consumption abroad, numerous subtle ways influence the media of the sparring partners. Given its dogmatic doctrine and the longevity of its dictatorship, the party has all the leisure time in the world to conceive and implement a continuous line of diplomacy; the best example of this is Andrei Gromyko's extraordinary tenure as foreign minister.

A Difference in Appraisal

More serious are the disparate assessments of the adversary, which has strongly colored the history of relations between the United States and the Soviet Union. As long as the United States—and, alas, the majority of other Western nations—considers that it faces one country, the USSR, and one people (in oversimplified terms, Russians or, by extension, Slavs), it will neither see nor recognize that its sparring partner is a system, Marxism-Leninism, that is spreading throughout the world to fulfill the mission of limitlessly expanding its influence. The United States views Soviet politics, strategy, and decisions—in short, all their methods of understanding the problem—to be false, incomplete, sterile, ineffective, and self-destructive.

As long as enunciating the word *communism* in the United States constitutes a serious lack of benevolence and of good education, all the finest analyses, like most onerous tasks, shall fall by the wayside. The USSR, on the other hand, is engaged in a merciless battle against a political and economic system, namely, *capitalism*. In fact, the USSR battles all forms of non-Marxist-Leninist political or philosophical expression with strict regulation of preference. Consequently, the Soviet battle is waged in all directions, throughout the world, and with fluctuations depending on events—but always according to a global strategy that is subservient to an omnipotent system.

Too often the U.S. responds to this global strategy in a piecemeal fashion, intervening in particular regions against particular governments. Lacking an apparent global strategy and a provision of unity, these individual responses unfortunately result in the United States' involvement at their adversary's chosen time and place. This leaves the adversary with the choice of the battlefield and arms—a serious flaw in strategy—and, in turn, prevents the U.S. from taking the initiative.

A DIFFERENCE IN MEANS

If the end justifies the means, then the USSR apparently uses several means, of which two are quite different in its practice of diplomacy. The Soviet Union uses the means commonly known as traditional diplomacy—that which is practiced between sovereign states and through peoples and institutions representing their respective elected governments. The second means, parallel diplomacy, is practiced efficiently by the pro-Soviet leanings of innumerable associations (for example, pacifist movements, terrorist organizations, liberation movements). In a more cordial milieu, this means of diplomacy is conducted by various friendship, charity, and social groups. To these categories must be added the formidable instruments of professional and labor movements, with particular ones reporting directly to Moscow.

In different countries each of these associations operates in an allegedly spontaneous way, without directly implicating the USSR in its actions or locations. This results in campaigns against missile deployment and for the withdrawal of Western Europe from NATO; various assassination attempts, curiously always directed against targets directly or indirectly related to the North Atlantic Alliance; regional conflicts and revolutions in Central and South America; repeated destabilization attempts in Africa, with particular relentlessness via-à-vis South Africa, an eminently important region of the world that supplies 75 percent of the West's strategic materials for high technology and defense; wars and constant turmoil in the Middle East and in countries bordering the Indian Ocean; and destabilization campaigns in the South Pacific, for example, in New Caledonia. These are but some of the results; an exhaustive list would be impossible. Each time that trouble explodes in some area of the world, the source usually is an organization or movement connected to Marxism-Leninism—although, perhaps, not initially evident—proving that behind this façade, the USSR pursues a well-defined policy that cannot be halted through the traditional channels of diplomacy.

By virtue of its democratic traditions and its respect for liberty, the United States, on the other hand, finds it repugnant to actively sustain anti-Marxist resistance movements within its own borders. Rather than aiding such organizations, the U.S. frequently ignores their information, advice, and more important, appeals for help when they crucially need the means to defend their endangered liberty. After having long evaded action and having been locked into long, vague diplomatic discussions—which gives mischief makers time to secure key positions in all respects—the United States too often rushes onto a battlefield where nothing officially obliges it to intervene, instead of supporting indigenous groups for whom resistance is a raison d'être. It thus runs the risk not only of embroiling itself in a situation without glory or issues but also of being denounced by its own media—media that have many victims, more or less consenting, and more or less unaware of a well-orchestrated disinformation campaign.

This contrast in the methods of disseminating and explaining information has forced the United States—a country in which all opinions have a right to be quoted, with a curious preference for those that are *anti*—in an unfavorable light vis-à-vis the USSR—a country in which only government or party information is released, required by and in the service of an ideology to wage psychological warfare that it conducts successfully according to the tenets of Marxism-Leninism. In this kind of war, semantics are undoubtedly the most efficient weapons; the use of clumsy language and ad hoc vocabulary has done more damage than the most sophisticated and expensive machines.

Alas, neither adequate time nor sufficient money has been spent in this veritable struggle against disinformation, a cancer that cunningly gnaws at the foundation of Western society and traditional human values. The most efficacious way to combat disinformation is to provide complete, honest, and more important, verifiable information. In international negotiations, it would be nice to envisage a true exchange of ideas, which presumes adversaries using words in the same sense and being familiar with the reasoning process of the opposing side. The United States should use the following simple rules as cornerstones in its dialogue with the Soviet Union:

- Utilize the same vocabulary and the same reasoning process (why not envision a school of rhetoric that would give form to such methods?).
- Do not hesitate to define precisely the meaning of words.
- Understand that clarity and firmness are essential qualities in conducting normal and satisfactory relations.

These are simple rules of common sense and abiding morality. Evidently, the USSR is not hindered by too many scruples and, thus, uses any available means to seduce the West under the guise of official discussions. Artists, intellectuals, and especially businessmen are always

tempted by the alluring prospect of important agreements and con-
tracts; in their shortsighted strategies, they seem to forget that Lenin
himself predicted the demise of capitalism as the day capitalists would
sell to the Marxist world the rope for hanging themselves.

The spirit of the Pilgrim fathers is instilled in the American soul and
outlook. Americans believe that the entire world is motivated by the
same benevolent sentiments and that it suffices to be good, indulgent,
and understanding in convincing others—even those who can be cruel,
malevolent, or dangerous—to adopt a wiser, more moral outlook. These
exemplary sentiments, the hallmark of a good and generous country,
become a lamentable deficiency in the face of determined and cynical
opponents who do not hesitate to profit from any occasion to appeal to
the hearts of others in order to promote their own goals, without the
least intention of fulfilling reciprocal commitments.

In this endless game—in the course of which the fate of the world,
our fate, is at stake—are there not more uniform rules? The Soviets play
chess, a game in which they are champions, and the Americans play
poker, a game that excites them. Currently, while important meetings
concerning the future of the free world convene or reconvene in various
capitals—under the leadership of a Soviet figure with a new profile,
more seductive perhaps, surely younger, but probably just as determined as his predecessors—it would be prudent for us to remember in
what spirit and by what means the USSR is waiting, as it has for a long
time, for the free world at the other side of the table.

12

PUBLIC DIPLOMACY AND THE FOREIGN SERVICE

Friedrich Hoess

Ever since the practice of diplomacy became a profession, nations have sought to sway the opinion of those whose judgment counted at home and abroad. The practice of public diplomacy in feudal times differs from its practice in the present Western world in the number of educated people exposed to print and electronic media in a way that warrants the term *universal media*. In the same way that public relations has become the primary task of political work, public diplomacy comprises an increasing portion of a diplomat's work.

This development should not, however, lead to the temptation to cause a spiritual split in the foreign service between those who must conduct existing classic diplomatic duties and those who should help to present the foreign policy of their country in an understandable manner to foreign publics. The final result of such a split would be the misconception in the minds of some politicians and government officials that public diplomacy is an adequate *Ersatz* in our time for the conduct of diplomacy as such, the latter being regarded as a relic of cabinet politics. This danger exists because in some countries politicians confound domestic public relations with productive work and action. Policy is thus formulated often by a given issue's chance acceptability to the media and not by its inner value, truth, or justice.

Public diplomacy not only complements political goals abroad but also supplements the foreign service; certainly, public diplomacy is the most ancillary service in the present. The responsible leader of a chief foreign office and heads of mission must always remain untouched and must retain the last word about the use of public diplomacy at any given time. This requires close cooperation at all levels among those responsible for public diplomacy and those formulating and executing foreign policy objectives. To establish effective teamwork, foreign service officers must not only view public diplomacy as helpful and necessary but also consider themselves as public diplomats.

This is a prerequisite for every foreign service officer today, because the recent transparency of the mass media has contributed to the disintegration of cabinet policy and cabinet diplomacy in favor of the reign of lobbies and anonymous corporations. Foreign service officers must therefore regard themselves as public diplomats, and many of them have conducted public diplomacy excellently—long before the term was coined. The nationalization of private, secret, and cabinet diplomacy by the mass media has exacerbated the necessity for diplomacy to be public. Presently, the media can play three basic roles:

1. To strengthen and secure freedom
2. To endanger freedom by fundamental criticism, which sells well to the public
3. To suppress freedom

In addition, published opinion (that is, press, radio, television) shapes, to a large degree, public opinion. Given the nature of the media and published opinion, public diplomacy is therefore a highly valuable means to achieve political goals abroad.

Despite the current necessity and the enormous possibilities of public diplomacy, well-trained, loyal, patriotic, dedicated, and motivated foreign service officers at all levels have an important role to play in the future. Their capacity to evaluate and critically analyze will remain indispensable in impressing their government's views upon its counterparts abroad and in formulating the political goals that can be achieved through the complementary use of public diplomacy.

13
SOVIET PROPAGANDA AND WESTERN SELF-INJURIES

Lucio Leante

Soviet propaganda is not irresistable; its effectiveness is often a consequence of Western leaders' mistakes. Despite some successes, the USSR can neither direct Western public opinion from outside nor divide it when and as it chooses. In terms of internal political and ideological differences, which are physiological in pluralistic systems, divisions among Western publics already exist. Westerners often mistrust and disregard Soviet propaganda and usually follow the cues from their political leaders; however, Western leaders sometimes echo USSR themes for internal reasons, disregarding the East-West implications in such cases.

Most Euro-American conflicts on dealing with the Soviet Union are rooted in the geopolitical and economic differences between Europe and the United States; however, many of them are not and are therefore avoidable. In their propaganda activities, the Soviets usually only have to utilize the most convenient among the already existing national and international disarrays in the West, to exploit them, and thereby enlarge the fractures between Western political elites. Some of these disarrays stem from the pluralistic nature of Western systems and from the structural differences between Europe and the United States and are therefore unavoidable. Many of them, however, could be avoided both internally and internationally through greater care in Western public diplomacy.

A Balance Sheet
of USSR Propaganda

When, how, and why has Soviet propaganda succeeded? One can draw a rough balance sheet as follows:

1. By imposing a veto over the neutron bomb debate, the USSR succeeded in squelching a major Western defense policy.

2. Although, as Iurii Andropov stated, the Soviets had hoped to win their battle in the streets of Western cities (as had already happened during the Vietnam War), they failed in a similar veto effort—the debate about intermediate nuclear-force (INF) missile deployments in Western Europe.

3. They succeeded, however, in exhorting a minority (*albeit* stable and influential), peace-loving network that rallied pacifists, environmentalists, unilateralists, neutralists, communists, and leftists on the basis of their scepticism of Western government reliability in preserving peace and security.

The Neutron Bomb Debate

In failing to deploy the enhanced radiation warhead (ERW), the Western weakness resulted primarily from the Carter administration's unsteadiness, rather than the effectiveness of USSR propaganda or the vulnerability of the West's open public opinion arena. The orchestration of Soviet and pro-Soviet propaganda started only after President Carter announced in June 1977 that he had not yet personally approved production of the ERW. In October 1977, when Defense Secretary Harold Brown declared that President Carter would approve production of the new weapons only after the NATO allies had agreed in advance to deployment on their respective territories, pro-Soviet activities and protests increased and spread worldwide.

After showing the USSR a Western window of vulnerability and shifting the entire burden of the decision to his allied European leaders, President Carter exposed himself and these leaders to intensified pressures. In fact, the propaganda campaign against the "hypocritical," "inhuman," and "capitalistic" neutron bomb soon became irresistable worldwide, rallying masses of unwitting protesters. Finally, on 7 April

1979, President Carter canceled the production of ERW without any reciprocal concession from the Soviet Union.

The Lessons of the INF Debate

The success of Western leaders in dealing with the Euromissile issue can be attributed more to the absence of the types of mistakes the Carter administration had made than to USSR ineffectuality. American and other Western leaders have been more committed in their resolve to deploy the ground-launched cruise missiles (GLCMs) and Pershing IIs. In addition, according to Western public preferences the necessity of the new missiles was properly presented in terms of not only the Soviet SS-20 threat but also the preservation of peace. It was accompanied by an offer to negotiate with the Soviets to reduce or eliminate INF missiles on both sides, based on NATO's dual-track decision. Thus, the official Western position harmonized well with public opinion.

Likewise, the erroneous shifting of political responsibility to the European allies was not repeated; and, despite many shadows, unity has been maintained in the Western camp. Although the dual-track decision was taken in 1979 at the insistence of Europeans, particularly West German Chancellor Helmut Schmidt, Soviet propaganda and pacifists mainly accused the Americans for the Euromissile decision. Indeed, West European governments often neglect to remind their respective populaces that the dual-track approach was taken because of European concerns about the INF imbalance in Europe. Had the Reagan administration vacillated or had it made a renewed demand on the Europeans in the way the Carter administration did, the West would probably now be viewing the ruins of NATO.

Western leaders have committed, however, some old and new mistakes. First, the tendency of NATO leaders to make statements designed for exclusive internal consumption often has been confirmed by both American and European leaders. Although a rhetorically hard-line image helped to re-establish the U.S. leadership's reliability among its allies, the Reagan administration promoted this image to an unnecessary degree during the period 1980–83. Words make a difference. The peaceful image of the United States, and thus that of NATO's policies, has suffered among Western public opinion. This, in turn, provides additional opportunities for the USSR to create strains within the Atlantic Alliance.

Second, beyond a certain threshold, insistence about the dreadful Soviet threat can be counterproductive. Although a threatening image of the USSR already exists among Western publics, it is not perceived as an immediate danger. For instance, rather than prompting an attitude of steady public resistance, evoking images of the Soviet Union as an "evil empire" only creates a hard-line image of the one invoking it. On the other hand, European leaders have indulged—sometimes for internal reasons—in often unjustified criticism of American foreign policy, which among European publics only fuels the Soviet-sponsored notion of the "moral equivalence" of the two superpowers.

Europe Between
the USA and the USSR

Both American hard-line rhetoric and European critical indulgence have contributed to spreading this Soviet notion of a moral and political equivalence between the two superpowers in Western Europe. This idea not only enhances the Soviet attempt to enlarge schisms in the Euro-American relationship but also reinforces the isolationist tendencies among those Americans who would otherwise favor a U.S. withdrawal behind fortress walls.

The Euro-American relationship is a difficult one because military dependence is, of course, not consistent with traditional European freedom of action. In addition, geopolitical and economic differences between Western Europe and the United States tend to accentuate conflicts about how to deal with the Soviet Union and Eastern Europe. Nonetheless, many misunderstandings of the early 1980s could have been avoided through more effective and careful public diplomacy, which too often does not focus adequately on the common interests and values of the Western community.

First, in the public debate on the sterility of East-West relations and the arms race, the core values of Western societies are often lost. To the contrary, the fundamental division between East and West, between totalitarian and democratic societies, is often forgotten, along with all the military and strategic differences that flow from this fundamental division.

Second, the fact that the USSR has a global strategy for the final victory of communism on a worldwide scale is often ignored. The United States and other Western countries, on the other hand, do not have such a mission; NATO merely has tactics for the containment of Soviet expansionism.

Third, in general, European critics of U.S. policies in Central America, the Middle East, and the Third World often neglect to consider that, like the United States, Western Europe has vital interests in containing Soviet attempts to control the raw material flow to the West and, hence, USSR expansionism worldwide.

Fourth, in retrospect, many areas of conflict about the meaning and implementation of détente could have been avoided. Whereas Americans have tended to underestimate the West European need for trade with Eastern countries and have overevaluated the danger of European dependence on Soviet energy sources, West Europeans have tended to ignore the long-term threat to Europe and beyond posed by the USSR interpretation of détente. As long as NATO remains in disagreement about East-West trade and détente, the Soviets will continue to reap direct and indirect political benefits within the realm of Western public opinion.

CREDIBILITY AND COORDINATION

The propaganda battle being fought on European soil, however, is not necessarily going to be won by the USSR; on the contrary, it is largely within the grasp of Western political leaders and opinion makers. This does not suggest, though, that technical problems are absent from the practice of Western public diplomacy. The practice of public diplomacy in the West is twofold, revolving around the strictly linked problems of credibility and coordination.

Since Western governmental sources are obviously committed to advocating the respective governments' policies, such sources have a credibility problem. This problem is magnified when a national information agency disseminates information to foreign audiences. Increased Euro-American coordination in this area would enhance the overall credibility of Western public diplomacy. Although such coordination is likely to be, for the most part, informal, NATO's information service could probably facilitate the process: The 1956 *Report of the Three on Non-Military Cooperation* (specifically Article 84) provided NATO with a formal role in allied cooperation to counter Soviet propaganda.

More than coordination per se, the core problem is credibility. It has been fallaciously asserted that, if more information could be more adequately communicated to Western populations, protests would disappear. There is, in fact, a superabundance of available information in the West. The public's confusion about whom to believe and how to view the issues clearly among this cornucopia of information is the real problem in the West. The West's true strength lies in the extraordinary variety, expertise, and reliability available at private research institutes on strategic and international studies. Few accounts are as convincing to the Western public as a scholar's or a journalist's independent conclusions.

Private institutes cannot substitute, however, for national public information agencies; they often further their own immediate aims instead of serving the purposes of public diplomacy. The presence of the private sector can, however, enhance the credibility of national information agencies. Despite unreconcilable differences between government and private viewpoints, a competitive collaboration between private and public sources should therefore be encouraged. As previously mentioned, Western governments obviously have an interest in advocating their own policies; but they also have a deeper interest in the pluralism, freedom, and credibility of Western channels of communication, even when individual positions oppose those of the government. To better utilize the expertise and credibility of the private sector, it should be the main priority of Western governments to foster a closer link among responsible private institutions and the Western media network.

14

RADIO POWER IN GERMANY: A NEGLECTED FIELD OF PUBLIC DIPLOMACY

Henning von Löwis of Menar
Translated from the German by Margit N. Grigory

In the Federal Republic of Germany (FRG), public diplomacy is not a topic! In escaping from its own history, the land that invented modern propaganda and developed it to a fine art has stricken the term *propaganda* from its vocabulary. Joseph Goebbels assembled an apparatus beyond compare. Using the German media to disseminate Hitler's message and thereby enhance his popularity, Goebbels clearly understood the power of the word. This same understanding led him to ban listening to foreign broadcasts.

After the end of World War II, the United States successively launched Radio in the American Sector (RIAS), the Voice of America, and Radio Free Europe to break the East bloc's monopoly of the airwaves. Although Radio Free Europe and Radio Liberty (RFE-RL) became major and important sources of information for the East bloc—with constant objections by the USSR and its allies about their existence and influence in the German Democratic Republic—over the years the FRG has given it only varying degrees of lukewarm support.

GERMAN SHORTCOMINGS IN THE CONTEST BETWEEN THE SYSTEMS

Although, as measured by the number of Western radio and television stations that broadcast into the Soviet bloc the FRG is the strongest anticommunist bulwark on the air, a discrepancy exists between the quantity and quality of its broadcasts. This is especially true of the West German stations, which for the most part are cautious on the air and decline to engage in aggressive confrontational activities. Praiseworthy exceptions include certain sections of *Deutsche Welle,* such as its East European edition, and the East-West edition of *Deutschlandfunk* (DLF) or its Berlin studio. Because of particular obstacles, which steer an appeasement course, dedicated individual journalists have a difficult time in their own studios.

In the first decade of its existence, the FRG did not have its own national radio station—like the East Berlin *Deutschlandsender,* today called the *Voice of the German Democratic Republic*—from which to address all German listeners. *Deutschlandfunk* (DLF) went on the air on 1 January 1962. In executing its mission "to report as much and as fairly as possible from and about East Germany," DLF is confronted with difficulties because of party politics.[1] As a radio bridge to the East, it has an editorial staff of three persons who are given only a few minutes of broadcast time per day. The commentaries, specifically for East Germany, are aired on weekdays at 4:05 A.M., when most listeners are asleep. Such scheduling is obviously not accidental. For example, at present there is no program for East German youth and no ultra-high-frequency network of stations, a basic necessity for stereo-quality broadcasting of music programs. According to available evidence, however, the DLF is the "most listened to" Western station throughout East Germany. East Berlin has accused it of "sowing suspicion about the politics of the SED [the ruling party] and encouraging subversive activities among certain segments of the East German population."[2]

In 1973 the director of the Hessen Radio, Werner Hess, submitted a confidential memorandum to cancel a DM 28 million subsidy paid by the national broadcasting institute to the DLF. He supported this recommendation by indicating that the DLF, following the renegotiation of relations with East Germany, would no longer have the task of addressing the question of united Germany: "The West German broadcast service to the East is to be regarded, after the expiration of the original treaty, [in the same way as] the provisions for the German-speaking neighbors of Austria and Switzerland."[3]

On the left side of the FRG political spectrum, there are influential forces that support one-sided Western disarmament on the air. The importance of the free flow of information from West to East is not given the attention it deserves. Well-made propaganda items, whose producers have to defend themselves from being called "cold warriors," or in Eastern parlance, "criminal perpetrators of the airwaves," are banned from program segments.

A showcase example of aggressive East-West journalism is a DLF press program called "From East Berlin Newspapers," the only press program from a West German broadcasting company, aired on weekdays at 7:35 A.M. The East's reaction to this program proves that a nerve, a weak point in the communist system, has been touched: "In an analysis of the program 'From East Berlin Newspapers,' it is clear that this is propaganda whose data are tightly paced, overlapped, and manipulated according to the desired effect. The real socialism of East Germany stands in the crossfire of falsification, deception, and defamation."[4]

A Cologne political scientist points out that journalists who produce certain programs for the East bloc attempt to inform without appropriate diplomatic considerations:

> Timidity, accommodation, and subservience in the face of complaints from Eastern regimes can be observed much sooner in the party political arena and among certain Western governments. The public, therefore, has the task to watch constantly over the many over-anxious politicians and bureaucrats, so that the informational programs that reach the socialist states may be kept free of every Eastern influence and may be secure in terms of finances, organization, and personnel.[5]

It is not easy to make it understood that the "war of the airwaves," the confrontation of systems via the media of radio and television, is a necessary and unavoidable component of the East-West conflict. Like children who were burned, the Germans fear fire; distancing themselves from National Socialism led to a downright criminal negligence of public affairs and propaganda—of public diplomacy. Situated on the seam between two antagonistic world systems, the Federal Republic has a special responsibility to inform, constantly and comprehensively, the people on the other side of the Iron Curtain about international events.

It is incomprehensible why *Deutsche Welle* broadcasts its programs for the Soviet Union exclusively in Russian; by doing so, it inadvertently boosts Moscow's russification campaign. For the peoples of the Baltic states, traditionally allied with German, programs should be aired in Estonian, Lithuanian, and Latvian. This type of broadcasting is not a technical or a financial problem, but a question of political will. This political situation, a superpower suppressing the freedom of the Baltic peoples, calls for action; there is no excuse for sitting idly by.

Sooner or later, the FRG cannot avoid to show its colors in a "war of the airwaves," use available means more effectively, or emphasize more clearly its programming contents. Until the present, those responsible have failed to formulate a clear concept and a convincing strategy for media politics vis-à-vis the communist-ruled states. Four decades after the end of World War II, during a period of embittered East-West confrontation, evidently we should make up for lost time. An ideological war cannot be won with military armaments. In the face of nuclear stalemate between the superpowers, the "war of words"—the struggle for the hearts and minds of people—is no longer just a sideshow but, rather, the central battlefield of East-West conflict, on which there will never be a ceasefire. There are situations in which microphones have a greater impact than rockets; microphones are guarantors of Western security—even if some politicians do not, or, do not want to, see this.

NOTES

1. Bernhard Wordehoff, "Das Aktuelle Program und sein Auftrag," in *Deutschlandfunk Jahrbuch 1976–78* (Cologne: Deutschlandfunk, n.d.), p. 14.

2. Manfred Klaus, "Der BRD-Auslandssender Deutschlandfunk," in *IPW Berichte*, no. 7 (1984), p. 51.

3. Herbert Kruse, ed., *Die Vierte Front: Zur Psychologischen Kriegführung der NATO* (Berlin, GDR, 1977), p. 97.

4. Willy Walther, *Der andere Krieg: Geiselnehmer und Animiermädchen in Weiss, Grau und Schwarz* (Leipzig/Jena/East Berlin, 1983), p. 106.

5. Hans-Peter Schwarz, *Zwischenbilanz der KSZE* (Stuttgart, 1977), p. 107.

15

PUBLIC DIPLOMACY AND THE SOVIET BLOC

Roger Scruton

Perhaps the major concern of public diplomacy toward the communist powers is how to make contact with the people of the Soviet bloc countries in such a way as to neutralize the hatred of our way of life that is constantly conveyed to them and in order to inspire in them whatever courage and conviction might be necessary to secure our long-term interests. It has been suggested that we should continue to broadcast, as often as possible using the best available means, the messages conveyed by Radio Free Europe and Radio Liberty (RFE-RL), the British Broadcasting Corporation (BBC), and the Voice of America (VOA). Every improvement in this means of communication should be actively encouraged. It is also important, however, to listen to any criticism that may be obtained from within the Soviet empire. I have often heard VOA compared unfavorably with the BBC and RFE by people whom I know in Eastern Europe. It is not necessary to think that VOA should, therefore, change its tune—provided the intellectual community is catered to by other services. But it is necessary to learn the lessons of Leninism: A society is more influenced, in the end, by its elite than by the mass of people whose instinct is not to lead but to follow.

Others have suggested that exchange programs, especially academic exchange, should be encouraged as a means of bringing "ordinary" citizens of both sides into contact. I have two reservations. First, no traveler from a Soviet bloc country (with certain important exceptions) is an "ordinary" citizen. As a rule, a citizen travels as the knowing but undisclosed agent of the communist party and receives permission to visit the West in exchange for services rendered in the past or to be rendered in the future. The visitor realizes that the West is a better place to live than his own country. Ideally he hopes for the freedom given to the higher ranks: the freedom to live in the USSR or Eastern Europe and travel freely to the West, earning hard currency and purchasing privileges that will enable him to lead the fully enriched life of the *nomenklatura*. Often he is required to pay, as the initial price of his privilege, his respects to the ruling purpose of the party. He will appear on television to spout "peace propaganda" to the Soviet or East European peoples in order to show them that a visit to the West has not blunted but, on the contrary, sharpened his awareness that American weapons and NATO belligerence are the principal causes of the present tension. In other words, his visit to the West gives him ambassadorial status: He speaks where we should speak, but only in order to convey the very same lies that we hoped to destroy by inviting him, and to whose power and persuasiveness we have merely added. These appearances on television are not often mentioned in the Western press; indeed, in Britain only the *Salisbury Review*, which maintains contact with writers behind the Iron Curtain, has so far pointed to this important instrument of Soviet diplomacy.

More important, however, is the fact that Western citizens who visit official Soviet bloc institutions travel to places that are (again, there exist important exceptions) totally unrepresentative of the society from which their membership is recruited. I am not speaking of scientific institutions; science has a universal character that makes it useful to all people everywhere; the CPSU has therefore encouraged such institutions, since it is in desperate need of scientific expertise if it is to realize its supreme purpose. I speak of humanities departments in universities, cultural and musical institutions, clubs, churches, and societies.

For instance, what meaning does a "cultural exchange" have with a Czech university, when the nature of the exchange is literary or cultural? The greatest Czech writer of this century, Franz Kafka, is officially unpublishable in Czechoslovakia; it is even forbidden to mention him in official publications, however scholarly. Other Czech writers of the earlier years in this century are either unpublished or published only in part. The very history of the first Czechoslovak republic has been suppressed and is not a possible subject of research at any Czech university. Of the most important writers, the playwright Vaclav Havel is unpublishable and has just served four years in prison for upholding the spirit of justice; the poets Bohuslav Reynek and Vladimir Holan are unpublishable; the most important prose writer, Ivan Klima, likewise; the most original political theorist, Milan Simecka, likewise. Jaroslav Seifert, the Czech poet who recently received a Nobel prize, was published only in *samizdat* until recently and has been subject to continual persecution. The greatest Czech philosopher of this century, Jan Patocka, a pupil of Edmund Husserl and a master of Central European thought, was interrogated to death by the secret police in 1977 and is now unmentionable. Patocka's pupils and friends, all expelled from their university positions, continue to meet—secretly and in constant fear of discovery. The children of all such "unmentionable" intellectuals are excluded from universities and condemned to lives of menial labor.

Furthermore, a vast number of the more important talents (for example, Milan Kundera, Pavel Kohout, Josef Skvorecky) have been forced into exile. Of the lively theater and cinema—important as they have been for contemporary culture—only fragments remain in Czechoslovakia. The ban extends to musicians who have displeased the authorities, including the celebrated pop group Plastic People, recently imprisoned for several years. Of my own colleagues, almost all have been forced out of their universities into degrading and miserable occupations, and almost nobody remains within the universities whom it would be instructive for me to meet.

I labor the point simply to raise the obvious question: Under these circumstances, what conceivable relation can exist between a Western and a Czechoslovak university that would benefit either the Western visitor or the true defender of Czech literature, art, and culture? In fact, to maintain official relations and to accept the humiliating terms imposed by them is, under these circumstances, simply to betray one's colleagues and to betray the culture that they have nobly fought to preserve but which only exists in persecuted form.

Two exceptions to the foregoing generalizations should always be borne in mind: namely, Poland and Hungary, in both of which the universities enjoy a degree of autonomy that allows the Western visitor to speak openly about his true intellectual concerns and permits the Polish or Hungarian visitor to come to the West without the party instantly turning him into an agent. But these exceptions should serve to remind us of another important truth: An immense amount of knowledge is necessary when dealing with the Soviet bloc countries; we must know the terrain and know *with whom we are dealing*. This means that we should always proceed cautiously with an eye for the real but hidden chance—the chance to speak the truth to the people of the land and, especially, to the educated, in whose mind truth may germinate.

In practical terms, this entails the following:

1. We should approach each country of the Soviet bloc individually, using whatever opportunities locally exist to communicate with the people of that country. We should see this communication as a major part of our diplomatic endeavor since, until it can be achieved, we shall always be at a gross disadvantage in our diplomatic relations with the bloc.

2. We should be wary of official exchanges and be especially careful of visitors coming from the USSR to the West. We should remember that such a visitor cannot effectively serve as an ambassador for the West on his return; on the contrary, he is likely to be used to add his voice to the propaganda war.

3. We should encourage those who go to official institutions (particularly, cultural institutions) to make contacts at unofficial gatherings, give lectures in private apartments, and offer what support they can to their colleagues who have been victimized for refusing to become agents of the system. (I will discuss *how* this can be achieved below.)

4. Our embassies should provide as many resources as possible (information, books, records, films) that can be used by the ordinary citizens of the countries in question, and every effort should be made to ensure that such citizens can have access to such resources without being in danger. (I also discuss this point below.)

5. In the event that a Western national is arrested—for giving a lecture in a private house, making contact with dissidents, carrying in books that the authorities (in violation of the Helsinki Accords) forbid to cross their borders—our embassies should react more strongly than they have in the past.

Recently, one of the most notable features of Western diplomacy in Eastern Europe has been the incredible feebleness and trepidation with which it has been conducted. In March 1985 an American military officer was actually shot dead in East Germany, and nothing perceivable has been done in response. Hundreds of others suffer harassment and persecution, with the full knowledge that, when the crunch comes, their embassies will only use low-level threats to secure their release.

In one case, however, a Western government behaved properly. This is the case of Jacques Derrida who, visiting Prague under the auspices of an educational foundation, gave a lecture to a private seminar at the foundation's request. He was arrested, and drugs were found in his luggage (they obviously had been planted there by the secret police). He was imprisoned, and criminal proceedings were begun against him, the outcome of which threatened to be extremely serious. Fortunately, the Czech police had not done their homework; they were ignorant of the fact that Derrida is regarded as France's most distinguished philosopher. President Mitterrand took the measures that under such circumstances should always be taken: He summoned the Czech ambassador and threatened to reconsider diplomatic relations if Derrida were not instantly released.

This threat of rupture should never be lightly made; however, it must always be contemplated, since diplomatic relations between East and West are *far more important* to the communist party and its global plan than they are to the West. Indeed, if these relations did not exist, we should be able to defend ourselves easily against Soviet subversion, terrorism, and disinformation, while the communist party would suffer an immense propaganda defeat in the eyes of its own subjects and would lose access to precious information and resources.

It is not necessary to resort to severance of relations as a deterrent to lawless behavior; it is possible, however, to act as rational people normally do, which is to reciprocate. Every time a citizen of a Western country is harassed in a Soviet bloc country for activities that are provably lawful (indeed, in the cases I have in mind, sanctioned by the Helsinki Accords), similar treatment should be meted out to a national of a bloc country in the West. Since such a national is likely to be an agent of the communist party (unless he is a Pole or a Hungarian), this would have immediate repercussions. I am only suggesting this; clearly the details of any incident should be carefully studied by those with the relevant competence before embarking on any action. However, diplomacy that denies itself the possibility of retaliation is, in the present case, powerless to influence the other side.

The above brief summary of positive suggestions for public diplomacy raises some important questions about (1) the extreme difficulty of making contact with unofficial organizations and cultural activities in the Soviet bloc, (2) the restrictions placed on our embassies, and (3) the dangers presented to the bloc citizen by the contacts that I have been contemplating. I will briefly deal with each of these in turn.

UNOFFICIAL CONTACTS

In the West there are several organizations and trusts that maintain unofficial contacts and lend support to those engaged in independent cultural, scholarly, and religious activities. Such trusts operate often with little financial help and only through the dedication of their members. Naturally, they cannot risk a high profile in the West for fear of endangering their contacts in the East. Nevertheless, they continue to operate and to use whatever links are available to send visitors and materials behind the Iron Curtain. Such groups deserve the support of Western governments, and their efforts should be regarded as necessary to a full diplomatic engagement.

Furthermore, the Helsinki Accords supposedly guarantee, under "Basket 3," the legality and security of the activities undertaken by these trusts and by those who make contact with them. Either this agreement means nothing—in which case it should be repudiated—or it means something—in which case, again, it must be invoked or enforced in the normal way by making its violation more costly than its implementation. Only an aggressive diplomacy can guarantee the protection offered by the accords; without such diplomacy the accords are nothing more than a shameful fraud.

It should always be remembered that communism has a fearful enemy that stalks its territories: religion. Under the present Roman Catholic pope, the citizens of Eastern Europe have woken to their ancestral religion and allegiances, and increasingly the subjects of the Soviet Union are recognizing the Orthodox Church and the official Moslem clergy for what they are—sophisticated KGB front men who have the control, rather than the propagation, of religious sentiment as their goal. Religion presents a vehicle for feelings, knowledge, and resolve that run counter to the Great Communist Plan, and our embassies should never neglect this vital link that ties us to the peoples of the East. Communist penetration of Western churches has indeed proceeded apace, but it is still possible to find the occasional churchman in the West who is prepared to make contact with the genuine congregations of the Eastern bloc, even if he has to meet them in cellars, barns, or fields.

Protection of Our Embassies

It has never ceased to amaze me that we tolerate the grossest asymmetries in treatment between our respective missions. In London the Soviet bloc embassies are entirely serviced by their own personnel and are utterly closed to outside interference. At the same time, trade, cultural, and sporting missions occupy premises scattered all over London and send their staffs on trouble-free errands about the country. Meanwhile, our embassies in the East are frequently serviced by local residents; their buildings are narrowly restricted and thoroughly bugged; and their staff are closely followed wherever they go. Obviously the status of an embassy as sovereign territory is a ruling principle of effective diplomacy; hence, our embassies in the Soviet bloc must be as well insulated from outside interference as possible.

Moreover, every effort should be made to ensure that a local citizen could visit some part of the mission (a cultural establishment, for example) without risking everything. For instance, the British Council enjoys a relationship with Poland that enables Polish citizens freely to use its library. This is a peculiarity that arises from unique historical circumstances. Nevertheless, every effort should be made to secure similar arrangements elsewhere.

PROTECTION OF THE
SOVIET BLOC CITIZEN

This is the most difficult task of all. However, unless we are able to consider it, we shall not have taken to its conclusion the public diplomacy that is truly beneficial to us.

The only protection that can be offered to the Soviet subject by a Western government is maximum publicity combined with diplomatic pressure. In both cases, we have been predictably feeble. Consider, again, the Helsinki Accords. In response to these accords, brave citizens in the Eastern bloc—notably, from the Helsinki Watch Committee in the USSR and Charter 77 in Czechoslovakia—undertook to do what could be done to ensure that the agreement was lawfully applied in their countries. In every case, those who have taken part in these organizations have been persecuted—often by imprisonment or, in the USSR, by psychiatric "treatment." The record of this event is one of the most depressing in the annals of modern history. There is only one correct Western response to the behavior of the Eastern bloc countries: Threaten total repudiation of the agreement if the persecutions did not stop. Not to make that threat is simply to connive at this new persecution—a persecution that the agreement itself had made possible.

In general, we have to be prepared to make maximum publicity for every case in which a citizen of the Eastern bloc countries is "unjustly prosecuted." The information is still gathered by VONS in Czechoslovakia, the Independent News Services in Poland, and similar organizations elsewhere in the bloc. This information should form an important part of our broadcasts to the East and should be made widely available to the citizens of the Soviet empire; that is, records of trials, names of victims, sentences bestowed. Presently, very little broadcasting time is devoted to this exercise, but it is certain to cause enormous discomfort to the communist parties and considerable relief to our persecuted friends.

16

PUBLIC DIPLOMACY, SOVIET-STYLE

Gerhard Wettig

According to the Soviets, international relations are subdivided into two categories: (1) interstate relations and (2) relations at the societal level. The first category refers to government-to-government contacts, that is, the generally accepted view developed in the modern age. Contacts at the societal level, on the other hand, constitute a mode of interaction that is peculiar to the Soviet Union and the countries within its power sphere. This second category is not familiar to analysts and politicians in the West and, therefore, tends to be overlooked—with dire consequences for Western policies vis-à-vis the USSR and its political clientele.

NATO's dual-track decision of 12 December 1979 provides a case in point. It all started when two social democratic leaders, James Callaghan and Helmut Schmidt, felt that the Soviet Union was about to upset the military equilibrium in the European theater by deploying numerous SS-20s and demanded that United States President Jimmy Carter do something about it. At the Guadeloupe summit in early January 1979, the two men finally succeeded. However, they did not favor Western counterarmament, since that would further escalate the arms race spiral. What they deemed appropriate was a serious attempt to negotiate the SS-20s away; it is this notion that sparked the dual-track approach.

The USSR would be confronted with the prospect that either NATO would follow the example of a Soviet buildup or Moscow would have to abandon its deployment program. Callaghan, Schmidt, and Carter were confident that, if it was faced with such a choice, the Kremlin would certainly prefer equilibrium at a lower level to one that would force both sides to higher levels, necessitating higher matériel and political costs.

The Western calculus seemed convincing, but it proved utterly wrong. The Soviet leaders felt that NATO had little chance to confront them with the intended dilemma, since they could undercut Western resolve to counter the SS-20 deployments. Moreover, Callaghan, Schmidt, and Carter seemed clearly disinclined to deploy the 572 missiles to counter the USSR buildup if need be. Soviet leaders were confident that they could prevent their Western counterparts from doing what the NATO alliance hesitatingly wanted, namely, by mobilizing sufficient Western public pressure against the venture so that the USSR would continue its arms buildup and NATO would be unable to initiate the envisioned countermeasures. If Western resolve were to prove stronger than anticipated and NATO's intermediate-range nuclear force (INF) modernization program should materialize—as was ultimately the case, contrary to Gromyko's forecasts—then the West would at least have to pay a high political price, in terms of considerably weakening its domestic support for defense.

If Western statesmen had studied more closely patterns in USSR foreign policy or had listened more attentively to expert advice, they would have known that Soviet leaders were unlikely to succumb to an undesired choice, offered at the diplomatic level, but would seek to circumvent their dilemma by promoting intra-Western mass action against those governments that attempted to impose the choice upon their respective publics. In general, USSR foreign policy attempts to supplement interstate relations with the West by means of concerted activities at the societal level in Western countries. As has been stated, the Soviet Union "does not address only one but two addresses," that is, "both governments and peoples" of the Western states in order to "further its political goals simultaneously *from above* and *from below*" (italics added).[1]

This dual foreign policy means that the Kremlin cultivates businesslike relations with Western governments (often termed "cooperative" relations), while the Western public is galvanized for pressuring those very governments. Soviet attitudes toward Chancellor Schmidt's government in the early 1980s are an example. The Brezhnev leadership was pleased that Helmut Schmidt was reluctant to join the United States in countering the USSR following the invasion of Afghanistan and that the social democratic leader wanted to "promote East-West dialogue in a period of speechlessness" (that is, he continued the policy of détente in spite of both the Carter and Reagan administrations' opposition). The Soviets did everything possible to organize societal forces in the Federal Republic against Schmidt's commitment to INF deployment and to weaken his government domestically; they believed that leftist "peace forces" would take over after Schmidt (a stunning miscalculation as it turned out).

The second level of USSR foreign-policy making ("from below") vis-à-vis the West is not public diplomacy as this concept is understood in the West. In Soviet parlance, the term *ideological struggle* is applicable; that is, to amplify rather than tone down relations under the auspices of "peaceful coexistence" and "relaxation of tensions." This is in complete opposition to the manner in which Western-style public relations is conducted. The USSR intention is to create a favorable public environment for Soviet policymaking at the intergovernmental level; in accordance with the principle of "unity of theory and practice," Soviet propaganda is viewed in Western societies as political action. Ever since the founding of Lenin's newspaper *Iskra* (The Spark), the organizing center of the political struggle waged by his party, Soviet-type communists have practiced propaganda as a political war against their opponents—termed "peaceful" only because armed force is not involved.

Such public diplomacy (a most inappropriate term in this case) means mobilizing, organizing, and as much as possible, controlling political forces in Western societies in order to exploit them for the attainment of definite Soviet purposes. The general goal is to promote conflict among Western countries and to weaken them internally vis-à-vis the USSR and its allies. The issue and government targets depend on the needs of Soviet foreign policy at a given moment. From the autumn of 1979 through the end of 1984, the central issue was prevention of United States INF deployments. Since then, protest against the American Strategic Defense Initiative (SDI) research program has been the target. Wherever and whenever possible, the Soviets and their local agents seek to convert contemporary protesters into organized followers who are under the reliable and permanent control of front organizations.

USSR propaganda in Western countries is a form of direct policy action. When Moscow's polemics concentrated on NATO's proposed INF deployments during the period 1979–1983, the practical purpose was to force the governments of the countries in which deployment was planned to abandon such plans. Soviet leaders did indeed feel that the West European peace movement, which they sought both to bols er and channel, would prevent deployment in key countries (particularly in West Germany), regardless of what respective governments wanted to do.

Already existing and ad hoc front organizations propagate the USSR viewpoint and press for its realization under the guise of independence. Disinformation is spread throughout noncommunist channels in order to mislead the Western public. Even more deceptive, however, is ideologically framed Soviet rhetoric itself. As perceptively described during the late 1940s in George Orwell's *1984*, key political terms are redefined by the USSR to convey a different, often completely opposite meaning to the Western public, which unlike communist cadres, is unaware of the intricacies of Soviet newspeak.[2]

For example, Moscow continuously asserted that it stood for parity while American bids for superiority endangered peace. To largely credit the USSR while blaming the United States was a crucial psychopolitical factor for the West European peace movement; on the basis of Soviet definitions, it was clear to initiated cadres that this meant that the Kremlin leaders were not willing to relinquish the superior military position they had previously claimed in Europe and actually sought to enhance that position.

As previously noted, Soviet propaganda in the West centers on an unrelenting struggle with the West; it implies alliance strategies, as prescribed in detail by any relevant Soviet textbook.[3] What emerges is always a dual-patterned strategy. On the one hand, the communists and their front organizations are not allowed to waver in the principled stand made obligatory for them by the USSR; that is, the goals and purposes underlying the allied common action may not be discussed, let alone questioned, or compromised. On the other hand, this is posited without an explanation of common ground between the communists and their noncommunist allies, which calls for some undefined common action.

Consequently, the communists (who, as Soviet textbooks incessantly emphasize, always take the lead and do their best to achieve that purpose through whatever means available and as inconspicuously as possible) never state the political motivations that underlie their actions and recommendations. Often their noncommunist allies do not really see the hidden rationale and allow themselves to be exploited for the attainment of goals with which they would otherwise not identify.

The illusion of common interests that the communists seek to convey to their Western "allies" allows the pro-Soviet side—even if it is infinitely inferior numerically, as it usually is—to control not only the political orientation but also crucial practical actions of its noncommunist "partners." In addition, superior organizational skills, maximum discipline, and vast financial resources provided by the USSR and other East bloc states contribute to the success of the pro-Soviet cadres vis-à-vis their "allies," particularly if these groups are as unorganized as most peace movements are.

Another asymmetry favoring the USSR is the basic pattern of the ideological struggle itself. As the late chief ideologue Mikhail Suslov noted, this struggle against Western democracies is waged between the East and West within Western societies but not within Eastern societies. Consequently, the USSR and other socialist countries must keep whatever influence from capitalist countries is deemed undesirable and dangerous out of their territories.[4] The concept of the ideological struggle to be fought in Western countries is supplemented by a concept of anti-Western seclusion for the Soviet power sphere. This is intended to provide an East-West political pattern that allows change to take place only at the expense of capitalism in favor of "socialism," but not vice versa. This is supportive of the Soviet thesis that history is setting the stage for the gradual worldwide transition to what Moscow calls socialism.

In contrast to public diplomacy as practiced by the West, USSR propaganda operations are not ventures that sell foreign policies after they have been decided upon. Instead, propaganda has been an integral part of Soviet foreign policy and the Kremlin's decisionmaking process from its inception. Officials responsible for intergovernmental and intra-Western societal action are represented in both the Politburo, which handles all relevant foreign policy decisions, and in the Defense Council, which, among other tasks, prepares all policies relating to arms negotiations. This same pattern is repeated down the bureaucratic ladder to the daily policymaking level.

For instance, the Soviet delegation at the Geneva INF negotiations during the period 1981–83 received its daily instructions from a body that was chaired by (then) Foreign Minister Gromyko and staffed by representatives from both the foreign and defense ministries; the head of the CPSU's International Information Department (responsible for open foreign propaganda); the deputy chairman of the CPSU's International Department (responsible for instructing communist parties and front organizations in the West and for any type of "gang" action conducted through them); and the head of the KGB's Directorate A (responsible for "black action" in Western countries).[5] In other words, the line adopted by Soviet arms negotiators was formulated by a committee that was bound to have considered not only the diplomatic advantages and disadvantages of certain negotiating stances but also the propagandistic pros and cons of whatever the Soviet delegation might have been ordered to do.

Such a pattern of decisionmaking implies that propaganda considerations can, and do, often take precedence over diplomatic needs, as evidenced by the INF negotiations. In July 1982 Soviet chief negotiator

Iulii Kvitsinskii returned to Moscow with a tentative compromise that he and his American counterpart Paul Nitze privately envisioned; he learned that his superior had rejected not only this compromise but also any conceivable compromise. Much to the chagrin of the Soviet military—who would have welcomed a "compromise" that would have helped the United States to save face but would have provided for a Soviet INF near-monopoly in Europe—the Politburo had ruled under Andropov's aegis (Brezhnev was no longer operative by that time) that no agreement that allowed for a single Pershing II or cruise missile to be deployed in Western Europe was acceptable. Instead, the Soviet leadership preferred no agreement whatsoever. The majority opinion concurred that the USSR had committed itself, vis-à-vis its "friends" in Western Europe (that is, communist parties and peace movements), not to accept the deployments of any American missiles in Western Europe.[6]

Moscow's propagandistic credibility was at stake, and consequently, the Soviet Union could not afford the slightest flexibility at the Geneva talks, despite the possible diplomatic benefits to be reaped from such flexibility. The underlying conviction shaped the decision to invest all Soviet hopes in the West European peace movement, which, as leading foreign affairs officials were increasingly confident, would force the West European governments to abstain from deploying American missiles in their respective countries.

A peculiar pattern of USSR foreign-policy making emerges. Diplomatic action and the political struggle within Western countries are the complementary parts of Soviet *Westpolitik*, which is devised and implemented as a concerted effort on two different levels of action. The obvious purpose is to expose Western governments to Soviet influence and bring pressure to bear from two directions: from the usual interaction between states and from the West's domestic front. In doing so, USSR leaders seek to exploit the vulnerabilities of the open nature of Western societies to the maximum benefit of the USSR; the Soviets correctly believe that the Western side is unable to reciprocate, given the tightly controlled, closed nature of societies within the USSR's orbit.

There is no panacea for the asymmetry dilemma confronting the West, but the problem could at least be eased if Western politicians and communicators would finally become cognizant of it and would be willing to take action. Western analysts should closely examine the overt and covert activities of the Soviets and their "stooges" in Western countries; expose them to the public eye wherever and whenever feasible; and deny them the benefit of unreciprocated forums for their propaganda actions. At the same time, Western governments should no longer devise policies without initially thinking about the propaganda implications.

The handling of President Reagan's Strategic Defense Initiative (SDI) provides a negative example. When the initiative was announced in March 1983, no allied government (and, indeed, hardly anyone within the Reagan administration) had been informed about the driving motive and the implied purpose of SDI. To make matters worse, there was a great deal of ambiguity and conflict about what was intended by the initiators. For two years, no consistent rationale emerged. Allied governments and their publics were kept in the dark about what to expect from SDI.

Consequently, it was a splendid opportunity to develop the "Star Wars" theme and the "Star Peace" postulate as instruments of a propaganda war with the objective of stopping SDI and thereby preserving a Soviet monopoly on strategic defense developments that the USSR had sought during the preceding decade. Before Washington had even charted a course of action and subsequently provided public explanation of SDI, Moscow's propaganda was already actively denouncing its adversary's new strategic defense concept by unilaterally "misdefining" what SDI allegedly meant and entailed. Hence, the Soviets exploited the period during which Washington was formulating its SDI program and public relations by successfully conveying to Western, primarily West European, audiences an offensive armament image of the United States. When the U.S. had finally developed its policy and explanation of SDI, public opinion already had been molded by the opposing side.

Presently, few West Europeans are aware that the USSR has heavily invested in antimissile and antisatellite programs since the conclusion of the ABM Treaty; that the United States, therefore, has every reason to be concerned about the possibility of a future Soviet breakout from the treaty; and that, consequently, something must be done to counter such a possibility. If one argues that the Soviets already are engaged in antimissile and antisatellite activities and that this constitutes a challenge requiring a response, one generally encounters utter incredulity, even among those who claim expert knowledge in the field.

The analysis of the preceding pages suggests some methods for Western governments to deal with Soviet foreign policy:

1. It should be recognized that relations with Western countries are seen and handled as an ongoing struggle by the Soviet leadership. Compromise and conciliation are not part of Moscow's pro-

gram of dealing with the Western "antagonist." Instead, unrelenting hostility is the basic underlying attitude toward Western democracies that, by their very existence, pose a fundamental and inescapable challenge to "socialism." Compromise and conciliation may be appropriate, and even necessary, at times but only at a tactical level, that is, as a temporary arrangement as a result of what is required by a momentary force relationship. Détente is viewed in that light, and Western nations should not expect otherwise from the USSR.

2. As the Kremlin operates at both the interstate East-West level and the societal intra-Western level, the governments of NATO and other Western countries should initially consider their actions and reactions within that dual context. Soviet propaganda should be viewed as a pervasive characteristic of USSR foreign policy that is interrelated with diplomatic moves. Any Western decision should be judged not only for its diplomatic merits but also with regard to the "ideological struggle" that Moscow wages against the West.

3. The Western response to this "struggle" cannot simply duplicate, in order to reciprocate, USSR goals in that realm. After all, there is a distinctive difference between Soviet communism and Western democracy. The West must never resort to Moscow's practice of manipulating unsuspecting audiences and societal forces by means of propaganda and fronts. Instead, Western governments should expose the transparency of Soviet political strategies and tactics.

4. At the societal level the Soviet Union enjoys a unilateral advantage over the West by virtue of the latter's open nature as opposed to the USSR's repressive and reclusive nature. This advantage must be reduced; however, the West cannot and will not use Eastern societies as a political battlefield comparable to the Kremlin's view of Western (notably, West European) societies. But the West can and should break the official Soviet information monopoly in the East to provide Eastern publics with officially withheld information that will, in turn, allow them to dispute the *nomenklatura*'s informational control over them. This can best be achieved by means of transgressing honest information across borders that will contrast with the manipulative content of Soviet propaganda.

5. In dealing with the USSR's confrontational stance, Western countries have an opportunity to transform fundamentally, in the long-term, the present East-West relationship into a more peaceful and conciliatory one. If the Soviet leadership realizes that its handling of the relationship is being effectively countered and, there-

fore, no longer offers success, it will gradually be induced to consider less frustrating alternatives.

NOTES

1. V. Kuznetsov, "Mir i demokratiia," *Novoe vremia* 13 (1983): 5.

2. See Gerhard Wettig, "Greetings from Big Brother: Orwellian Patterns of the Soviet 'Struggle for Peace and Disarmament,'" in Shlomo Giora Shoham and Francis Rosenstiel, eds., *And He Loved Big Brother* (London: The Council of Europe, Macmillan, 1985), pp. 53–62.

3. The basic textbook for societal action in Western Europe was written after the international communist party conference of 1969: V. V. Zagladin, ed., *Mirovoe kommunisticheskoe dvizhenie* (Moscow: Politizdat, 1970). This book has been translated into most relevant West European languages and has been re-edited and used by communist parties loyal to Moscow. It has been recurrently updated with supplementary information.

4. Speech by M. Suslov, published in *Pravda*, 14 July 1973.

5. Paul H. Nitze, "Living with the Soviets," *Foreign Affairs* 63, no. 2 (Winter 1984–85): 362.

6. See Paul H. Nitze, "Negotiating with the Soviets," *Department of State Bulletin* 84, no. 2089 (August 1984): 36.

Concluding Remarks

Philip Habib

Having attended the sessions of this workshop, I have a fair appreciation of the talents of this distinguished group. I am personally delighted that a meeting of this sort has included several active bureaucrats, so that a degree of responsibility is represented—instead of the usual occurrence in such intellectual halls where those who *don't* or *can't* or *haven't* or *don't want to* sit back and criticize those who *do*. It is a pleasure, therefore, to find that those of us who are not out of the business do not have to defend the bureaucracy—the bureaucracy is with us. This is a good thing; those of you who are returning to campuses and think tanks should keep that in mind. In some of my other functions since retiring, I have kept this in mind.

My first exposure to public diplomacy was in 1950–51, when I was serving at my first post. I was the third secretary at the American embassy in Canada—the last person on the list in the diplomatic corps. I was the assistant agricultural attaché. Evidently, the ambassador liked the way I wrote about the egg and poultry situation in Ontario, and he dragooned me into being one of his speech writers. A secretary in the political section and I traveled with the ambassador, Stanley Woodward, a political appointee and a marvelous old fellow who had been a former foreign service officer. Stanley loved to travel and make speeches throughout Canada. In the period 1950–51 (the beginning of the Cold War and the Korean War) American diplomats abroad were busy explaining United States policy, as they still are today, but in a context of the Cold War's beginnings. Stanley was such an inveterate traveler that he gave a lot of speeches; his public diplomacy consisted of traveling around the country and attempting to convince Canadians (there were many critics of the United States) that what we were doing in the world was right.

Well, after we had written ten to fifteen speeches, we had depleted our supply of things to say. But one day I told my fellow speech writer that I had a solution; I had found something in my reading that we could use. I had been reading the *Philippics* of Demosthenes: If we inserted the Soviet Union in place of Macedonia, and instead of Phillip, we inserted Stalin, we could crib paragraphs. (And if one does that, there is nobody better than Demosthenes.) So, I cribbed entire paragraphs, stuck them into Stanley's speeches, and he gave them across Canada—nobody ever caught on to it. Well, that was my first exposure to public diplomacy.

During the course of this workshop, there has been a certain feeling among practitioners of the art of public diplomacy that, somewhere along the line, foreign policy rather than public diplomacy is lacking. At this meeting I have heard the following refrain: "Somebody ought to tell us what the issues are." (This was in one paper—I could not believe it.) If you do not know the current issues in foreign policy, I do not know where the hell you have been.

There has been a constant preoccupation with definitions: How do we define public diplomacy? There is a distinct difference between public diplomacy and public affairs. The word *diplomacy* means "outside" and has nothing to do with what you are trying to do with the American people, which is altogether different. Gaining the support of the American people for U.S. foreign policy initiatives is entirely different from attempting to pursue the interests of the United States in the foreign arena. This is what diplomacy is all about—that is, the representation of the national interest abroad.

Modern diplomacy is distinct from classical diplomacy. The diplomat as the courtier at the court, representing one sovereign to another, no longer exists. He represents his nation, his nation's people, his nation's ideals, and his nation's point of view. That is what diplomacy has become in the modern sense.

I would like to discuss the policymaking process as it affects foreign policy and as it affects public diplomacy. In our nation, the U.S. Constitution tells us that the foreign policy process starts with the presidency; the president is the arbiter of foreign policy. On the other hand, in the formulation and decisionmaking process, the executive branch *under* the direction of the president has a certain constitutional responsibility, deriving from *his* constitutional responsibility. On top of this, of course, we have the constitutional responsibilities of Congress and other government institutions. But in the manner in which our administrations develop foreign policy, the role of the executive is primary, particularly in the formulation of the decisionmaking. Within the executive, the role played by the Department of State is primary at the implementation stage.

Other agencies of the United States government have a role in the process of policymaking and implementation. The United States Information Agency (USIA) has a very clear mandate in terms of public diplomacy, which has been well emphasized at this workshop. There is no question that the National Security Council (NSC)—which includes the secretary of state, the secretary of defense, and occasionally, other cabinet members—has a very clear role in the formulation of foreign policy. And in their own special way, other departments are involved in implementation: the Department of Defense and the armed forces, the Central Intelligence Agency, the Agency for International Development, the Department of the Treasury, the Department of Agriculture, and other parts of the executive branch.

This distinction must be clarified in terms of formulation of decisionmaking and, then, implementation. When you get to the field of public diplomacy, in effect you take foreign policies as they have been formulated and translate them into some form of persuasion, education, and influence on foreign nations, and in support of the policies as they attempt to deal with the issues. But where and how does public diplomacy (or the public affairs component, if you are dealing with your own public) enter into the foreign policy process? Well, it does so at every level. Any rational policymaking process among experienced and competent people takes into account whether the policymakers have weighed the public diplomacy aspect of a decision on a given issue and whether they have considered how well it is going to play in Peoria as well as how it is going to sell in Petrograd. But what is the process that is taken into account? That is a question of how the departments are organized and how the authority asserts itself through the reaches of government.

Nobody working at the lower levels in the Department of State can think of everything. So, when it comes to the final level of decisionmaking, and the process that produces the final decision, along the line all relevant factors become involved. Anybody who does not think that happens has not watched it done. Why would you expect, or suspect, that a secretary of state with a staff would not have taken into account either the public diplomacy aspect or the public affairs counsel? It is inherent, instinctive, and involved. In addition, there are institutional ways in which that kind of consideration comes to bear. This is another futile argument that has been made over the past few days. Of course, the secretary of state considers how the thing is going to play abroad or at home, and so does everyone else with a responsible place in the process. It is a *process* that produces foreign policy; the aspects of public affairs and public diplomacy that come to fruit in the formulation of foreign policy must be translated into some kind of implementation, which requires organization.

From our discussion at this conference, the organization for the normal aspects of public diplomacy is clearly adequate. Undoubtedly, National Security Decision Directive 77 (NSDD-77) includes the organizational framework. Now whether we use it, or how we use it, can be argued. A possible additional element to the structural system in Washington might deal with the gray or black types of Soviet activity in the field of public diplomacy. This has not been adequately explored: We have sufficient means to deal with the overt aspects, but we need an instrument to contend with covert Soviet public diplomacy. We do not have a sufficiently institutionalized instrument for coping with that problem, in part because it is probably going to take more than people and thought to develop the necessary counteractions. One man, or a subcommittee of the NSC meeting, sporadically thinking about the problem is not the way we should deal with it.

During the 1950s and early 1960s I had some experience that might serve as a lesson in this regard. You may recall when we became aware of what was then known as "Soviet economic penetration" of the Third World. It was an explosive item in the intelligence community. I was involved in the first report drafted by that community during the early 1950s that attempted to catalog and analyze Soviet activity around the world in terms of economic penetration. We formed a small staff, consisting of about ten to twelve people, to decide what we were going to do about it. Divided geographically, the staff had certain capabilities. Most important, it worked for powerful men: This group started out under Douglas Dillon and ended up under George Ball. So there was access to the upper echelons.

The ideas that we originated to counter the USSR were easy to translate into policy at a high level. We had few successes and many failures—obviously because that was not the way to deal with the problem. Our group formulated the policy to deal with the Congo's independence (1960–61); although the chances of the Congo going the other way were great at that time, our policy turned out to be successful. We were not prepared, the Congo was not prepared, and Western Europe was not prepared to deal with the problem when the Belgians were pulling out. I mention this because it is an example of a public diplomacy issue that required a form of specialized action, and the specialized group that exists under NSDD-77 has not viewed the problem in an issue-by-issue manner on a regular seven-day-a-week basis. You cannot do this in committee—at least not from my past experience.

Turning to the present, what kind of world are we likely to face in the foreseeable future? Well, obviously, in terms of foreign policy, we will face continuing competition between the Soviet Union and the United States. This competition is not going to disappear; I prefer to use the term *competition* as opposed to *confrontation*. It does not have to be thought of as conflict in the sense of ongoing hostility, but rather as an ongoing competition for influence and presence throughout the world. Its fundamental nature will not change.

The foundation of American foreign policy is easily stated: the pursuit of peace, not simply the absence of conflict since that is not our definition of peace. You have to consider how nations live together in some degree of harmony, so that they have mechanisms to avoid conflict. And thus in their activities, they contribute to some sense of world order as well as to the social, economic, and political development of their own people. This is what peace means to me. That is the foundation, the basic objective, of American foreign policy.

The issues with which this policy has to deal in the future are clear. First, the United States and its allies have to find a means of managing their relations with the Soviet Union. This is not just a question of strategic arms reduction, of East-West commercial relations, or of linkage in the Middle East. It is a question of how to manage the totality of the relationship in order to pursue the basic purposes of American foreign policy outlined above; that is, not simply to avoid conflict but to build something that allows us to move in a direction with some degree of orderliness in a world devoid of conflict. A great deal more could be done about our relationship with the Soviet Union than is being done presently. I want to emphasize the phrase, *management of the relationship;* I use *management* deliberately because it is a question that has to be managed on a daily basis.

The second issue involves maintaining and strengthening our alliances. We have to be concerned about certain geopolitical issues. Regional, local, and bilateral disputes (wherever they occur) are undoubtedly going to be a problem that concerns the United States, because in almost every case these disputes affect our interests. We can avoid neither the relationship of our interests nor that of our allies. And we cannot avoid a sense of responsibility for trying to do something about regional, local, and bilateral disputes.

All issues involving the international economic structure are problems we must face—whether they be debt burden, financial problems, trade, economic development, the North-South issue, or the haves versus the have-nots. That great rubric of economic issues will be with us during the foreseeable future. There are other functional issues that we must also deal with: nuclear proliferation, environmental problems, terrorism, human rights, technology transfer (both in economic and security terms). Finally, we will have crises and crisis management to contend with. It is inevitable that somewhere there will be another crisis that is going to be a part of the foreign policy problem. How will this crisis be dealt with, and how will the structural requirement in Washington grapple with it?

In all of this, public diplomacy and public affairs play a role if you accept, define, expand, refine the elements of risk involved. As we pursue our national interests and those of our allies in the field of foreign policy, these are the kinds of issues with which public diplomacy must deal.

Public diplomacy is not confined to how we treat the Soviet Union, because public diplomacy is applied on a global scale. It is probably just as important to have a rational policy of public diplomacy toward the Third World as it is to have one toward the USSR. Part of the struggle (that is, the competition) with the Soviet Union is going to be universal; the capacity of Moscow to reach almost anywhere in the world with its military power, and its political and economic capabilities, is such that competition in any corner of the world is clearly to be anticipated.

As we approach the problem of "how do we deal?" and the explanation of "what we are up to as a nation," I would say that, internally, the public affairs aspect is easy to define. We must keep the American public informed, in both the implementation and the formulation of foreign policy, since we must have an informed and willing American public. President Harry Truman used to say that the foreign policy of the United States rests upon the support of the public. Fortunately, our public has that capability; it is neither naive nor innocent. In the mass, the American people usually come down on the right side in foreign policy. When based upon whatever degree of information has been handed to them, they manage to accumulate enough knowledge to see what the issues are. It is not a question of whether some redneck in North Carolina or some logger in Idaho understands the ramifications of foreign policy—that is not public opinion. Public opinion is a *national* response to knowledge and events.

As I have traveled around this country for the past year and a half since my retirement, I have probably spoken to 50,000 or 60,000 people across the United States. I do not find ignorance out there; I do not find any lack of interest. I have spoken to all sorts of audiences: trade union-ists, university students, special interest groups, business groups, pub-lic organizations, and churches. The capacity of the American people to deal with these issues is much greater than intellectuals are likely to give them credit for.

Their confidence that they understand what they are being told and have the ability to react to it is only shaken by one thing—their lack of confidence in elected and appointed officials. This is a fact. I am not sure what the polls show these days, but there is no doubt in my mind—and it is not simply a Vietnam syndrome. It is partly a result of the fact that we do not have any bipartisanship of the sort we used to have in foreign policy, which affects the public perception of how the government runs. In part, it is Watergate, Vietnam, Abscam, and Koreagate. But you scratch that thing out there, and you find it is a lack of confidence not only in officials but also in what government is doing, which is even worse. This is something that those of us in the field must try to do something about.

About the Contributors

Elie Abel, Chandler Professor of Communication at Stanford University, had been a working journalist for a quarter century before he entered teaching, coming to Stanford after nine years as dean of journalism at Columbia University. Among his other books, he is the author of *The Missile Crisis* and editor of *What's News: The Media in American Society.*

Catherine P. Ailes manages the science policy and strategic economics program at SRI International in Washington, D.C. She is coauthor of *The Science Race: Training and Utilization of Scientists and Engineers, U.S. and USSR* and, most recently, of *Cooperation in Science and Technology: An Evaluation of the U.S.-Soviet Agreement.*

Kathleen C. Bailey is a consultant specializing in international affairs, public diplomacy, and arms control issues. Previously, she served as deputy director for the office of research at the U.S. Information Agency and, before that, as associate division leader for international assessments at the Lawrence Livermore National Laboratory. Her doctoral dissertation was based on research at the National Iranian Oil Company in Tehran.

James H. Billington has been director of the Woodrow Wilson International Center for Scholars in Washington, D.C., since 1973. He previously taught at Harvard and Princeton, and has been chairman of the Board of Foreign Scholarships (the Fulbright Program). His publications include *The Icon and the Axe: An Interpretative History of Russian Culture* and *Fire in the Minds of Men: Origins of the Revolutionary Faith.*

Richard E. Bissell is executive editor of *The Washington Quarterly* and adjunct professor of government at Georgetown University. Formerly, he served as director of research and of program development at the U.S. Information Agency. He is author or editor of *Strategic Dimensions of Economic Behavior* and three books on Africa.

Mark Blitz is a senior professional staff member for the Committee on Foreign Relations of the United States Senate. Previously he had been director at the office of private sector programs, U.S. Information Agency and, before that, assistant director of ACTION. He is author of *Heidegger's "Being and Time" and the Possibility of Political Philosophy.*

Stanton Burnett is counselor of the U.S. Information Agency. Previously he had worked for NBC and several radio stations as well as newspapers, and taught political science at Hobart and William Smith Colleges. Among his other government assignments, he had been counselor for public affairs in Rome and at the U.S. Mission to NATO. In Washington, D.C., he also served as director for European affairs and director of research at USIA.

John R. Clingerman has been director for African affairs at the U.S. Information Agency since June 1983. A career foreign service officer, he served overseas as economic officer in Kinshasa and principal officer in Kisangani, Zaire; deputy chief of mission in Cotonou, Benin, and Lusaka, Zambia; political officer in Brussels, Belgium; and U.S. ambassador to Lesotho.

John J. Dziak has served at the Defense Intelligence Agency since 1965, specializing in Soviet political-military affairs. A member of the senior executive service, currently he is on leave-of-absence as director of DIA's international applications office to write a history of the Soviet intelligence and security services. His other books include *Soviet Perceptions of Military Doctrine and Military Power.*

Hugh Fallis joined the staff of Radio Liberty in 1964 and was appointed vice president for engineering and technical operations at Radio Free Europe/Radio Liberty (RFE-RL, Inc.) four years ago. Recently, he directed development of a ten-year plan for modernizing transmitting stations to improve and establish new coverage.

Robert B. Fenwick is chairman of the board and former president of BR Communications in Sunnyvale, California, with which he has been associated since 1966. For his doctorate at Stanford, he specialized in high-frequency "shortwave" radio propagation. This interest has continued, both professionally for military and diplomatic communications and in a National Research Council study on the Voice of America's system upgrade program.

Edwin J. Feulner, Jr. has been president of The Heritage Foundation in Washington, D.C., since 1975 and is chairman of the U.S. Advisory Commission on Public Diplomacy. Formerly, he served as executive director of the Republican Study Committee in the U.S. House of Representatives, confidential assistant to Secretary of Defense Melvin R. Laird, and administrative assistant to Congressman Philip M. Crane. His numerous publications include *Congress and the New International Order, U.S.-Japan Mutual Security,* and *China: The Turning Point.*

Monique Garnier-Lançon resides in Paris, France, and is vice president and director of foreign relations at the European Institute for Security, co-president of the Western European Defense Association, and special adviser for Europe to the American Foreign Policy Council.

Philip C. Habib joined the U.S. Foreign Service in 1949. He served in Canada, New Zealand, Trinidad, Korea, and France. Ambassador Habib has been under secretary of state for political affairs and special presidential envoy to the Middle East. After retirement, he became a senior research fellow at the Hoover Institution and currently is president of the World Affairs Council of Northern California.

Walter Hahn is editor-in-chief of *Strategic Review* and vice president of the United States Strategic Institute. Formerly, he worked at the Institute for Defense Analyses in Washington, D.C., and the Foreign Policy Research Institute at the University of Pennsylvania.

Ronald H. Hinckley, senior fellow at The National Strategy Information Center, previously had served as director of special studies for the National Security Council's crisis management center; chairman of the foreign opinion review advisory group (1983–85); and special assistant to the director of the White House office of planning and evaluation. He has published in the areas of public opinion and decision support systems for national security decisionmaking.

Friedrich Hoess, former Austrian ambassador to Australia and New Zealand, is a member of parliament in Vienna. He is doctor of laws from the University of Vienna and specializes in international law and the German question.

Walter Jajko did graduate work in East European studies at Columbia University. Since 1980, he has been involved with policymaking to counter Soviet active measures and currently is director of the special advisory staff, office of the deputy under secretary for policy, Department of Defense. He holds the rank of brigadier general, U.S. Air Force (Reserve).

Lisa Jameson is senior political commentator at the Voice of America and previously served as deputy chief in its USSR division, responsible for planning and programming broadcasts to the Soviet Union. A specialist in foreign relations, she has graduate degrees in Slavic languages and history. Her essays, articles, and translations have been widely published.

Michael S. Joyce is executive director and trustee of the John M. Olin Foundation. Previously, he had been director of the Institute for Educational Affairs; executive director of the Morris Goldseker Foundation; and assistant director at the Educational Research Council of America. He has served on the executive committee of the President's Private Sector Survey on Cost Control, the National Productivity Advisory Committee, and the presidential Task Force on Private Sector Initiatives.

Lucio Leante is an Italian journalist specializing in East-West issues, notably in Soviet foreign policy. He holds a NATO fellowship for research on Soviet indirect strategies toward Western Europe and is analyzing Soviet propaganda. He is a staff editor for the Italian news agency ANSA and contributes regularly to the monthly magazine *Mondo Operaio*. He also contributed to the Italian weekly magazine *Il Mondo* from 1980 to 1984 when he was based in Paris.

Michael A. Ledeen, senior fellow in international affairs at the Center for Strategic and International Studies in Washington, D.C., previously served as special adviser to the secretary of state. He edited a volume of Grenada documents and wrote *Grave New World*.

Richard C. Levy is deputy director of USIA-TV and a principal architect of WORLDNET, the first global satellite television network. A former special assistant to the president of Paramount Pictures International, he later served as director of foreign advertising and publicity for Avco Embassy Pictures. Among his books are *Plane Talk: The Consumer's Air Travel Guide.*

Carnes Lord is director of international studies at the National Institute for Public Policy in Fairfax, Virginia. During 1981–84, he served on the senior staff of the National Security Council as director of international communications and information policy. He has written extensively about nuclear strategy, arms control, and public diplomacy.

Henning von Löwis of Menar is a researcher, journalist, and consultant. He works for West Germany's international broadcasting stations, *Deutschland-funk* and *Deutsche Welle,* apart from teaching international relations at the University of Cologne. He is Bonn correspondent for SWABC/Windoek and author of *Namibia in the East-West Conflict.*

Gifford D. Malone, a former senior foreign service officer, retired from the Department of State in 1985. He was twice detailed to the U.S. Information Agency, first as deputy assistant director for the Soviet Union and Eastern Europe, and later as deputy and then acting associate director for programs. He is currently writing a book on public diplomacy for the Miller Center of Public Affairs at the University of Virginia.

Sig Mickelson, research fellow at the Hoover Institution, is an adjunct professor at San Diego State University. He serves on the boards of directors for Stauffer Communications Inc., Satellite Education Services Inc., and the RFE-RL Fund Inc. His previous positions included president of CBS News, director of international broadcast operations for Time Inc., and president of RFE-RL, Inc. He is author of *America's Other Voice: The Story of Radio Free Europe and Radio Liberty.*

Alfred H. Paddock, Jr., has been the military member of the policy planning staff in the Department of State since July 1984. His career included command and staff assignments in Korea, Laos, Okinawa, and Vietnam. Colonel Paddock coauthored *Organization, Missions and Command and Control of Special Forces and Ranger Units in the 1980s* and is the author of *U.S. Army Special Warfare: Its Origins.*

Jack R. Perry is director of the Dean Rusk Program in International Studies and professor of political science at Davidson College. A retired diplomat, he served as political officer in the embassies at Moscow and Paris and on the international staff of NATO; as deputy chief of mission in the Prague and Stockholm embassies; and U.S. ambassador to Bulgaria.

Allen M. Peterson serves as professor of electrical engineering at Stanford University, codirector of its Center for Radar Astronomy, and senior scientific adviser to SRI International. In addition, he is a consultant at the jet propulsion laboratories of the California Institute of Technology (NASA/JPL Advisory Council).

Bernard Roshco is director, office of opinion analysis and plans, bureau of public affairs, U.S. Department of State. He formerly edited *Public Opinion Quarterly*. In addition to numerous articles on news media and polling, Dr. Roshco is the author of a sociological study about news reporting entitled *Newsmaking*.

Alan A. Rubin serves as president for Partners of the Americas, the largest private voluntary organization promoting economic and social development and people-to-people activities in the Americas. He also is on the boards of directors for the Peace Corps Twenty-Fifth Anniversary Foundation and the Consortium for International Citizen Exchange. Since 1976, he has been a member of the United States–Mexico Bilateral Education and Cultural Commission.

Harriet Fast Scott, a consultant on Soviet military affairs, is a member of the U.S. General Advisory Committee on Arms Control and Disarmament and a senior research associate of the Advanced International Studies Institute in Washington, D.C. Her translation and analysis of Marshal V. D. Sokolovskii's *Soviet Military Strategy* is a standard reference work, as are three of her other books, coauthored with her husband, Dr. William F. Scott: *The Armed Forces of the USSR* (3d rev. ed.), *The Soviet Art of War,* and *The Soviet Control Structure: Capabilities for Wartime Survival*.

Roger Scruton, professor of aesthetics at the University of London, is a regular columnist for *The Times* and author of *The Meaning of Conservatism* and *From Descartes to Wittgenstein,* among other books.

Wallace H. Spaulding, Colonel USAR (ret.), a specialist on communist parties and front organizations for the Central Intelligence Agency, is a regular contributor to the Hoover Institution's *Yearbook on International Communist Affairs* as well as *Problems of Communism.*

Richard F. Staar coordinates the international studies program at the Hoover Institution and, since 1983, has been a consultant to the U.S. Arms Control and Disarmament Agency. He took leave of absence for public service as U.S. ambassador and head of delegation at the Mutual and Balanced Force Reduction talks in Vienna, Austria. His latest books are *Communist Regimes in Eastern Europe* (4th rev. ed.) and *USSR Foreign Policies After Detente.*

John D. Sullivan has been at the Center for International Private Enterprise since its inception as director for public and congressional affairs and as special assistant to the executive director. During 1982, he served as associate director of business programs for the study that led to establishment of the National Endowment for Democracy. He is the author of several books on public affairs and economic education.

James D. Theberge is chairman of the National Committee on Central America in Washington, D.C., and an international management consultant. He previously served as director of Latin American and Iberian studies at the Center for Strategic and International Studies, Georgetown University; in the U.S. embassy to Argentina (1961–1964); as U.S. ambassador to Nicaragua (1975–1977); and as U.S. ambassador to Chile (1982–1985). He was a special adviser on inter-American affairs to the Department of Defense (1981–1982), and to the National Security Council (1983–1984). Author or editor of ten books on Latin America and Spain, his most recent publication is *Reflections of a Diplomat: United States and Latin America* (1985). He is a senior counselor of the Atlantic Institute.

Hans N. Tuch retired from the foreign service in 1985 as senior career minister with the U.S. Information Agency. His positions included press and cultural attaché in Moscow, USIA director for Soviet and East European affairs, deputy and acting director at the Voice of America. In addition to articles on public diplomacy and U.S.–West German relations, he coauthored *Atoms at Your Service.*

Oswald G. Villard, Jr. is professor of electrical engineering at Stanford University and senior scientific adviser for the engineering research group at SRI International. He is a recipient of the Medal for Outstanding Public Service, awarded by the U.S. Secretary of Defense.

Nils H. Wessell currently serves as director in the office of research at the U.S. Information Agency. Previously, he had been editor of *Orbis* and director of the Foreign Policy Research Institute in Philadelphia. Among other books, he has coauthored *Ground Rules for Soviet and American Involvement in Regional Conflicts* and coedited *The Soviet Threat: Myths and Realities*.

Gerhard Wettig is a senior staff member and acting head of the foreign policy research section at the Federal Institute for Eastern and International Studies in Cologne, West Germany. His books include *Community and Conflict in the Socialist Camp* and *Broadcasting and Détente* in English. He is coeditor of the journal *Aussenpolitik*.

APPENDIX

UNCLASSIFIED
NATIONAL SECURITY DECISION DIRECTIVE 77 (NSDD-77)
JANUARY 14, 1983

MANAGEMENT OF
PUBLIC DIPLOMACY RELATIVE
TO NATIONAL SECURITY

I have determined that it is necessary to strengthen the organization, planning and coordination of the various aspects of public diplomacy of the United States Government relative to national security. Public diplomacy is comprised of those actions of the U.S. Government designed to generate support for our national security objectives.

A Special Planning Group (SPG) under the National Security Council will be established under the chairmanship of the Assistant to the President for National Security Affairs. Membership shall consist of the Secretary of State, Secretary of Defense, the Director of the United States Information Agency, the Director of the Agency for International Development, and the Assistant to the President for Communications or their designated alternates. Other senior White House officials will attend as appropriate. Senior representatives of other agencies may attend at the invitation of the chairman.

The SPG shall be responsible for the overall planning, direction, coordination and monitoring of implementation of public diplomacy activities. It shall ensure that a wide-range program of effective initiatives is developed and implemented to support national security policy, objectives and decisions. Public diplomacy activities involving the President or the White House will continue to be coordinated with the Office of the White House Chief of Staff.

Four interagency standing committees will be established, and report regularly to the SPG. The SPG will ensure that guidance to these committees is provided, as required, so that they can carry out their responsibilities in the area of public diplomacy. The SPG will further periodically review the activities of the four permanent coordinating committees to ensure that plans are being implemented and that resource commitments are commensurate with established priorities.

The NSC Staff, in consultation with the regular members of the SPG, will provide staff support to the SPG and facilitate effective planning, coordinating and implementing of plans and programs approved by the SPG. The NSC Staff will call periodic meetings of the four committee chairmen or their designates to ensure intercommittee coordination.

- *Public Affairs Committee:* This coordinating committee will be cochaired by the Assistant to the President for Communications and the Deputy Assistant to the President for National Security Affairs. This group will be responsible for the planning and coordinating on a regular basis of U.S. Government public affairs activities relative to national security. Specifically, it will be responsible for the planning and coordination of major speeches on national security subjects and other public appearances by senior officials, and for planning and coordination with respect to public affairs matters concerning national security and foreign policy events and issues with foreign and domestic dimensions. This committee will coordinate public affairs efforts to explain and support major U.S. foreign policy initiatives.
- *International Information Committee:* This committee will be chaired by a senior representative of the United States Information Agency. A senior representative of the Department of State shall serve as vice chairman of the committee. The body will be responsible for planning, coordinating and implementing international information activities in support of U.S. policies and interests relative to national security. It will assume the responsibilities of the existing "Project Truth" Policy Group. The committees shall be empowered to make recommendations and, as appropriate, to direct the concerned agencies, interagency groups and working groups with respect to information strategies in key policy areas, and it will be responsible for coordinating and monitoring implementation of strategies on specific functional or geographic areas.
- *International Political Committee:* This committee will be established under the chairmanship of a senior representative of the Department of State. A senior representative of the United States Information Agency shall serve as vice chairman of the committee. This group will be responsible for planning, coordinating and implementing international political activities in support of United States policies and interests relative to national security. Included among such activities are aid, training and organizational support for foreign governments and private groups to encourage the growth of democratic political institutions and practices. This will require close collaboration with other foreign policy efforts—diplomatic, economic, military—as well as a close relationship with those sectors of the American society—labor, business, universities, philanthropy, political parties, press—that are or could be more engaged in parallel efforts overseas. This

group will undertake to build up the U.S. Government capability to promote democracy, as enunciated in the President's speech in London on June 8, 1982. Furthermore, this committee will initiate plans, programs and strategies designed to counter totalitarian ideologies and aggressive political action moves undertaken by the Soviet Union or Soviet surrogates. This committee shall be empowered to make recommendations and, as appropriate, to direct the concerned department and agencies to implement political action strategies in support of key policy objectives. Attention will be directed to generate policy initiatives keyed to coming events. Close coordination with the other committees will be essential.

• *International Broadcasting Committee:* This committee will be chaired by a representative of the Assistant to the President for National Security Affairs. This committee will be responsible for the planning and coordination of international broadcasting activities sponsored by the U.S. Government consistent with existing statutory requirements and the guidance established by NSDD-45. Among its principal responsibilities will be diplomatic and technical planning relative to modernization of U.S. international broadcasting capabilities, the development of antijamming strategies and techniques, planning relative to direct radio broadcast by satellite and longer-term considerations of the potential for direct T.V. broadcasting.

Each designated committee is authorized to establish, as appropriate, working groups or *ad hoc* task forces to deal with specific issues or programs.

All agencies should ensure that the necessary resources are made available for the effective operation of the interagency groups here established.

Implementing procedures for these measures will be developed as necessary.

Full text of NSDD-77

INDEX